# Child Support Handbook

**26th edition**

Mark Brough

Child Poverty Action Group

Child Poverty Action Group works on behalf of the more than one in four children in the UK growing up in poverty. It does not have to be like this. We use our understanding of what causes poverty and the impact it has on children's lives to campaign for policies that will prevent and solve poverty – for good. We provide training, advice and information to make sure hard-up families get the financial support they need. We also carry out high-profile legal work to establish and protect families' rights. If you are not already supporting us, please consider making a donation, or ask for details of our membership schemes, training courses and publications.

Published by Child Poverty Action Group
30 Micawber Street, London N1 7TB
Tel: 020 7837 7979
staff@cpag.org.uk
www.cpag.org.uk

*This book is sold subject to the condition that it shall not, by way of trade or otherwise, be lent, resold, hired out or otherwise circulated without the publisher's prior consent in any form of binding or cover other than that in which it is published and without a similar condition including this condition being imposed on the subsequent purchaser.*

A CIP record for this book is available from the British Library

ISBN: 978 1 910715 37 6

Child Poverty Action Group is a charity registered in England and Wales (registration number 294841) and in Scotland (registration number SC039339), and is a company limited by guarantee, registered in England (registration number 1993854). VAT number: 690 808117

Cover design by Colorido Studios
Internal design by Devious Designs
Content management system by Konnect Soft
Typeset by DLxml, a division of RefineCatch Limited, Bungay, Suffolk
Printed in the UK by CPI Group (UK) Ltd, Croydon CR0 4YY

# The author

**Mark Brough** is a freelance writer. He previously worked for many years as a welfare rights adviser for people with learning disabilities.

# Acknowledgements

A huge debt is owed to Nick Turnill for checking the text of this edition, and to all the authors of previous editions and, in particular, to Will Hadwen.

Many thanks to Alison Key for editing and managing the production of the book, Anne Ketley for compiling the index, and Kathleen Armstrong for proofreading the text.

Finally, thanks are also due to officials at the Department for Work and Pensions for patiently answering queries and providing helpful information.

The law described in this book was correct at 1 June 2018.

# Contents

**Appendices**

# Abbreviations

| | |
|---|---|
| CMS | Child Maintenance Service |
| CSA | Child Support Agency |
| DfC | Department for Communities (Northern Ireland) |
| DLA | disability living allowance |
| DWP | Department for Work and Pensions |
| ECHR | European Convention on Human Rights |
| ESA | employment and support allowance |
| EU | European Union |
| HMCTS | HM Courts and Tribunals Service |
| HMRC | HM Revenue and Customs |
| IB | incapacity benefit |
| ICE | Independent Case Examiner |
| IS | income support |
| JSA | jobseeker's allowance |
| NI | national insurance |
| PAYE | pay as you earn |
| PC | pension credit |
| PIP | personal independence payment |
| UC | universal credit |

# Chapter 1

## Introduction

**This chapter covers:**
1. What is child support (below)
2. The statutory child support scheme (below)
3. Responsibility for the child support scheme (p3)
4. Arrangements in Northern Ireland (p4)
5. Using this *Handbook* (p5)

## 1. What is child support

All parents have a legal responsibility to support their children financially until they are 16 (sometimes 20).[1] Child maintenance paid by parents who do not live with their children is intended to reflect this. Some people make voluntary arrangements to pay maintenance, others have arrangements made by a court order, and some people have maintenance calculated and enforced under the statutory child support scheme run by the Department for Work and Pensions. Some people may pay or receive child maintenance in more than one of these ways.

This *Handbook* explains how the statutory scheme operates. We use the term **'child support'** to refer to maintenance calculated and enforced under the statutory scheme. **'Child maintenance'** is used as a generic term for all types of child maintenance, including child support, voluntary agreements and payments made under a court order.

## 2. The statutory child support scheme

The statutory child support scheme calculates the amount of child support people have to pay. It has been in operation since 1993, but has changed significantly since then.

The current system of calculating child support was introduced on 10 December 2012. Since 25 November 2013, all new applications have been dealt with under this system. It is sometimes referred to as the **'2012 rules'** or the 'gross income' scheme. There are four rates of child support, depending on the parent's gross income (see Chapter 4). The calculation can be varied in certain circumstances (see Chapter 5). Fees may be charged in certain circumstances (see p23, p135 and p180).

There are two previous schemes. The original scheme, introduced in 1993, is usually referred to as the **'1993 rules'**. In 2003, this scheme was replaced by a simpler calculation, usually referred to as the **'2003 rules'**.

Both these schemes are now closed – ie, it is not possible to make new applications under these schemes. Most cases begun under these schemes have now closed, and all remaining cases are due to close by the end of 2018 (see below). All child support cases will then be dealt with under the '2012 rules'.

For full details of any remaining cases under the '1993 rules' and '2003 rules', see previous editions of this *Handbook*. Child support is calculated differently under each of these schemes, and there are differences in how other aspects of child support apply – eg, rules on enforcement. The legislative sources are also different.

## Closing old cases

Following the introduction of the '2012 rules', all existing child support cases under the '1993 rules' and '2003 rules' schemes are being closed. Most cases are now closed or in the process of being closed. All remaining cases are expected to be closed by the end of 2018.[2]

The process of closing existing cases has taken place in stages. Some existing cases have not been dealt with in this staged transition process – ie:

- cases that are due to close anyway before the end of 2018 – eg, because a child becomes too old to count as a 'qualifying child' (see p8); *or*
- where a new application is made under the '2012 rules' during the transition period and this triggers the closure of an existing 'related' case.

*Related case*

A **'related case'** is one where the non-resident parent in the new application:[3]

– is also a non-resident parent in an existing case with a different person with care; *or*

– has a partner who is a non-resident parent in an existing case, and either one (or both) of the non-resident parents receives income support, income-based jobseeker's allowance, income-related employment and support allowance, pension credit or universal credit calculated on the basis that s/he does not have any earned income.

Parents whose case is being closed will be notified in writing of the date that existing liability for child support ends – ie, the date the case will close. The notice must include information on how to choose to stay in the statutory scheme.[4] Parents must then choose either to make their own private family-based arrangements for child maintenance or make a new application to the statutory scheme under the '2012 rules'.

If the parties in a case that is being closed want to stay in the statutory scheme with no break in child support liability, they must apply under the '2012 rules' before the date the existing case is due to close.[5] The application is treated in the same way as any other new application (see Chapter 2). The application fee applies (see p23).

**Note:** parents who opt to stay in the statutory scheme may find that their child support liability under the '2012 rules' is considerably higher than under the previous scheme (some cases were calculated several years ago and have not been changed since). However, there is no provision to phase in the new child support liability. In other cases, liability under the '2012 rules' may be lower because of changes in the way income is calculated.

For full details of the transition to the '2012 rules' scheme and the process of closing existing cases, see Chapter 5 of the 2017/18 edition of this *Handbook*.

---

# 3. **Responsibility for the child support scheme**

The Department for Work and Pensions (DWP) is responsible for the statutory child support system in Great Britain.

The child support scheme is administered by the **Child Maintenance Service** (CMS), staffed by the DWP. The CMS deals with all cases under the '2012 rules'.

The DWP is also responsible for the **Child Maintenance Options** service (see below), which provides information and support.

**Note:** previous cases were dealt with by another service, the Child Support Agency (CSA). The CSA continues to deal with existing '1993 rules' and '2003 rules' cases until they are closed.

## The Child Maintenance Service

The CMS is responsible for calculating child support payments and, in some cases, collecting and enforcing them. This includes tracing non-resident parents and investigating parents' means.

The CMS has wide powers to gather information. These are covered in Chapter 3. If you are unhappy with the service provided by the CMS, you can make a complaint (see Chapter 11). If you are unhappy with a child support decision, you may also be able to challenge it (see Chapters 9 and 10).

## Child Maintenance Options

The DWP is responsible for the Child Maintenance Options service, which is intended to be the first port of call for anyone seeking information on child maintenance. Parents must contact Child Maintenance Options before making an application for child support (see p23).

Child Maintenance Options offers information and support to help parents make informed choices about child maintenance arrangements. It can be used by separating and separated parents, as well as by family, friends, guardians and anyone with an interest in child maintenance.

Child Maintenance Options can provide information and assistance with:[6]

- setting up a child maintenance arrangement following separation;
- establishing child maintenance arrangements for parents who are not in a relationship;
- switching from a private arrangement to an application under the statutory scheme, or vice versa;
- situations in which an existing child maintenance agreement has broken down or is not working well.

The service is free and is delivered by telephone, via a website and through a face-to-face service if required. See Appendix 1 for contact details. It aims to encourage voluntary maintenance arrangements by providing estimated calculations based on the statutory scheme, and other guidance to help parents decide on maintenance arrangements and amounts. It also provides information on other related areas, such as housing, employment and money, and can put people in touch with specialist advice agencies.

Child Maintenance Options can be used anonymously and records are not linked, so if two parties contact the service independently in relation to the same child(ren), no information about one party will be divulged to the other. The website includes leaflets explaining how personal information is used[7] and how to complain about the service (see Chapter 11).[8]

# 4. **Arrangements in Northern Ireland**

The child support system is largely the same throughout the UK, but Great Britain and Northern Ireland are treated as two separate territories for child support purposes.

There is a separate agency for Northern Ireland, also known as the Child Maintenance Service. It is part of the Department for Communities (DfC), and has the same powers as the Child Maintenance Service in England, Scotland and Wales. There is also an information and support service, known as Child Maintenance Choices, providing impartial information and support in a similar way to Child Maintenance Options.

If this *Handbook* is being used in Northern Ireland, references to the Department for Work and Pensions should be read as references to the DfC. **Note:** some legislative references are different in Northern Ireland.

If an application is made to the statutory child support scheme and the person with care, non-resident parent and qualifying child do not all reside in the same territory, there are special rules to determine how the application is dealt with.

New applications are generally dealt with by the agency of the territory where the non-resident parent named in the application lives. They are dealt with by the territory in which the applicant lives until the address of the non-resident parent is verified and, if the applicant lives in Great Britain, any application fee due is paid.

**Note:** if the non-resident parent in a new application is also named in an existing '1993 rules' or '2003 rules' case, or if a '2012 rules' application is being made as part of the case closure process (see p2), the new application is transferred to the territory in which the non-resident parent lives once the existing case has closed.[9]

Remaining cases under the '1993 rules' and '2003 rules' are dealt with by the agency of the territory where the person with care lives.[10]

Any calculation made must take into account the rules of the other territory.[11] Because the rules for calculating child support in the two territories are very similar, this should not, in practice, make any difference.

# 5. Using this *Handbook*

This *Handbook* explains the rules of the statutory child support scheme and how it is administered by the Child Maintenance Service (CMS). It is intended to help parents who use this scheme and their advisers. It covers the child support scheme in England, Wales and Scotland as at 1 June 2018.

This *Handbook* deals mainly with the current '2012 rules' scheme. In a few places, it highlights important older rules where these are different. For full details of the previous '1993 rules' and '2003 rules' schemes, see the 2014/15 edition of this *Handbook*.

Much of the caselaw relevant to child support was established under the '1993 rules' and '2003 rules'. However, many of the principles still apply to '2012 rules' cases. Where there are likely to be differences in interpretation or difficulties in applying previous caselaw to the '2012 rules', this is explained.

Around 95 per cent of people who apply for child support are women. However, the rules apply in the same way whatever the gender of the person with care of the child or the paying parent, including if both parents are men or both are women. The various parties are therefore referred to in a gender-neutral way in this *Handbook* wherever possible.

## Structure of the book

**Chapter 1** is an introduction to child support. It explains how to use this *Handbook*. **Chapter 2** explains how applications are made and **Chapter 3** covers how the CMS seeks information. Once all the information is available, the amount of child support can be worked out. **Chapter 4** explains how this is done, and **Chapter 5** explains how the amount can be varied in certain circumstances. **Chapter 6** covers decisions. **Chapter 7** explains how child support is collected and paid. **Chapter 8** explains how child support arrears are dealt with and enforced. **Chapters 9 and 10** explain how to change, query or challenge a decision. **Chapter 11** explains how to complain about anything to do with child support.

The **appendices** contain useful addresses and information about reference materials.

The best way to find the information you need is to use the **index** at the back of the book.

## Endnotes

Each chapter has endnotes that contain the legal sources, relevant caselaw and other information that support the text. These can be quoted to the CMS if the statement in the text is disputed. Appendix 5 explains the abbreviations used in the endnotes, with information on how to obtain the sources.

The Department for Work and Pensions (DWP) does not currently publish the guidance used in making child support decisions. As the guidance is not readily available, this *Handbook* generally avoids using it as a source. The guidance can, however, be obtained by making a request to the DWP under the Freedom of Information Act 2000. Anyone concerned about the application of a particular aspect of the law may wish to ask the CMS to provide a copy of any guidance it has taken into account when making the decision.

# Notes

**1. What is child support**
1 s1(1) CSA 1991

**2. The statutory child support scheme**
2 Reg 4(1) CS(ELEC) Regs; DWP, *Child Support Scheme for Timing and Related Matters in Relation to Ending Liability in Existing Cases ('the ending liability scheme)*, October 2017
3 Regs 1(3) and 4(2) CS(ELEC) Regs; Sch 1 para 4(1)(c) CSA 1991; reg 44(2) CSMC Regs
4 Sch 5 para 1(1) CMOPA 2008; reg 5 CS(ELEC) Regs
5 Reg 5(5) CS(ELEC) Regs

**3. Responsibility for the child support scheme**
6 Child Maintenance Options, *Information for Parents Living Apart From Their Child*, August 2015
7 Child Maintenance Options, *How Child Maintenance Options Uses Your Personal Information*, August 2015
8 Child Maintenance Options, *How to Complain about Child Maintenance Options*, November 2013

**4. Arrangements in Northern Ireland**
9 Sch 1 Art 5(8)-(8D) CS(NIRA) Regs, inserted by Sch 1 CS(NIRA)(A) Regs 2014
10 Sch 1 Art 5(5) CS(NIRA) Regs
11 Sch 1 Art 5(4) and (7) CS(NIRA) Regs

# Chapter 2

**· · · · · · · · · · · · · · · · · · · · · · · · · · · · · · · · · · · · · · · · · · · · · · · · · · · · · ·**

# Applications

**This chapter covers:**
1. Who can apply for child support (below)
2. When an application can be accepted (p15)
3. How to apply (p23)
4. Withdrawing or cancelling an application (p27)
5. Multiple applications (p28)
6. Communicating with the Child Maintenance Service (p29)

## 1. Who can apply for child support

Both parents (see p9) of a child have a legal duty to contribute to the maintenance of that child.[1] A parent who is not living in the same household as her/his child (a 'non-resident parent' – see p12) may be required to pay child support to the person who is the child's main carer. In most cases, this is the child's other parent, but could be another person – eg, the child's grandparent.

The following people can apply to the Child Maintenance Service (CMS) for child support for a 'qualifying child' (see p8):
• a person with care (see p10);
• a non-resident parent (see p12);
• in Scotland, a child aged 12 or over (provided no application has been made, or is treated as having been made, by the person with care or the non-resident parent).[2]

Child support can only be paid to one person with care of a qualifying child. If there is more than one person with care and they both/all apply for child support, the person whose application is accepted (see p28) receives all the child support. The CMS has an order of priority to decide which application to accept (see p28).

If two or more people in different households care for a qualifying child and at least one, but not all, of them has parental responsibility (see p10) for the child, only those with parental responsibility can apply for child support.[3] For example, if a child is cared for partly by her/his mother who has parental responsibility and partly by her/his grandmother who does not have parental responsibility, only the mother can apply. This means that if the person with parental responsibility decides not to apply, another person with care could lose out on child support.

## Who is a qualifying child

Child support is only payable for a 'qualifying child'. A child is only a **'qualifying child'** if one or both of her/his parents are non-resident parents (see p12).[4]

A **'child'** is defined as a person who is:

- under 16 years of age; *or*
- a young person aged 16–19 inclusive and:[5]
  - child benefit is payable in respect of her/him; *or*
  - receiving full-time, non-advanced education (see below).

Even if someone is in one of the above groups, s/he is not a child if s/he is, or has been, married or in a civil partnership. This applies even if the marriage or civil partnership has been annulled or was never valid – eg, because s/he was under 16.[6]

**Note:** child benefit has to be 'payable' for the young person, not actually paid. If a person has elected not to receive child benefit for a young person because s/he would be liable for the 'high income child benefit charge' in income tax, child benefit is still treated as payable in respect of her/him. 'Payable' means properly and lawfully payable, so a young person may not be a qualifying child if child benefit is being paid for her/him in error.[7]

See CPAG's *Welfare Benefits and Tax Credits Handbook* for full details of the rules on child benefit.

### Full-time, non-advanced education

A course is **non-advanced** if it is up to A level or Higher or Advanced Higher Scottish National Qualifications, or NVQ and SVQ level 3 and below. Courses of degree level and above, Diploma of Higher Education, Higher National Diploma or Higher National Certificate, Diploma of Higher Education, or NVQ and SVQ level 4 and above count as advanced education.[8]

The young person must attend a recognised educational establishment (such as a school, college or university) or the education must be recognised by the CMS. The CMS can only recognise such education if it was being provided for the young person immediately before s/he reached 16.[9]

The CMS must treat a young person as receiving **full-time** education if s/he attends a course with more than 12 hours of weekly contact time. 'Contact time' includes teaching, supervised study, exams and practical or project work which are part of the course. It does not include meal times or unsupervised study, whether on or off school premises. It is the hours of education received that count, not the hours of attendance.[10]

If a young person is not attending such a course (eg, if the contact time is 12 hours or less), the CMS must look at all the facts and decide whether the education is full time.[11]

After leaving school or college, a young person still counts as being in full-time education until child benefit stops being paid.

A young person at school or college can still count as a qualifying child if there is a temporary break in full-time education. It does not matter whether s/he is under or over 16 when her/his education is interrupted. A break of up to six months can be allowed. The CMS can allow longer if the break is due to an illness or disability of the young person. For someone to continue to count as a qualifying child, any breaks in full-time education must not be followed by a period during which child benefit stops being payable.[12]

## Who is a parent

A **'parent'** is a person who is legally the mother or father of the child.[13] This includes:
- a biological parent;
- a parent by adoption;[14]
- a parent under a parental order (used in surrogacy cases).[15]

If a child was conceived by artificial insemination or in vitro fertilisation:
- the mother is the woman who gave birth to the child, unless an adoption order or parental order is made;[16]
- the father is the man who provided the sperm (but see below).

If the insemination or in vitro fertilisation took place on or after 1 August 1991 but before 6 April 2009, the father is:
- the mother's husband, unless he did not consent to,[17] or died before, insemination;[18] *or*
- if the insemination was during licensed treatment services provided for the mother and a man, that man.[19] The man and woman must have received treatment services together.[20] This rule does not apply if the woman was inseminated or fertilised outside the UK.[21]

From 6 April 2009, in the case of assisted reproduction:[22]
- a man who is married to the mother is the father, unless he did not consent;
- if a man and woman are not married and the woman has a child as a result of licensed treatment, the man is the father if there is a notice of consent between them.

Two women who are married or civil partners are treated in the same way as a man and woman who are married – ie, if one partner gives birth to a child as a result of donor insemination, she is the mother of the child and her partner is automatically the other parent, unless she did not consent to the mother's treatment.[23]

An **adoption order** means the child is legally the child of the adopter(s).[24] The liability of a biological parent to maintain her/his child ends on adoption, and the parent(s) by adoption become the only person/people liable to maintain the child.

**Note:** a person who has legal parental responsibility (see below)[25] is not necessarily a parent for child support purposes.[26] For example, a step-parent who has acquired parental responsibility (except one assumed to be a parent – see p43) cannot be required to pay child support.[27] However, the courts could order her/him to pay maintenance.

A **foster parent** is not a parent for child support purposes because the child has been placed with her/him by a local authority (see below).

## Parental responsibility

A mother automatically has parental responsibility for her child from birth. Parents who were married to each other when the child was born both automatically have parental responsibility. This continues even if they later divorce.[28] If the parents are not married, the mother can make a formal agreement giving the father parental responsibility.[29] In addition, in England and Wales, if a child's parent is married to (or in a civil partnership with) someone who is not the child's other parent (ie, a step-parent), s/he (or if both biological parents have parental responsibility, both parents) can make a parental responsibility agreement with the step-parent, giving her/him parental responsibility for the child.[30] The courts can also give parental responsibility to a person (including a non-parent or step-parent) who applies for it.[31]

In England and Wales, if an unmarried father's name appears on a birth certificate on or after 1 December 2003, he has parental responsibility.[32] In Scotland, this applies if an unmarried father jointly registers a birth on or after 4 May 2006.[33] Unmarried fathers who signed a birth certificate before these dates cannot acquire parental responsibility without going through one of the other routes – ie, arranging a formal agreement with the mother or applying for a court order.

A female partner of the mother of a child conceived on or after 6 April 2009 automatically has parental responsibility if her details are included in the birth registration on or after 1 September 2009.[34]

If a birth certificate was issued before these dates, a female partner can only acquire parental reponsibility through one of the other routes.

## Who is a person with care

A **'person with care'** is the person with whom a child has her/his home (see below) and who usually provides 'day-to-day care' (see p11) for the child.[35]

*Home*

A **'home'** is the physical place where the child lives. It is different from a household (see p12). Although there is no specific definition of 'home' in the child support rules, the child's home is usually clear. A child may have more than one home – in which case, the CMS decides which is her/his principal home.

The person with care is usually the child's parent or another individual who provides day-to-day care for her/him, but could also be, for example, an organisation such as a children's home. However, a local authority *cannot* be a person with care, nor can someone who is looking after a child who has been placed with her/him by the local authority (including, in Scotland, someone who is providing 'continuing care' to a young person after s/he reaches age 16),[36] unless in England and Wales that person is the child's parent and the local authority has allowed a child it looks after to live with her/him.[37]

If the person with care is the child's parent, s/he is known as the **'parent with care'**.[38]

In some situations, the day-to-day care of a child is shared and a parent who provides some care may nevertheless be treated as a non-resident parent (see p13).

**Note:** the CMS uses the term **'receiving parent'**, rather than 'person with care', in its leaflets and letters.

## Day-to-day care

**'Day-to-day care'** is not specifically defined in the rules. The ordinary meaning of the phrase should be used when deciding who is a person with care and who can, therefore, receive child support. In most cases, it is clear who has day-to-day care.

Two or more people living in different households may each provide day-to-day care for the same child.

In deciding whether a person has day-to-day care of a qualifying child, the CMS should consider the overall care arrangements. The number of nights a year for which a person provides care may be a guide, but should not be the only consideration. If a mother provides care during the day but her children sleep at their father's home, both may be regarded as providing day-to-day care.[39]

A person who is responsible for a child's daily routine may be providing day-to-day care, even if some things are done by another person – eg, a childminder. It may not be necessary for someone to be *with* the child if s/he is nevertheless the person responsible for her/his overall care during that time. What matters is the degree to which a person continues to have control over the child and to be responsible for her/his behaviour and protection.[40]

If a child is placed with her/his parent by a local authority in England and Wales, even though the local authority is legally responsible, the parent is treated as providing day-to-day care.[41] If a child is a boarding school boarder or a hospital patient, the person who would otherwise provide day-to-day care is treated as still doing so.[42] The person who is treated as having day-to-day care while a child is at boarding school need not be the person who pays the school fees.[43]

Although it is not explicitly stated in the rules, if a child is temporarily in someone else's care, whoever would otherwise have day-to-day care is treated as providing care.[44]

If a change in the pattern of care occurs, the CMS should be informed, as this may affect the amount of child support payable and may be grounds for a supersession (see p196). However, the CMS is likely to take an overall view of the care arrangements rather than make separate decisions for different periods of time.

## Who is a non-resident parent

A 'non-resident parent' is a parent (see p9) who is not living in the same household (see below) as her/his child, and the child has her/his home with a person with care (see p10) – eg, where the parents of a child have separated.[45] Only a non-resident parent can be required to pay child support. However, if people share the care of a child, a parent who provides some care for the child may be treated as a non-resident parent (see p13).[46]

Both parents can be non-resident parents, in which case they can both be required to pay child support to the person with care – eg, to a grandparent who provides day-to-day care for a child.[47]

If a step-parent adopts a child and, therefore, legally replaces a biological parent, there may be no non-resident parent.[48]

If separated parents reconcile and live together, the non-resident parent is no longer non-resident and the child support calculation ceases to have effect. How soon this happens depends on the circumstances – eg, the nature of the reconciliation and the intentions of the couple. It may mean that the calculation ceases to have effect immediately.

**Note:** the CMS uses the term **'paying parent'**, rather than 'non-resident parent', in its leaflets and letters.

## Household

'Household' is not defined in the child support legislation. A household is something abstract, not something physical like a home (see p10). It is either a single person or a group of people held together by social ties.[49] In many cases, whether or not people are members of the same household is obvious. If it is not obvious, the CMS considers other factors. No one factor on its own should be conclusive. There does not need to be any settled intention about future arrangements for a household to exist.[50]

The meaning of household has been considered in family law and social security cases as well as child support cases, and this caselaw may be used to help make child support decisions. For some of the social security caselaw, see CPAG's *Welfare Benefits and Tax Credits Handbook*.

Caselaw has established the following.
- There can be two or more separate households in one house.[51]
- One or more members of a household can be temporarily absent from the home without ending their membership of the household.[52]

- There does not need to be a relationship like marriage for people to share a household – eg, two sisters can form a household.[53]

If there is a polygamous marriage, the CMS decides whether the qualifying child lives in a different household from at least one of the parents when establishing whether there is a non-resident parent. There can only ever be two legal parents, regardless of the number of partners either parent may have.

A couple may become members of the same household even if they get back together only briefly, assuming that they are hoping the relationship and their domestic arrangements will be indefinite.[54] In this case, a new household could be formed immediately, whether or not it then ceases to exist a few weeks or months later. A household can be formed as soon as people live together intending to form a household, and before they have arranged joint domestic and financial matters.

**Note:** a decision by the CMS or First-tier Tribunal that the couple share a household for child support purposes is likely to mean that they share a household for benefit or tax credit purposes. For more information about cohabitation decisions for benefits and tax credits, see CPAG's *Welfare Benefits and Tax Credits Handbook*.

### When a parent with care is treated as a non-resident parent

If both parents share the care of a child for whom a child support application has been made and the CMS accepts that both have 'day-to-day care' (see p11), one of the parents must be treated as the non-resident parent in order for there to be liability to pay child support.[55]

If one parent is treated as a non-resident parent (see p12), s/he is liable to pay child support, and the entire amount is paid to the other parent (or person with care).

If one or both parents share the child's care with a person with care who is not a parent of the child (eg, a grandparent), at least one of the parents must be treated as a non-resident parent in order for there to be a liability to pay child support. Both parents may be treated as non-resident and liable to pay child support to the person with care.

The person who receives child support could decide on an informal basis to pass some of the child support to the other person with care, but this cannot be enforced.

A parent with care who applies to the CMS for child support from the non-resident parent but ends up being deemed the non-resident parent and being required to pay child support can request that the application be withdrawn (see p27).

If a parent with care is treated as a non-resident parent, the amount of child support s/he must pay is worked out as usual. However, see p79 for how the amount of care she provides affects her/his liability.

If both parents share the care of a qualifying child equally, no one is liable to pay child support (see below).

*Example*

Susan and her partner Geoff are separated. Their daughter Katherine lives with Susan three nights each week. Susan works some night shifts, so Katherine stays with her grandmother two nights each week. Katherine stays with Geoff for two nights each weekend.

Susan applies for child support. Although Geoff also provides day-to-day care of Katherine, he provides care to a lesser extent than Susan. He is deemed to be the non-resident parent (see below) and is liable to pay child support (adjusted under the shared care rules for the care he provides). All the child support is paid to Susan. She decides to pay two-fifths of it to Katherine's grandmother to reflect the regular care she provides.

### Who is treated as the non-resident parent

A parent with care is treated as the non-resident parent if s/he provides care to a lesser extent than the other person with care.[56] A 'lesser extent' could mean either fewer nights a week on average or fewer hours, but the overall pattern of care arrangements should be considered.

The CMS usually assumes that the parent who does not receive child benefit is providing the lesser amount of care, and s/he is therefore treated as the non-resident parent.[57] This may lead to competing claims for child benefit. If more than one person who is entitled makes a claim for child benefit, an order of priority is used to decide who receives it.[58] For example, the person with whom the child is living has priority over other claimants. If the priority rules do not decide the matter and the claimants cannot come to an agreement, HM Revenue and Customs makes the decision. Priority can be conceded by a higher priority claimant to someone else, in writing.

**Note:** if a person has elected not to receive payments of child benefit because s/he would be liable to the 'high income child benefit charge' in income tax, child benefit is still treated as payable in respect of the child.[59] See CPAG's *Welfare Benefits and Tax Credits Handbook* for full details of the rules on child benefit.

If you think a decision that you are a non-resident parent is wrong, get advice. You may need to provide the CMS with evidence (eg, a diary), showing the pattern of care.

If the evidence shows that day-to-day care is shared equally between a qualifying child's parents, neither parent is treated as non-resident and so there is no liability for child support. This is the case, even if the two parents have significantly different levels of income. The CMS must consider the *overall* care arrangements when deciding whether day-to-day care is shared on a practically equal basis. It should not focus solely on whether or not the number of nights of care provided by each is equal.[60] So a child being cared for by one parent for a few days more or less than an absolutely equal pattern does not necessarily prevent the CMS from deciding that care is shared equally.

*Example*

Marcia and Nathan are divorced. They have two children, Oscar (7) and Patrick (5). Every fortnight the children spend five nights with Nathan. The rest of the time they live with Marcia.

Marcia has the children nine out of every 14 nights = approximately 234 nights a year.

Nathan has the children five out of every 14 nights = approximately 130 nights a year.

Both parents have day-to-day care.

Because Nathan looks after the boys to a lesser extent, he is treated as a non-resident parent and a calculation is carried out to decide how much child support he should pay to Marcia.

Marcia remains the parent with care and has no liability to pay child support.

A year later, Nathan has moved onto shift work. One week he has the children four nights, the second week three nights. Marcia cares for the children the rest of the time. They now share care equally. As Marcia receives child benefit, Nathan is still treated as the non-resident parent.

However, the CMS accepts that care is now shared equally and cancels the calculation.

There may be cases where each child of a family spends a different amount of time with the two parents – ie, the mother may be treated as the non-resident parent for one child, and the father for the other. If this is the case, the situation is similar to that of a divided family in which different children live full time with different parents (also known as '**split care**' – see p66). Two separate calculations are carried out. For example, a couple have two children, a boy and a girl: if the mother cares for the daughter for the greater amount of time, the daughter's child support is worked out with the father treated as the non-resident parent; child support for the son, who spends more time with the father, is worked out with the mother treated as the non-resident parent.

## 2. **When an application can be accepted**

People are not obliged to apply to the Child Maintenance Service (CMS) for child support. Parents can make an informal arrangement or draw up a written maintenance agreement that may be formalised. The government intends the statutory child support scheme to be the option that parents choose only if other arrangements cannot be agreed.

There are certain circumstances in which the CMS does not have jurisdiction or cannot accept an application.

The CMS cannot make a child support calculation unless the person with care, non-resident parent and qualifying child are all 'habitually resident' in the UK (see below). If the CMS decides that it no longer has jurisdiction because one of the parties is no longer habitually resident in the UK, the decision on child support liability should be superseded and the calculation cancelled (see p128).

The CMS also cannot accept an application for child support if there are certain maintenance orders made by a court or certain written maintenance agreements for the child(ren) concerned (see p18). **Note:** if the CMS has jurisdiction to make a calculation, however, the child support scheme has priority over the court system and there are limits on the role of the courts in relation to child maintenance (see p20).

A CMS decision on whether it has jurisdiction can be revised (see Chapter 9) and subsequently appealed to the First-tier Tribunal (see Chapter 10).[61] A court ruling that the court has no jurisdiction can be appealed or judicially reviewed (see p190).[62] No case should be outside the jurisdiction of both the CMS and the courts.

## Habitual residence

The CMS cannot make a child support calculation unless the person with care, non-resident parent and qualifying child are all 'habitually resident' in the UK.[63]

Other children who affect the child support calcualtion ('relevant other children' – see p64) do not have to be habitually resident in the UK.[64] The person with care does not have to be habitually resident if that 'person' is an organisation.[65]

The UK means England, Scotland, Wales and Northern Ireland (including coastal islands like the Isle of Wight). It does not include the Isle of Man or the Channel Islands.[66]

If a person is not habitually resident in the UK, see p22.

### What is habitual residence

A person is habitually resident if s/he is ordinarily resident in the UK and has been for an appreciable period of time.[67] 'Ordinary residence' means 'residence for a settled purpose'.[68]

There is no comprehensive list of factors that are relevant to deciding whether a person is habitually resident in the UK. A decision must take into account all the person's circumstances and intentions. Some of the most important factors that are considered include:

- the person's usual centre of interest or connections to a particular place;
- the length, continuity and purpose of residence in the UK;
- the length and purpose of any absence from the UK; *and*
- the nature of the person's work.

The following principles are some of those that have been established by caselaw. Cases that do not relate directly to child support are 'persuasive', but do not necessarily have to be followed.

- A person can habitually reside in more than one country, or in none.[69]
- Habitual residence can continue during an absence from the UK.[70] A person may be habitually resident in the UK even though s/he has employment and accommodation elsewhere.[71]
- A person cannot be habitually resident in the UK if s/he has never been here.
- A person who leaves the UK intending never to return to reside stops being habitually resident in the UK on the day s/he leaves.[72] The intention never to return must be a settled intention and not to see how things will work out in another country.[73]
- A person held in a country against her/his will may not be habitually resident there, even after long residence (but see below).[74]
- A person unlawfully in the UK may be habitually resident.

If a non-resident parent is not habitually resident in the UK, the CMS can still make a calculation if s/he is employed by the civil service, the armed forces, a UK-based company (ie, a company which employs a person to work outside the UK but which makes payment arrangements in the UK ), a local authority or the NHS.[75]

A person returning to the UK after an absence may have remained habitually resident in the UK during her/his absence.[76] When deciding whether a person has ceased to be habitually resident in the UK for child support purposes, the emphasis should be on the nature and degree of her/his connections with the UK, and any future intentions.[77] If the non-resident parent requests a supersession of the calculation because s/he is no longer habitually resident in the UK, the onus is on her/him to prove that this is the case.[78]

## Children

Whether or not a child is habitually resident is a question of fact that depends on her/his age and circumstances. The assessment of habitual residence should be centred on the child. Her/his place of habitual residence should reflect a degree of integration in a social and family environment.[79]

The habitual residence of the parent or person with whom a child lives, and the intentions of that person for the child, are relevant but they do not determine the habitual residence of the child. If there are two people with parental responsibility who live in different countries, the habitual residence of the child depends on the circumstances. Any existing residence order, or order for custody or care and control, is an important factor.

If both parents have parental responsibility for a child, it is possible for one parent to cause the child's habitual residence to change by moving the child to another country without the consent of the other parent. The assessment must be about the life of the child and not about the dispute between parents.

If there is only one parent or person with parental responsibility, the child's residence is most likely to change with that person's or to be determined by where that person allows the child to live.[80]

## Written maintenance agreements and court orders

**Note:** it is advisable to obtain legal advice about any court proceedings. The following is not intended to be a comprehensive guide to the law.

### Written maintenance agreements

Even if an application could be made to the CMS for child support, parents can still choose to make a maintenance agreement.[81] Maintenance agreements made on or after 5 April 1993 cannot prevent a parent, or any other person, from applying to the CMS for child support for a child who is the subject of the agreement, except if the agreement has been endorsed by a court (see below). Any clause included in the agreement that claims to prevent someone from applying to the CMS is void.[82]

If a maintenance agreement was endorsed by a court in a consent order (or a registered minute of agreement in Scotland) before 3 March 2003, it prevents an application from being made to the CMS (see p19). If it is made on or after 3 March 2003 and has been in force for less than one year, it prevents an application from being made to the CMS.[83]

---

*Maintenance agreements and consent orders*

'**Maintenance agreement**' means an agreement for making (or securing the making of) periodic payments of maintenance (or aliment in Scotland) to, or for the benefit of, a qualifying child.[84] This does not include any agreement to make a lump-sum payment (a 'capitalised payment'), even if this is intended to be the equivalent of regular child maintenance payments for a future period.[85]

A '**consent order**' is an order made by the court with the written consent of both parties. It is legally binding and can be enforced like any other court order and cannot be changed by one party without the court's permission.

---

Parents who want a consent order should obtain assistance from a family law solicitor to turn their agreement into a draft order to be submitted to the court. This is because a consent order must be made as part of a formal application to the court and must refer to the family law provisions under which it is made. The wording of the order is important – eg, a consent order containing an order to provide maintenance for the parent with care, and undertakings to provide maintenance for the children, may not prevent a calculation by the CMS.[86]

The court can also use its powers to vary an existing agreement (whenever made) by increasing the periodic child maintenance payments due under that agreement,[87] but not by adding a requirement to pay periodic child maintenance, unless the parties to the agreement give their written consent.[88] A person who does not want to apply to the CMS, or who is waiting for a CMS decision, can go back to court to increase (or reduce) maintenance. This is especially important if it is unclear whether the CMS has jurisdiction (eg, if the non-resident parent may no longer be habitually resident in the UK), as it allows the level of child maintenance to be reconsidered quickly by the court and not left unchanged until any CMS decision is finally made.

## Court orders

A maintenance order made by a court before 3 March 2003 prevents an application for any child to whom it relates – ie, the CMS will refuse to make a calculation.[89] If the order was made on or after 3 March 2003 and has been in force for less than one year, it also prevents an application.[90] If a child support application is made within a year of an order made after 3 March 2003, the CMS may hold it until after the one-year period expires and then treat it as an application rather than insist that a new application be made.[91]

A court order only counts for these purposes in the following circumstances.

- It requires periodic payments of maintenance (or aliment in Scotland) to be made to, or for the benefit of, a qualifying child.[92] However, because an order only prevents an *application* to the CMS, an order made *after* the application (eg, a 'top-up order' – see below) does not stop the CMS making a calculation, or prevent the CMS from revising or enforcing an existing calculation. A court order directing capital payments (ie, not periodic payments) does not count as an order for these purposes.[93]
- It must be in force. The meaning of 'in force' is not defined in the legislation, and so you may wish to obtain advice, as this can be a complex issue. The fact that parties may have waived their rights under an order, or agreed to make different arrangements, does not affect the status of the order itself.[94] It may be arguable that an order is in force only if it is still relevant – eg, the non-resident parent against whom the order was made is still a non-resident parent.[95] An order is in force if some undertakings or arrangements, such as for residence of the child, are still in effect, even though there is no further liability for maintenance payments[96] or the liability for child maintenance under the order has not yet begun.[97] If a court decides that it has no power to vary or enforce an order, an application can be made to the CMS.[98]
- It must be made under one of certain legal provisions (see Appendix 2).[99] The order usually states the legal provision under which it was made.

These rules also apply to consent orders (see p18) and to a registered minute of agreement (a form of enforceable legal agreement in Scotland) in relation to child maintenance in the same way as to maintenance orders made by a court.[100]

An application to the CMS is not prevented by the existence of a type of order known as a 'Segal order'. This is one that makes specific provision for an award of maintenance to reduce at a later date because a child support calculation is made.[101]

If you cannot apply to the CMS because of an order, you can ask the court to:

- vary or enforce the amount of maintenance under the order;
- revoke it so that a CMS application can be made (but see p22).

Although the courts can revoke child maintenance orders, this is not usually done simply to allow an application to be made to the CMS.[102] If revocation is being considered, advice should be obtained on the likely child support calculation.

People with court orders can use the CMS's collection and enforcement service for amounts due under these orders, provided child support is also being collected (see p142).

## The role of the courts if the Child Maintenance Service has jurisdiction

In general, the courts cannot make, vary or revive an order for periodic payments of child maintenance if the CMS has jurisdiction to make a child support calculation. The courts can still, however, revoke a maintenance order and have the power to enforce payment of any arrears arising from a period before the CMS had jurisdiction.[103] The CMS has jurisdiction if a child is a 'qualifying child' and all the relevant parties (child, person with care and non-resident parent) are habitually resident in the UK, even if the CMS *would not* in fact make a calculation.[104]

However, the courts can make certain orders in relation to maintenance (eg, consent orders, orders on special expenses and maintenance orders) for a young person who is no longer considered to be a qualifying child by the CMS. Courts can also vary orders in situations where an application to the CMS cannot be accepted (see p22).

Even if the CMS has jurisdiction, the courts may still be able to make maintenance orders for:[105]

- any stepchildren of the non-resident parent – ie, children who were accepted by that parent as members of her/his family when they used to live with her/him, but who are not qualifying children;[106]
- the expenses of a child's education or training;[107]
- the expenses of a child's disability. A child counts as disabled if s/he is getting disability living allowance (DLA) or personal independence payment (PIP), or does not get DLA/PIP but is blind, deaf, without speech or is substantially and permanently disabled by illness, injury, mental disorder or congenital deformity.[108] The courts can extend payments beyond the age at which the child may no longer be a qualifying child for child support purposes;[109]
- a spouse or civil partner;

- the person with care;[110] *and*
- a qualifying child in excess of the maximum worked out under child support rules.[111]

The courts can backdate these maintenance orders to the effective date (see p127) of a child support calculation, if the application is made within six months of that date.[112] Backdating is at the court's discretion and can ensure that other maintenance is in step with child support.

The court's power to make a lump-sum award for a child should not be used to provide regular support for the child in place of child support, but only to meet a need for a particular item of capital expenditure – eg, acquiring a home.[113]

The child support scheme does not change the court's powers in relation to other aspects of relationship breakdown (eg, contact and residence orders, maintenance for a spouse or civil partner and the division of property) or the court's jurisdiction to deal with parentage disputes (see p43).

If a court order is cancelled because it was made by mistake when a CMS calculation was in force, any payments made under it are treated as payments of child support.[114]

If a court order ceases to have effect because of a child support calculation, but the CMS revises the decision and decides no child support is payable as the previous decision was made in error, the court order revives and any child support already paid counts as maintenance paid under that order.[115]

## The effect of child support on existing court orders and agreements

When a child support calculation is made, any existing court order or maintenance agreement either ceases to have effect or has effect in a modified form in relation to periodic payments.[116]

These rules apply even to 'clean break' orders or agreements. There are conflicting court decisions on whether the child support scheme allows the court to reopen the capital or property part of such an order.[117] The arrangement may be self-adjusting to address the effect of a child support calculation. This could mean, for example, a legal charge on the transferred home so that the non-resident parent could recover any child support paid from the transferred property.[118] It could also mean an order that the non-resident parent top up any future child support to a certain total amount of maintenance.[119]

If a child support calculation is made for all the children still covered by a court order, that order ceases to have effect on the effective date of the calculation (see p127).[120]

If the order includes provisions for additional maintenance (eg, for a child's education or training expenses or for a disabled child's special needs), only the elements for periodic maintenance payments for a qualifying child should cease to be in force. If the order is made solely for these additional expenses, it remains in force.[121] Parts of the order for matters other than periodic maintenance for the children named in the calculation (eg, other children or spousal maintenance) remain in force.[122]

In Scotland, if the CMS ceases to have the power to make a calculation in respect of a child, the original order revives from the date the CMS ceases to have that power.[123] The same is not explicitly stated for England and Wales, which means that the original order does not revive when CMS involvement ceases. However, it could be argued that it should apply, since the court order has not been revoked but simply ceased to have effect for the duration of a child support calculation. If the original order does not revive, a new agreement or consent order needs to be negotiated.

Maintenance agreements are unenforceable from the effective date of the child support calculation.[124] Again, this only affects the part of the agreement to pay periodic maintenance for the children named in the calculation. The agreement remains unenforceable until the CMS no longer has the power to make a calculation.[125]

If the CMS is aware that an order is in force, it must notify all the parties and the relevant court about the calculation.[126] Similarly, if a court makes an order which affects, or is likely to affect, a child support calculation, the relevant court officer (see p36) must notify the CMS of this if s/he knows a calculation is in force.[127]

## The role of the courts if the Child Maintenance Service has no jurisdiction

If the CMS does not have jurisdiction (eg, because one parent or the qualifying child is not habitually resident in the UK), the courts may make, vary or revive a maintenance order. If there is a pre-3 March 2003 court order for child maintenance, or an order made on or after 3 March 2003 which has been in force for less than a year, the courts have the power to vary such orders.[128]

The courts may use the child support scheme as a guide when setting levels of child maintenance. This may avoid child support applications being made as soon as the order has been in force for a year. Parents seeking a variation of an order can ask their solicitors to prepare a calculation. An online calculator is available on the gov.uk website. The '2012 rules' calculation is likely to be seen as 'highly persuasive', but not legally binding on courts (as the '1993 rules' formula was in the past).[129] This principle has been emphasised in Scotland.[130] The courts also have the power to enforce orders and agreements, including those made by courts in other countries.[131]

In England and Wales, applications for maintenance are made to the family court or High Court. In Scotland, they are made to the sheriff court or Court of Session.

If a child support calculation is cancelled because the non-resident parent moves abroad (see p128), an application for maintenance can be made to the court. The person with care can apply for a 'reciprocal enforcement of maintenance order'.[132] If the application is made within six months, the order can begin from the date that child support ended.[133]

# 3. How to apply

Before applying to the Child Maintenance Service (CMS), a parent must contact the Child Maintenance Options service (see p3) and take part in a 'gateway' conversation. Child Maintenance Options is normally contacted by telephone or an online chat service, or face-to-face if required.

The gateway conversation is intended to encourage parents to consider the range of child maintenance options available before applying to the statutory scheme and, in particular, to consider making a private family-based arrangement. It is also intended to provide details of other support and information services. An applicant who states that s/he has experienced domestic violence (see p24) is fast-tracked through the gateway process to apply to the statutory scheme, rather than being encouraged to consider an unsuitable family-based arrangement.

## Application fees

There is a fee of £20 for making an application to the CMS.[134] The fee is payable whether or not a child support calculation is actually made as a result of the application. An application is not treated as properly made until the fee is paid or is waived by the CMS.

The application fee can be waived if:[135]

- the applicant is aged 18 or under on the date of the application; *or*
- the CMS accepts that the applicant has experienced domestic violence or abuse.

The CMS accepts that an applicant has experienced domestic abuse or violence if s/he:

- has reported the violence or abuse to an 'appropriate person'; *and*
- informed the CMS that s/he has experienced domestic violence or abuse and that s/he has reported this to an appropriate person. The CMS must be informed at the time of making the application or in a written declaration that the CMS may ask the applicant to complete (provided the application fee has not already been paid before the declaration has been returned).

If an application does not proceed because a qualifying child has died before the calculation is made, the fee must be refunded.[136]

2

*Domestic violence*

The CMS has published guidance on how it decides whether a person has experienced domestic violence or abuse.[137]

**'Domestic violence'** is defined as 'any incident or pattern of incidents of controlling, coercive or threatening behaviour, violence or abuse towards the applicant which is between persons aged 16 or over who are or have been intimate partners or family members, regardless of gender or sexuality. This can encompass, but is not limited to, the following types of abuse: psychological, physical, sexual, financial, emotional.' Abuse can include a person witnessing the abuse of her/his child by a current or previous partner.

The CMS has also published guidance on who is accepted as an **'appropriate person'** for these purposes.[138] These are:

– a court;
– the police;
– a medical professional;
– social services;
– a multi-agency risk assessment conference;
– a specialist domestic violence organisation or service, including a refuge;
– an employer;
– educational services;
– a local authority;
– a legal professional;
– specialist support services.

**Note:** an application fee is not expected to be introduced in Northern Ireland.[139]

## Making the application

After the gateway conversation with Child Maintenance Options, if a parent wishes to apply to the statutory scheme, s/he is given a unique 12-digit reference number that allows an application to be made. Child Maintenance Options does not deal with applications for the statutory scheme, but transfers a parent to the CMS at the end of the gateway conversation or provides a contact number for making an application to the CMS at a later date. If you do not have a reference number or you have lost or forgotten it, you are usually told to contact Child Maintenance Options first before the CMS proceeds with an application.

The CMS can determine how an application should be made and what information must be provided to process it.[140] In practice, this means that applications usually begin by contacting the CMS by telephone. Applications can also be made in writing. Contact details for the CMS can be found on the gov.uk website and in Appendix 1.

The CMS can require the applicant to provide any evidence or information reasonably needed to process the application (including sufficient information to allow the non-resident parent to be identified).[141] The application is treated as having been properly made when any information required to process it has been provided to the CMS.[142] In most cases, the CMS expects to gather information by telephone and paper application forms are not routinely issued. An application by a child in Scotland is always dealt with by telephone.

The reference number given by Child Maintenance Options is used to verify identity and personal details when contacting the CMS about the application.

## Information required for an application

An applicant is likely to have to provide the following information in order for the CMS to process an application:

- personal details – eg, name, address, national insurance (NI) number, date of birth, phone numbers and the best time to ring, and armed forces service number;
- child(ren) being applied for – eg, name, date of birth, NI number if 16 or over, who gets child benefit for the child, maintenance arrangements and any shared care arrangements (or local authority care);
- if the parent/person with care is applying, whether the non-resident parent knows that s/he is named as the parent and whether s/he knows where the applicant lives;
- the child's education (if aged 16–19) – eg, school/college, course, type of course and hours;
- local authority details (if the child is being cared for);
- the non-resident parent's details – eg, name and other names used, address or last known address and when s/he lived there, NI number, date of birth, employment details, phone numbers and whether the parent is the father or mother of the child;
- payment details – eg, whether child support is to be collected by the CMS, the preferred method and frequency of payment to the person with care and bank/building society details;
- details of any representative – eg, name, address, phone numbers and the best time to ring. If the representative is a solicitor, an attorney under a power of attorney, Scottish mental health guardian, mental health appointee or receiver, the representative can apply on behalf of the applicant.

The CMS may wish to see original documents to confirm certain details – eg, any relevant court order or a power of attorney document.

There are penalties for knowingly providing false information (see p38).

## Applications with more than one non-resident parent

An applicant can choose from which non-resident parent s/he wishes to apply for child support. So, if someone is a person with care of qualifying children of more than one non-resident parent, s/he could apply for child support from one (or more), but not necessarily all, of them.

## When to apply

There are no time limits for applying to the CMS. An application can be made as soon as someone becomes a person with care or a non-resident parent, or at any later date.[143] Liability to pay child support usually starts from two days after the date notification of the application was sent to the non-resident parent, and the CMS cannot do this until it receives an effective application (see below). This means that delaying the application may delay the start of liability. The parent with care should be aware that this is the case even if the reason for the delay is that s/he has been in touch with the Child Maintenance Options service and is considering alternatives, such as setting up voluntary maintenance arrangements. There is no provision for applying in advance – eg, before the birth of a baby.

## If an application is refused

The CMS may refuse to accept an application – eg, because it believes an existing maintenance order prevents an application or because it does not have jurisdiction (see p15). If this happens, you should explain to the CMS why you believe you are entitled to apply and ask for a written CMS decision. If a written decision is issued, you can try to challenge this by seeking a revision (see Chapter 9) and then appealing to the First-tier Tribunal (see Chapter 10). If this is not successful or if the CMS refuses to respond in writing, a complaint (see p235) and/or judicial review (see p190) could be considered.

## Effective applications

The CMS can only make a child support calculation if the application is 'effective'.[144] All applicants must provide information to enable the non-resident parent to be identified and traced and the amount of child support payable to be calculated and recovered (see Chapter 3).[145] If an applicant does not supply the information, the CMS may refuse to process the application (see p27).

Once an effective application has been made, the address of the non-resident parent has been verified and any application fee due has been paid, the CMS must notify the non-resident parent in writing as soon as possible and ask her/him for any information required to determine her/his child support liability. (This applies even if the non-resident parent is the applicant.) S/he is informed of the 'effective date' of the application (see p127), that the CMS can estimate income in certain circumstances and of the rules on 'default maintenance decisions' (see p125).[146]

The CMS cannot refuse to deal with an effective application, even if it considers that processing it would be against the welfare of the children concerned.[147] If it refuses to accept an application, see above.

For delays in dealing with applications, including if the non-resident parent is not co-operating, see p123.

## Amending the application

An application can be amended at any time before a child support calculation is made, but not to take into account a change which occurs after the effective date. For details of this and of changes after the effective date, see p124.

# 4. Withdrawing or cancelling an application

## The applicant no longer wants to proceed

An applicant can request that the Child Maintenance Service (CMS) cancel her/his application for child support. The request can be made at any time, whether or not a calculation has been made. The CMS cannot refuse this request.[148] For more information on cancelling calculations, see p128. Requests can be made by telephone or in writing to the CMS office processing the application, or to the regional centre if it is not clear which office has responsibility.

## The Child Maintenance Service withdraws or cancels an application

The CMS may withdraw or cancel an application before a calculation is made if the applicant does not provide information (see below).

The rules are different if the qualifying child dies before the calculation decision is made (see below).

### An applicant does not provide information

If a person with care does not provide sufficient information, the CMS can close the case and s/he will not receive child support.

Cases can only be cancelled if no effective application has been made (see p26). If there *is* an effective application, a decision must be made and notified, even if it is a decision not to make a calculation (see p124). If an effective application is cancelled against your wishes, get advice.

### The qualifying child dies

If a qualifying child dies before a calculation has been made, a decision on liability is still made for the period up to the date of her/his death. If the child was the only child named in the application, the decision is then cancelled with effect from the date of death; otherwise, it is changed (superseded) with effect from that date.[149]

# 5. Multiple applications

If more than one person applies for child support in respect of the same qualifying child before the decision on how much child support is payable is made, only one application can go ahead (see below).[150]

If one application is given priority, information provided in the other application that the Child Maintenance Service (CMS) does not proceed with may still be taken into account to help make a decision.

**Note:** once a calculation is in force, any subsequent application for child support made in the same circumstances in respect of the same person with care, non-resident parent and qualifying child(ren) may be treated as a request for a supersession (see p196) or, depending on the circumstances and information contained in the application, as a request for a variation (see Chapter 5).[151]

## Which application goes ahead

The CMS decides which application goes ahead, using the following order of priority.[152]
- In Scotland, an application from a person with care or a non-resident parent has priority over an application from a child.
- In other circumstances, an earlier application has priority over a later one.

In the following circumstances, the CMS treats the applications as a single application in relation to the qualifying child.[153]
- An application is made and both parents of a qualifying child are non-resident – eg, an application made by a person with care who is not the parent of the qualifying child, or by a child in Scotland whose parents are both non-resident.
- Both parents of a qualifying child are non-resident and both apply for child support.

Although the law does not state this explicitly, if more than one application is made by the same person in the same circumstances, they are likely to be treated as if they were a single application if the calculation decision has not been made.

## Applications for additional children

If there is an existing child support calculation and an application is made for an additional child of the same non-resident parent cared for by the same person with care, this is a relevant change of circumstances. A new calculation is made which supersedes the existing one (see p196).

# 6. Communicating with the Child Maintenance Service

Most contact with the Child Maintenance Service (CMS) is by telephone. This is the CMS's preferred method of communication. Parents must make a request if they wish to be contacted by letter instead. Details of the relevant office handling the case are on any letters received from the CMS.

The CMS should answer telephone calls promptly. It should reply to letters, resolving the issue or agreeing what will happen next, within three weeks. If you have difficulty in contacting the CMS, or obtaining a response within a reasonable time, complain (see Chapter 11).

The CMS does not normally offer face-to-face interviews, but these may be arranged if the CMS considers that the case involves complex issues and an interview may help to resolve them more quickly. An interview may also be considered if someone has communication difficulties which make other methods problematic. A request for a face-to-face interview by anyone involved in a case should be considered seriously if the CMS agrees that it is the most effective way to make contact or if all other ways of progressing the case have been exhausted.

The CMS should also meet any accessibility or language needs of the applicant – eg, if English is not her/his first language or if s/he has difficulty using the telephone.

Once an application is made, applicants can register with the government 'gateway' to manage their case through an online account.[154] This allows applicants to check the progress of an application, opt in or out of a text messaging service, report changes in their circumstances, upload documents and personal details, make one-off payments and view calculation details and payment history.

It is advisable to keep copies of letters and make a note of the date, time and content of telephone calls.

## Dates of postage

A document sent to the CMS is treated as being sent on the day the CMS receives it.[155] If the CMS posts a document to a person's last known address (or the address the person last notified to the CMS), it is treated as being received two days after the day it was posted.[156] It is understood that this is intended to exclude Sundays and bank holidays. A document is likely to be treated as having been 'sent' by the CMS if it was properly addressed, pre-paid and posted. Evidence that it was not received does not show that it was not sent.[157]

It is important to bear these rules in mind, especially where time limits are concerned.

**Note:** if no statutory timescale applies for a particular action to be done or for information to be provided, the CMS generally allows 14 days to provide information, and extends this to 16 days to allow for the time taken for information to reach the CMS by post.

## Representatives

Anyone dealing with the CMS can appoint a representative to act on her/his behalf.[158] If the person is not legally qualified, authorisation for her/him to act needs to be confirmed in writing, although if you are with the representative during a telephone call, you can authorise the representative verbally for the duration of the call. An authorised or legally qualified representative can complete forms, receive documents and supply information. A person with care may also choose to have payments of child support made to a representative.

A representative who understands the law and/or is experienced in dealing with the CMS may find it easier to get a quick response and clearer information from the CMS, and can advise about rights and options. For information about how to find independent advice, see Appendix 3.

Representatives with legal authority to act for a CMS client (eg, someone with power of attorney, a receiver or a mental health appointee or Scottish mental health guardian) can act for the client in every respect, as if they were the client.

The legal advice and assistance scheme in Scotland may help to cover costs in child support cases.

# Notes

**1. Who can apply for child support**
1. s1 CSA 1991
2. s7(1) CSA 1991
3. ss5(1) and 54 CSA 1991
4. s3(1) CSA 1991
5. Reg 76 CSMC Regs; s142(2) SSCBA 1992; regs 2-7 CB Regs
6. s55(2) and (3) CSA 1991
7. *JF v SSWP and DB (CSM)* [2013] UKUT 209 (AAC), reported as [2014] AACR 3; *DJ v SSWP and TJ (CSM)* [2017] UKUT 83 (AAC)
8. Reg 76 CSMC Regs; s142(2) SSCBA 1992; reg 1(3) CB Regs; CCS/12604/1996
9. Reg 76 CSMC Regs; s142(2) SSCBA 1992; reg 3 CB Regs
10. CCS/1181/2005

11. Reg 76 CSMC Regs; s142(2) SSCBA 1992; reg 1(3) CB Regs; *CF v CMEC (CSM)* [2010] UKUT 39 (AAC); CCS/1181/2005
12. Reg 76 CSMC Regs; s142(2) SSCBA 1992; reg 6 CB Regs
13. s54 CSA 1991
14. s39 AA 1976; s39 A(S)A 1978; s26(2) CSA 1991, Case A
15. s54 HF&EA 2008; s26(2) CSA 1991, Case B
16. ss27(2) and (3) and 29(1) HF&EA 1990
17. s28(2) HF&EA 1990; *Re CH (Contact: Parentage)* [1996] 1 FCR 768, [1996] 1 FLR 569, [1996] Fam Law 274
18. s28(6) HF&EA 1990
19. s28(3) HF&EA 1990

20  See *Re D (A Child Appearing by her Guardian Ad Litem)* [2005] UKHL 33
21  Because such a clinic would not have a UK licence: *U v W (A-G intervening)* [1997] 3 WLR 739, [1997] 2 CMLR 431, [1997] 2 FLR 282
22  ss35-37 HF&EA 2008
23  s42 HF&EA 2008
24  **EW** s67 A&CA 2002
   **S** s40 A&C(S)A 2007
   **Both** s54 CSA 1991, definition of 'parent'
25  **EW** CA 1989
   **S** C(S)A 1995
26  **EW** s3(4) CA 1989
   **S** s3(3) C(S)A 1995
27  R(CS) 6/03
28  s2(1) CA 1989; s3(1) C(S)A 1995
29  s4(1)(b) CA 1989; s4(1) C(S)A 1995
30  s4A CA 1989, as amended by s75 CPA 2004
31  ss4(1)(c), 4ZA(1)(c), 4A(1)(b) and 5(6) CA 1989; s11 C(S)A 1995
32  s4(1)(a) CA 1989
33  s3(1)(b)(ii) C(S)A 1995
34  s4ZA(1)(a) CA 1989; s3(1)(c) and (d) C(S)A 1995
35  s3(3) CSA 1991
36  s3(3)(c) CSA 1991; reg 78(1) CSMC Regs
37  Reg 78(1)(b) and (d) CSMC Regs
38  s54 CSA 1991
39  *GR v CMEC (CSM)* [2011] UKUT 101 (AAC)
40  R(CS) 11/02; *GR v CMEC (CSM)* [2011] UKUT 101 (AAC)
41  Reg 51 CSMC Regs. This applies if a child is placed under s22C(2) CA 1989 or s81(2) Social Services and Well-being (Wales) Act 2014.
42  Reg 55 CSMC Regs
43  R(CS) 8/98
44  This principle was explicitly stated for the '2003 rules': reg 1(2)(b)(i), definition of 'day-to-day care', CS(MCSC) Regs
45  s3(2) CSA 1991
46  Reg 50 CSMC Regs
47  s1(3) CSA 1991
48  *RW v SSWP (CSM)* [2013] UKUT 576 (AAC)
49  *Santos v Santos* [1972] 2 WLR 889, [1972] All ER 246 (CA)
50  CCS/2318/1997
51  CSB/463/1986
52  R(SB) 4/83
53  R(SB) 35/85
54  CCS/2332/2006

55  Reg 50 CSMC Regs
56  Reg 50(2) CSMC Regs
57  Reg 50(3) CSMC Regs
58  s144(3) and Sch 10 SSCBA 1992
59  Reg 50(4) CSMC Regs
60  *JS v SSWP and Another (CSM)* [2017] UKUT 296 (AAC)

## 2. When an application can be accepted

61  R(CS) 3/97
62  rr8.1(2)-(6), 10.24 and 10.25 Family Proceedings Rules 1991, No.1247
63  s44(1) CSA 1991
64  CCS/2314/2008; *AF v SSWP* [2009] UKUT 3 (AAC)
65  s44(2) CSA 1991
66  Sch 1 Interpretation Act 1978
67  *Nessa v Chief Adjudication Officer* [1998] 2 All ER 728, [1998] 2 FCR 461, [1998] 1 FLR 879, [1998] Fam Law 329 (CA), applying *Re J (A Minor) (Abduction: Custody Rights)* [1990] 2 AC 562, [1990] 3 WLR 492, [1990] 2 All ER 961, [1991] FCR 129, [1990] 2 FLR 442, [1991] Fam Law 57 (HL); *Cruse v Chittum* [1974] 2 All ER 940; *Brokelmann v Barr* [1971] 3 All ER 29; *Langford Property Co v Athanassoglou* [1948] 2 All ER 722
68  *Shah v Barnet LBC* [1983] 2 AC 309, [1983] 2 WLR 16, [1983] 1 All ER 226 (HL)
69  CCS/2314/2008; *AF v SSWP (CSM)* [2009] UKUT 3 (AAC); *Armstrong v Armstrong* [2003] EWHC 777 (Fam), [2003] 2 FLR 375
70  *Lewis v Lewis* [1956] 1 WLR 200, [1956] 1 All ER 375
71  *CJ v SSWP and VW (CSM)* [2017] UKUT 498 (AAC); *Arthur v HMRC* [2017] EWCA Civ 1756
72  *Re J (A Minor) (Abduction: Custody Rights)* [1990] 2 AC 562, [1990] 3 WLR 492, [1990] 2 All ER 961, [1991] FCR 129, [1990] 2 FLR 442, [1991] Fam Law 57 (HL)
73  CCS/3574/2008; *H v CMEC* [2009] UKUT 84 (AAC)
74  *Shah v Barnet LBC* [1983] 2 AC 309, [1983] 2 WLR 16, [1983] 1 All ER 226 (HL); *Re Mackenzie* [1940] 4 All ER 310
75  s44(2A) CSA 1991; reg 7A CS(MAJ) Regs
76  R(CS) 5/96
77  R(CS) 5/96
78  CSCS/6/2006

79 *B (A Minor: Habitual Residence)* [2016]
EWHC 2174 (Fam) and *SR (A Child:
Habitual Residence)* [2015] EWHC 742
(Fam), citing and summarising the
following UK Supreme Court
judgments: *A v A (Children: Habitual
Residence)* [2013] UKSC 60; in *Re L (A
Child) (Custody: Habitual Residence)
(Reunite International Child Abduction
Centre intervening)* [2013] UKSC 75; in
*Re LC (Children) (Reunite International
Child Abduction Centre intervening)*
[2014] UKSC 1; in *Re R (Children)
(Reunite International Child Abduction
Centre and others intervening)* [2015]
UKSC 35; *Re B (A Child) (Habitual
Residence: Inherent Jurisdiction)* [2016]
UKSC 4.
80 *Re J (A Minor) (Abduction: Custody Rights)*
[1990] 2 AC 562, [1990] 3 WLR 492,
[1990] 2 All ER 961, [1991] FCR 129,
[1990] 2 FLR 442, [1991] Fam Law 57
(HL)
81 s9(2) CSA 1991
82 s9(3) and (4) CSA 1991
83 ss4(10) and 7(10) CSA 1991; reg 2
CS(APD) Regs
84 s9(1) CSA 1991
85 *SJ v SSWP (CSM)* [2014] UKUT 82 (AAC),
reported as [2014] AACR 32
86 CCS/316/1998; CCS/8328/1995
87 s9(6) CSA 1991
88 ss8(5) and 9(5) CSA 1991
89 ss4(10)(a) and 7(10)(a) CSA 1991; reg 2
CS(APD) Regs
90 ss4(10)(aa) and 7(10)(b) CSA 1991; reg
2 CS(APD) Regs
91 *YW v CMEC (CSM)* [2011] UKUT 176
(AAC)
92 s8(11) CSA 1991
93 CCS/4741/1995, upheld by the Court
of Appeal in *AMS v CSO* [1998] 1 FLR
955
94 CCS/4049/2007

95 CCS/4049/2007. This and other cases
have disagreed with the conclusions
reached in R(CS) 4/96. The Court of
Appeal in *Kirkley v Secretary of State for
Social Security* ruling on an application
for leave to appeal against R(CS) 4/96
also disagreed with the reasoning.
Authorities differ as to whether changes
in child(ren)'s residence (eg, from the
parent with care to the non-resident
parent) mean that an order ceases to
have effect (CCS/3127/1995) or not
(CCS/2567/1998). In the latter case, the
commissioner suggested that it would
instead be grounds to seek to vary the
court order.
96 CCS/4741/1995
97 CCS/11364/1995
98 Reg 9 CS(MAJ) Regs
99 s8(11) CSA 1991; reg 2 CS(MAJ) Regs.
Provisions repealed before 1 April 1980
are not listed.
100 Reg 26(1)(c) CS(MCP) Regs
101 CCS/4047/2007, citing *Dorney-Kingdom
v Dorney-Kingdom* [2000] 2 FLR 855
102 s8(4) CSA 1991; *B v M (Child Support:
Revocation of Order)* [1994] 1 FLR 342,
[1994] 1 FCR 769, [1994] Fam Law 370
103 s8(1), (3) and (4) CSA 1991. It has been
decided that this lack of access to the
courts is not inconsistent with Art 6(1)
European Convention on Human Rights.
See *R v SSWP ex parte Kehoe* [2005]
UKHL 48.
104 s8(2) CSA 1991
105 s8 CSA 1991
106 **EW** MCA 1973
**S** FL(S)A 1985
107 s8(7) CSA 1991
108 s8(8) and (9) CSA 1991
109 Sch 1 para 3(2)(b) CA 1989. In *C v F*
[1997] 3 FCR 405 the court held that
where s8(1) CSA 1991 applies, s8(8)
CSA 1991 limits this power to children
aged under 19. However, this seems to
be wrong because the fact that the CSA
1991 only applied at the time of the
judgment to those aged under 19
cannot prevent an order being made
under the CA 1989 for a person aged 19
or over.
110 s8(10) CSA 1991
111 s8(6) CSA 1991
112 s29(7) MCA 1973; s5(7) DPMCA 1978;
Sch 1 para 3(7) CA 1989, as amended
by Sch 3 paras 3, 5 and 10 CSPSSA 2000
respectively

113 Sch 1 CA 1989; *Phillips v Pearce* [1996] 2 FLR 230
114 Reg 8(2) CS(MAJ) Regs
115 Reg 8(1) CS(MAJ) Regs
116 s10(1) and (2) CSA 1991
117 *Crozier v Crozier* [1994] 1 FLR 126; *Mawson v Mawson* [1994] 2 FLR 985
118 *Smith v McInerney* [1994] 2 FLR 1077. However, an arrangement like this might be void under s9(4) CSA 1991 because it would 'restrict the right to apply for a maintenance assessment', though the commissioner in CCS/2318/1997 thought not.
119 See the arrangement in CCS/2318/1997.
120 Reg 3(2) CS(MAJ) Regs
121 Reg 3(3) CS(MAJ) Regs
122 Reg 3(2) CS(MAJ) Regs
123 Reg 3(4) CS(MAJ) Regs
124 Reg 4 CS(MAJ) Regs
125 Reg 4(3) CS(MAJ) Regs
126 Reg 5(1) CS(MAJ) Regs
127 Reg 6 CS(MAJ) Regs
128 ss8(3A) and 9(6) CSA 1991; *McGilchrist v McGilchrist* [1997] SCLR 800
129 *E v C* [1996] 1 FLR 472; *GW v RW* [2003] EWHC 611 (Fam), [2003] 2 FLR 108
130 *Sutherland v Sutherland* [2004] GWD 20-436
131 MO(RE)A 1992
132 **E&W** HMCTS, *A Guide to Reciprocal Enforcement of Maintenance Orders*, June 2015
    **S** www.scotcourts.gov.uk/taking-action/frequently-asked-questions/reciprocal-enforcement
133 s29(7) MCA 1973; s5(7) DPMCA 1978; Sch 1 para 3(7) CA 1989

**3. How to apply**
134 s6 CMOPA 2008; reg 3 CSF Regs 2014
135 Reg 4(1)-(3) CSF Regs 2014
136 Reg 5 CSF Regs 2014
137 DWP, *Guidance on Regulation 4(3) of the Child Support Fees Regulations 2014: how the Secretary of State will determine if an applicant is a victim of domestic violence or abuse*, July 2017, available at www.gov.uk
138 DWP, *Guidance on Regulation 4(3) of the Child Support Fees Regulations 2014: list of persons to whom an applicant must have reported domestic violence or abuse*, 2 December 2013, available at www.gov.uk
139 Department for Communities Press Release, 20 September 2013

140 Reg 9(1) CSMC Regs
141 Reg 9(1) CSMC Regs
142 Reg 9(2) CSMC Regs
143 R(CS) 10/02
144 Reg 9(2) CSMC Regs
145 ss4(4), 6(7) and 7(5) CSA 1991
146 Reg 11 CSMC Regs
147 R(CS) 4/96; CCS/14/1994; CCS/17/1994; CCS/16535/1996

**4. Withdrawing or cancelling an application**
148 ss4(6) and 6(5) CSA 1991
149 Reg 18(3) CSMC Regs

**5. Multiple applications**
150 s5(2) CSA 1991
151 *DB v CMEC* [2010] UKUT 356 (AAC). This decision relates to a '2003 rules' case. However, the same principle should apply to the '2012 rules', although this is not explicitly stated in those rules.
152 Reg 10(2) CSMC Regs
153 Reg 10(3) CSMC Regs

**6. Communicating with the Child Maintenance Service**
154 www.gateway.gov.uk
155 Reg 7(1) CSMC Regs
156 Reg 7(2) CSMC Regs
157 R(CS) 1/99
158 Reg 8 CSMC Regs

**3**

# Chapter 3

# Information

**This chapter covers:**
1. Information-seeking powers (below)
2. Contacting the non-resident parent (p38)
3. Parentage investigations (p41)
4. Further investigations (p50)
5. Change of circumstances (p51)
6. Disclosure of information (p52)

## 1. Information-seeking powers

The Child Maintenance Service (CMS) has wide powers to obtain information from (among others) parents, employers, local authorities and HM Revenue and Customs (HMRC).[1] It can require information to be provided in order to make any child support decision.[2]

In addition, the CMS can appoint inspectors who have extensive powers to obtain information (see p51). In general, CMS staff seek information by telephone, but may also carry out face-to-face enquiries.

### When information can be requested

After a child support application has been made, the non-resident parent is notified in writing (see p38). The date this notice is issued sets the 'effective date' for the calculation (see p127). This notice is followed up by a telephone call to the non-resident parent to gather and confirm information.

The CMS can request information in order to:[3]
- determine an application for child support and any issues that arise from it – eg, to establish which parent receives child benefit and so who is the child's main carer if care is shared (see p14);
- make any other decisions – eg, to determine the income of the non-resident parent;
- enable child support to be calculated, collected and enforced.

See below for who can be required to give information, and p38 for what happens if someone fails to provide it.

## What information can be requested

The CMS can request information on many issues, including:
- the habitual residence of the person with care, the non-resident parent and any child covered by the application, to determine whether the CMS has jurisdiction;
- the name and address of the person with care and non-resident parent, their marital or civil partnership status, and the relationship of the person with care to any child covered by the application;
- the name, address and date of birth of any child covered by the application, the child's marital or civil partnership status and details of the child's education;
- if there is more than one person with care:
  - who has parental responsibility (or parental rights in Scotland) for any qualifying child; *and*
  - how much time is spent by that child with each person with care;
- if parentage is disputed, whether someone can be assumed to be a parent (see p43) and, if not, who is the parent of a child;
- the name and address of any current or recent employer of a non-resident parent and her/his gross earnings from that employment;
- if the non-resident parent is self-employed, the address, trading name, gross receipts and expenses, other outgoings and taxable profits of the trade or business;
- any other income of the non-resident parent;
- how much is paid or payable under a court maintenance order or maintenance agreement;
- details of anyone who lives in the same household as the non-resident parent, their relationship to her/him and to each other, and the date of birth of their child(ren);
- details and statements of any account in the name of the non-resident parent, including bank and building society accounts;
- whether someone counts as a qualifying child for child support purposes (see p8);
- information to decide whether a calculation should end (see p127).

## Who must provide information

Information can be required from the following, if they have the information or evidence in their possession or can reasonably be expected to acquire and provide it:[4]

- a 'relevant person' – ie, the person with care, non-resident parent or child applicant in Scotland (see below);
- someone who denies parentage of a child (see below);
- court officials (see below);
- the Department for Work and Pensions (DWP – see p37);
- HMRC (see p37);
- others, including employers, local authorities and banks (see p37).

Information or evidence can also be given to the CMS when there is no obligation to provide it – eg, from a relative, neighbour, GP or landlord. For information on disclosure by the CMS, see p52.

## A relevant person

All child support applicants must provide information required by the CMS to:[5]

- identify and trace a non-resident parent; *or*
- calculate, collect or recover child support.

The person with care and non-resident parent (or a parent treated as non-resident – see p13) must provide the information listed on p35, if requested.[6] A child applicant in Scotland must provide the same information, except information enabling the non-resident parent to be identified.[7]

If information is not provided by a person with care (or child applicant in Scotland), the application may be treated as withdrawn (see p27). If a non-resident parent does not supply the requested information, a 'default maintenance decision' may be made (see p125).

## Someone who denies parentage of a child

Someone who denies parentage of a child named in an application is required to give information:[8]

- to identify a non-resident parent; *or*
- to decide whether or not all the relevant people are habitually resident in the UK and, therefore, whether the CMS has jurisdiction.

This means, for example, that if the CMS only wants to identify someone as the non-resident parent, her/his employment details would not normally be necessary and so should not be requested until parentage is established.

## Court officials

Certain court officials can be required to give information for the purposes listed on p35 – eg, to allow the CMS to:[9]

- identify how much is payable under a court maintenance order;
- collect child support or maintenance under a court order;
- identify any proceedings about a court maintenance order;

- decide whether a maintenance order is in force that may affect whether an application can be made (see p18); *or*
- decide who has parental responsibility for the qualifying child if there is more than one person with care (see p10).

## The Department for Work and Pensions

Any DWP agency or anyone providing services to the DWP may give information held for benefit purposes to the CMS.[10]

## HM Revenue and Customs

There are specific arrangements for passing information about the non-resident parent's gross income from HMRC to the CMS (see p68).

In addition, HMRC can be required to disclose information or evidence for the purposes listed on p35.[11] Information provided can be used for any function related to child support. If a parent is self-employed, this also includes details of her/his taxable profits, gross receipts and expenses. It is unlawful for HMRC to give the CMS any other information.[12]

## Others

The CMS can also require the following to provide information for the purposes listed on p35:

- current or previous employers of the non-resident parent;[13]
- people or organisations for whom the non-resident parent provides, or has provided, goods or services under a contract.[14] This could include individuals, a company or partnership, or a government department, and means, for example, that a self-employed consultant could be traced and have her/his income investigated through companies for which s/he has provided services;
- a person who acts, or has acted, as the non-resident parent's accountant;[15]
- credit reference agencies;[16]
- the local authority in whose area either the non-resident parent or person with care lives or has lived.[17] The CMS may require the local authority to provide information, such as address and bank account details, relating to, for example, rent and council tax or a housing benefit claim;[18]
- the Driver and Vehicle Licensing Agency. In particular, it may be asked for information needed to trace the non-resident parent, and to collect and enforce payments;[19]
- prison authorities;[20]
- banks and building societies;[21]
- gas and electricity suppliers.[22]

## When must the information be provided

A person who has been requested to provide information must do so if that information or evidence is in her/his possession or s/he can reasonably be expected to acquire and provide it.[23]

The information must be provided as soon as it is reasonably practicable.[24] The CMS can allow information to be provided by a later date if it is satisfied that the delay is unavoidable.

See p29 for when documents are treated as having been sent and received.

## What happens if the correct information is not provided

It is a criminal offence for a person, without reasonable excuse, to fail to provide information, or to provide false information or allow false information to be provided.[25] All requests for information issued by the CMS must state this.[26]

If someone fails to provide information or provides false information, the CMS may decide not to process the application (see p27). If s/he is a non-resident parent, a default maintenance decision may be made (see p125). A decision based on her/his estimated income could be made in certain circumstances instead (see p72).

The CMS may also go to court, and a fine (currently up to £1,000) can be imposed. This is paid to the court, not to the CMS. A non-resident parent who fails to provide information may have both a default maintenance decision and a fine imposed. If a non-resident parent makes an application and the parent with care fails to provide information, the parent with care can be fined, although this would be rare.

If a parent does not give the required information, the CMS may ask another person for it – eg, her/his employer or accountant. As certain other people also have a duty to give information, the criminal sanctions also apply to them.

### Disputing the information required

A request for information can be challenged (see p190) if:
- it is not relevant to the reason for the request;
- it is of a very different kind from the examples given in the regulations;
- it is made to a person who cannot be required to give it; *or*
- the CMS has sufficient information to make a full calculation.

If this applies to you, explain this, preferably in writing, in order to avoid a penalty. A complaint could also be made (see Chapter 11).

# 2. Contacting the non-resident parent

When a new child support application is made, the applicant must verify the address of the non-resident parent and pay the application fee (see p23). The

Child Maintenance Service (CMS) must then notify the non-resident parent in writing as soon as reasonably practical. The notification asks about any information needed to make the calculation. The non-resident parent may dispute any of the facts relating to the application at this point (see p38). The date on which liability for child support usually starts (known as the 'initial effective date' – see p127) is specified in the notice. The CMS may telephone the non-resident parent on or before the initial effective date and then confirm this in writing to the parent's last known address. If the CMS does not telephone the parent, it must send written notice to her/his last known address at least two days before the initial effective date.[27] The initial effective date is usually expected to be two days after the written notice is issued.

If there is a long delay by the CMS in starting this process, the person with care could complain (see Chapter 11).

## Tracing the non-resident parent

The CMS can use its information-seeking powers (including contacting the people and agencies on pp35–37) to identify and trace the non-resident parent.

### Finding a reliable address

The CMS seeks to confirm the identity and address of the non-resident parent from information given by the person with care, Department for Work and Pensions (DWP) computer records and other methods. The CMS can decide that an address it holds for the non-resident parent can reliably be used as her/his current address, without having to establish it beyond all reasonable doubt.[28] If the DWP computer gives the non-resident parent's address and it is the same as that of the person with care, this is not considered reliable.

### Information from the person with care

When s/he applies for child support, the person with care is asked for the address of the non-resident parent, or for any information that could help trace her/him. This could include:

- her/his middle name(s) and any other names by which s/he may be known;
- other addresses at which s/he may have lived;
- her/his place of work and any previous employers;
- the name and address of her/his accountant;
- any benefit claims made; *and*
- if s/he has a car, the registration or make, model, colour and other details.

The CMS may contact the person with care again if additional information is required – eg, if parentage is disputed. A parent may be asked to provide a recent photograph of the non-resident parent if DNA testing may be involved, and to provide any relevant documents, such as a marriage certificate or expired passport. A person with care could also be asked other detailed questions – eg, whether the non-resident parent has ever lived with her/him. The CMS may contact friends and relatives with whom the non-resident parent may be living. If it does this, it must preserve confidentiality and should not disclose its interest.

The CMS does not normally offer face-to-face interviews (see p29), but these may be arranged if the CMS considers that the case involves complex issues and an interview may help to resolve them more quickly.

## Initial contact with the non-resident parent

The initial notification (see p38) to the non-resident parent that an application has been made includes a provisional child support calculation, based on the details provided by the applicant and information received by the CMS from HM Revenue and Customs (HMRC) or other parts of the DWP.[29] This is not a decision, but an illustration of the non-resident parent's child support liability based on the information the CMS currently has. It takes account of any information about shared care provided by the applicant.

The notification advises the non-resident parent of any information that s/he is required to provide for the child support calculation decision to be made. Details of the non-resident parent's income is normally provided to the CMS automatically by HMRC (see p68), unless HMRC has no income data or is unable to supply it, in which case the non-resident parent is asked for this.

A few days after issuing the notification, the CMS phones the non-resident parent to obtain information for the calculation decision. If the CMS is unable to contact the non-resident parent by telephone, a reminder notice is issued in writing. If there is no response from the parent after 14 days, the CMS may then make a default maintenance decision (see p125) or, in certain circumstances, a calculation based on estimated income (see p72).

**Note:** the CMS intends to obtain all (or most) of the information needed to work out child support by phone. If a non-resident parent prefers to be contacted in writing, s/he must request this.

If the parent is unaware of the child or is not named on the birth certificate, the CMS may try to arrange a face-to-face interview, although this is not expected to be done often.

There are special rules for young non-resident parents (see p41).

During the initial phone call, the non-resident parent may be asked questions in order to obtain or confirm any information needed to make a calculation. This information can also be provided by the parent in writing if s/he wishes.

For example, the non-resident parent may be asked to confirm:
- personal details – eg, name, address, other names used, phone number(s), national insurance (NI) number, date of birth and best contact times;
- details required to confirm whether the CMS has jurisdiction;
- whether s/he accepts parentage for the named qualifying child(ren);
- any means-tested benefits being claimed by, or for, her/him;

- student details, if appropriate – eg, name of college, course and qualification, and whether it is full or part time (evidence is requested);
- children who live with her/him – eg, date of birth, NI number (if appropriate) and who gets child benefit for the child (evidence is requested);
- details of any shared care and other special arrangements;
- employment details – eg, job title, employer (name, address and phone number), and start and end dates (if appropriate);
- income details – eg, frequency of pay, gross pay, bonuses and expenses (pay slips are requested);
- self-assessment form or tax calculation notice if the parent is self-employed;
- any other income – eg, pensions;
- payments made to a personal or private pension;
- collection details – eg, when the CMS will collect the child support and bank details, such as account number and sort code;
- representative details – eg, name, address, phone number and best contact times (signed authorisation is needed in certain circumstances).

The non-resident parent should be warned that a default maintenance decision (see p125), or in certain circumstances, a calculation based on an estimate of income, may be made if s/he fails to provide sufficient information to make a calculation. At various stages, s/he is given the opportunity to provide more information within at least seven days.

S/he must also be informed that failure to provide the information requested, or knowingly to provide false information, is a criminal offence (see p38).

Information given can be amended at any time before a calculation is made. See p196 for what happens if there is a change in circumstances after the effective date.

## Young non-resident parents

A face-to-face interview is likely to be arranged with a young non-resident parent – ie, one under 16 years of age (or aged 16–19 and treated as a child – see p8). No calculation can be made until the non-resident parent ceases to be treated as a child, but s/he is asked to confirm parentage for future reference. An adult must be present at the interview.

---

# 3. **Parentage investigations**

Disputes about whether someone is the parent (see p9) of a qualifying child can arise both before and after a child support calculation is made. The dispute can be about one or all of the qualifying children. Parentage is most commonly disputed by alleged non-resident fathers.

If the parentage of a qualifying child is denied or is in doubt, a child support application cannot be decided unless the Child Maintenance Service (CMS) can assume parentage (see p43) or parentage is determined.

An alleged non-resident parent may deny parentage during the initial phone contact with the CMS or in writing before a calculation is made.

The CMS can proceed with the calculation for any children for whom parentage is accepted or assumed while investigations are taking place for others.

The CMS carries out investigations to determine whether parentage may be established or assumed. Both the non-resident parent and person with care can submit evidence to resolve the matter, and may be interviewed (see p44). The qualifying child's other parent may also be interviewed if s/he is not the person with care. The CMS may seek a DNA test or court action to establish parentage. The person with care or alleged non-resident parent may also pursue court action at any time.

If an alleged non-resident parent accepts parentage when responding to CMS enquiries, neither the CMS nor the First-tier Tribunal can then cancel the child support calculation, unless a court decides that s/he is not, in fact, the parent.[30]

Once a calculation has been made, a non-resident parent who disputes parentage can request a revision (see Chapter 9). However, s/he must still pay child support until s/he provides conclusive evidence that s/he is not the parent.[31] At this stage, it is not sufficient to deny parentage: evidence must be provided to raise doubt – eg, if the parent with care was having another relationship when the child was conceived.

If the alleged non-resident parent provides evidence in the form of a previous negative DNA test or a declaration/declarator of parentage, this is sufficient proof.[32] The child support calculation is then cancelled and any payments made may be refunded. Whether or not all payments made are refunded may depend on how long after the calculation was made the parent disputed parentage, and a refund may only be made from the date when parentage was denied.[33]

If evidence provided by the alleged non-resident parent is not conclusive but raises a doubt about parentage, the parent with care is contacted by the CMS for comments on the non-resident parent's evidence.

• If the parent with care accepts that there may be doubt about parentage, a DNA test may be offered.

• If the parent with care disputes the non-resident parent's evidence, the decision is not revised. The non-resident parent is advised to obtain a DNA test or declaration/declarator of non-parentage; the CMS does not offer a DNA test in this case. The alleged non-resident parent is informed of her/his right to appeal to a court.

If a decision is not revised, the alleged non-resident parent may have to apply to the family court (in England and Wales) or the sheriff court (in Scotland) for a declaration/declarator of parentage. A decision to refuse to revise can be challenged (see Chapter 10), but parentage can only ultimately be established by the court.

## When someone is assumed to be a parent

If a person denies being the parent of a child, in certain circumstances the CMS must assume that s/he is the parent. (This does not apply if the child has subsequently been adopted by someone else.) S/he must then co-operate with the CMS, unless the CMS accepts proof that s/he is not, in fact, the parent of the child. The CMS must assume parentage if:[34]

- in England, Wales or Northern Ireland, a declaration of parentage or, in Scotland, a declarator of parentage, is in force for that person, including if the person with care or the CMS has applied to court for a declaration on whether the person is a parent of the child;[35]
- in Scotland,[36] England and Wales,[37] the person is a man who:
  – was married to the mother at any time between the child's conception and birth; *or*
  – acknowledged his paternity *and* was acknowledged by the mother *and* was named as the father on the birth certificate issued in the UK;
- the person is a man who was found to be the father by a court in England or Wales in proceedings under certain legal provisions (see Appendix 2). The court decision usually states the legal provision under which it was made;[38]
- the person is a man who was found by a court in Northern Ireland to be a father in proceedings under similar legal provisions to those in Appendix 2;[39]
- the person is a man who was found by a court in Scotland to be the father in any action for affiliation or aliment;[40]
- the person is a man who refuses to take a DNA test, or if the result of a test shows that he is the father (even if he refuses to accept it);[41]
- a parental order has been made in favour of that person following an application made within six months of a birth which is the result of a surrogacy arrangement;[42]
- certain types of fertility treatment have been carried out by a licensed clinic and the person is treated as a parent of the child under the Human Fertilisation and Embryology Acts 1990 and 2008.[43]

If none of the above applies, the CMS cannot make a calculation until parentage is admitted by a person or decided by a court.

If the alleged non-resident parent disputes that the rules apply (eg, s/he says the person named in a court order is someone else), s/he can appeal against the CMS decision. This appeal is dealt with by a magistrates'/sheriff court rather than by the First-tier Tribunal.[44]

If the alleged non-resident parent accepts that the rules apply, but disputes the correctness of the court order referred to by the CMS (eg, the court declaration/

declarator of parentage was wrong), s/he should consider applying to the court to set aside its order and/or making a late appeal against it. It is not possible to challenge a decision about parentage through the revision and and appeals process outlined in this *Handbook*.

If no one can be assumed to be a parent under these rules, the CMS usually attempts to arrange voluntary DNA testing or applies to court for a declaration/declarator of parentage.

## Interviews if parentage is disputed

If parentage is denied after the CMS's initial contact, the parent with care may be interviewed in order to establish the case to be put to the alleged non-resident parent. In other cases, sufficient information may already be available to contact the non-resident parent. However, both parties are interviewed before offering DNA tests (see p48) and, even if the parent with care has already been interviewed or parentage is assumed, s/he may be reinterviewed to see how s/he responds to the alleged non-resident parent's version of events. If the parent with care has already completed a parentage statement, s/he is only reinterviewed if the alleged non-resident parent has new evidence.

Interviews are usually conducted by phone. If someone does not want to be interviewed in this way, an interview may be conducted in the CMS office or at her/his home. It is not compulsory to take part in any interview, but see p35 for who can be required to provide certain information.

If the parent with care or alleged non-resident parent is under 16 (or 16–19 and treated as a child – see p8), her/his parent or guardian must consent to the application progressing. The young person must have a face-to-face interview in the presence of a parent or guardian. A child support calculation is not made for a young person in these circumstances, but a parentage statement is required for future use. Additional information may be sought about a young alleged non-resident parent to determine whether or not s/he should be treated as a child – eg, details of her/his current education or training.

### Interviewing the alleged non-resident parent

If the alleged non-resident parent denies parentage, s/he is asked whether s/he has evidence that s/he is not the parent. S/he may ask for further time to obtain documentary evidence: seven days is usually allowed.

If documentary evidence cannot be supplied, the person with care may be interviewed to gather her/his evidence. If no evidence can be provided to establish or assume parentage (see p43), the case may progress to DNA testing.

In an interview with an alleged father, the CMS could ask:

* whether he was in the country at any time between the date of conception and the child's birth;
* whether he had sex with the mother and, if so, over what period of time;

- if conception was assisted, whether he agreed to the treatment;
- how long the relationship lasted and whether he lived with the woman as husband and wife;
- whether or not he has had any contact with the child(ren);
- his reasons for thinking that he is not the father; *and*
- whether there is any other information that might support his view.

This is not an exhaustive list. The alleged non-resident parent need only answer such questions if he denies parentage and the information is needed to decide the issue.

The alleged non-resident parent is sent information about disputing parentage and the reduced-cost DNA test (see p46) before the interview. At the interview, the possibility of DNA testing is explained and his agreement sought.[45]

Interviewing officers should take notes, and details of the interview (including any statement made by the non-resident parent) should be recorded.

If the alleged non-resident parent does not comply with requests to be interviewed, the CMS may consider a home visit or court action.

If the alleged non-resident parent accepts parentage, the CMS proceeds to make a child support calculation.

## Interviewing the parent with care

If someone has been named as the parent of a qualifying child and denies it, the CMS informs the parent with care of this and explains the procedures that follow.

The parent with care is asked for any documentary evidence from which the CMS could assume parentage – eg, a birth or marriage certificate.[46] S/he is also questioned about her/his relationship with the alleged non-resident parent.

If no evidence can be provided to establish or assume parentage, the parent with care is asked whether s/he is willing to take a DNA test (see p46).

The CMS asks about the alleged relationship and the circumstances of conception and birth. A mother who is the parent with care is likely to be asked personal questions including:

- the place the child was born and whether the pregnancy was full term;
- who are named as the child's parents on the birth certificate;
- the man's reaction to the pregnancy;
- whether she and the alleged non-resident parent ever lived together and, if so, when and where;
- whether she considered them to be a couple at the time the child was conceived;
- whether the alleged non-resident parent has ever acknowledged the child;
- whether the alleged non-resident parent has ever paid any maintenance;
- whether there is, or has been, any contact with his family;
- whether she has any letters or cards acknowledging the child, or witnesses to her association with the alleged non-resident parent;

- whether the child's conception was assisted and, if so, whether the man agreed to the treatment and gave notice of this;
- whether she has any photographs of him; *and*
- whether she is willing to give evidence in court.

If you are a parent with care and consider the question(s) inappropriate, you should question their relevance. If the interviewer insists, you could ask to end the interview to consider whether or not to provide the information. You can ask the interviewer to write down the questions and the reason for them. If, at the interview or later, you refuse to answer any of the questions, you should indicate that you have given all the information that is necessary to trace and identify the father.

A parent with care may also be asked to make a parentage statement. You can refuse to sign this and the refusal forms part of the evidence, along with any reasons given. You may ask for a copy of the parentage statement and your reasons for not signing it. The statement is added to the report of the interview and can be used in court proceedings (see p48).

### Interviewing a person with care who is not the parent
If both parents are non-resident and an alleged non-resident parent continues to deny parentage after an interview, the person with care may be interviewed. The questions depend on the person with care's relationship with the alleged parents – eg, a grandparent may know the length of the relationship between the parents. S/he is asked for the addresses of both parents, and any letters or cards from them. S/he is also asked why s/he is looking after the child(ren), whether there is any documentation about the care arrangements and whether s/he gives her/his consent for the child(ren) in her/his care to undergo a DNA test (see below) if s/he has parental responsibility.

## DNA testing
DNA testing involves taking a cell sample from the parent with care, alleged non-resident parent and qualifying child. The test establishes the genetic fingerprint of the individual and is virtually conclusive. The test is usually done by taking a cheek cell sample from the inside of the mouth using a swab. It is possible for blood to be taken for the DNA test instead, but all parties must use the same method. If young children are involved, a cheek cell sample is usually preferred.

DNA testing is used when parentage cannot be assumed and the parties involved give their consent. If the CMS has applied to a court for a declaration/declarator of parentage, the court may order DNA testing.

The CMS arranges the DNA test. An alleged non-resident parent can also choose to arrange his own test (see p48).[47]

## Consent

If there is a dispute about parentage, both the parent with care and the alleged non-resident parent are asked to agree to a DNA test. Written consent must be obtained before a test can be carried out. If the qualifying child is under 16, her/his parent or guardian must give consent.

There are consequences if someone refuses to take the test.

- If the parent with care accepts DNA testing, but refuses consent for the child, a court can direct DNA testing if it is in the best interests of the child, but it cannot force the child to take the test.
- An alleged non-resident parent may be assumed to be the parent (see p43).[48]
- If a non-resident parent already assumed to be the parent refuses to take a test, the CMS does not revise the calculation.
- If a child support applicant refuses consent for her/himself and/or a qualifying child, the case may be closed.
- There is no guidance on what happens when a parent or guardian of a child applicant in Scotland refuses consent, but Department for Work and Pensions policy indicates that action may be taken to get a declarator of parentage.

The reason for any refusal must be explored. As the DNA test usually involves taking a cheek cell sample, any objections (eg, to blood tests on medical or religious grounds) may not be viable.

If the alleged non-resident parent agrees to the test, but fails to attend the appointment, parentage is assumed unless there are good reasons – eg, he was in hospital, did not receive the test notification or was ill.

If a qualifying child aged 16 or over refuses consent, the non-resident parent must apply to the court for a declaration/declarator of non-parentage.

## Paying for a DNA test arranged by the Child Maintenance Service

If he is found to be the father, an alleged non-resident parent is responsible for the costs of tests arranged by the CMS. He is responsible for the costs for himself, the parent with care and the child(ren). If he is found not to be the father, a full refund of the cost of the test is made.[49]

At the time this *Handbook* was written, the fee for a test arranged by the CMS was £239.40. The fee is higher if more than one child is tested.[50]

If the alleged non-resident parent says he cannot afford to pay for the test before a calculation is made, the CMS may pay for it, provided he agrees to accept the results and to repay the fee should the test show that he is the father. If he still refuses to take the DNA test, parentage may be assumed (see p43).

The CMS can recover the costs of the test from the alleged non-resident parent if the test does not exclude him from being the father and:[51]

- he does not now deny that he is the father; *or*
- a court has now made a declaration/declarator of parentage.

## Private testing

An alleged non-resident parent may choose to arrange the test himself. In the meantime, the CMS may still assume parentage if the CMS test has been refused.[52] Prices vary depending on which company is used, but are likely to be higher than for a test arranged by the CMS. If the alleged parent has arranged a test himself, the fee is not refunded if the test proves negative.

The test must be carried out by an approved agency and proper security measures must be in place; otherwise, even if the test is negative, the CMS and court may not accept the result.[53]

Tests must involve the parent with care; a test with only the alleged non-resident parent and the qualifying child is not accepted. No action can be taken against a parent with care who does not consent to a private test. If the alleged non-resident parent cannot arrange a private test because he does not know the address of the parent with care, the CMS does not provide contact details.

## DNA test results

Once the DNA-testing company has received all the samples, the test usually takes 10 days. The results are sent by post to the parent with care, the alleged non-resident parent and the CMS. The results are confidential and are not given by phone.[54]

If the alleged non-resident parent is shown to be the parent, he is also sent notification by the CMS. The CMS also asks for any additional information needed. (The 'effective date' of liability for child support remains the date two days after the original notification of the application was sent – see p127.) If the alleged non-resident parent still does not accept parentage, he must take court action to obtain a declaration/declarator of non-parentage. The CMS may make a calculation (or, if already made, refuse to revise one) because a positive DNA test is grounds to assume parentage.

If the DNA tests confirm that the person who took the test as the alleged non-resident parent is not the parent, action is taken to confirm the identity of the person tested. If the alleged non-resident parent sent someone else to take the test, the CMS passes the case to the fraud team. If the wrong person has been traced, the CMS pursues further tracing. If the identity is confirmed, the parent with care may be reinterviewed about any other possible non-resident parent.[55]

## Court proceedings

When all possible action and investigations have been completed, the CMS decides whether to apply to a court for a declaration/declarator of parentage.[56] Court action is rare, as there are other ways of being able to assume parentage (see p43). Examples of situations where court action may be taken include:

* if a DNA test is inconclusive;
* cases involving fertility treatment where an alleged non-resident father denies he consented to the treatment;

- if the parent with care disputes the non-resident parent's non-conclusive evidence after a child support calculation has been made. In this case, the non-resident parent must apply to court (the CMS may not be involved in this action, but may be informed of the outcome).

If the CMS decides not to take court action, the person with care may initiate proceedings her/himself.[57] The person with care or non-resident parent may start court proceedings at any time.

The CMS or the person with care can apply to court for a declaration/declarator of parentage. If the CMS is willing to do so, usually the person with care should not also apply, because s/he will probably have to pay her/his own legal costs (and those of the alleged non-resident parent) if s/he loses (see below). If the CMS suspends the case, but the person with care wants to go to court her/himself, s/he should obtain legal advice.

Only the courts have the power to order blood tests (including DNA tests – see p46) in any civil proceedings in which parentage is an issue.[58] If convinced that blood testing would be against the child's interests, the court should not order it.[59] A court can direct that blood tests be used to establish whether or not someone is a parent of the child, but cannot force anyone to give a blood sample. It can, however, overrule a child's lack of consent if it believes it is in the child's interests.[60] However, the court may draw its own adverse conclusions if a person fails to comply, depending on the circumstances of the case.[61] The costs of testing ordered by the court are treated as the costs of the party who applied for the testing.[62] However, if that person wins the case, the court usually orders the losing party to pay costs, which can include the costs of any test. In Scotland, if an alleged non-resident parent applies for a declarator of non-parentage and the CMS does not defend the action, no expenses can be awarded against the CMS.[63]

## Outcome of the court proceedings

If no child support calculation has been made, once a declaration/declarator of parentage is issued, the CMS contacts the non-resident parent to gather the information needed to make it.[64]

If the court finds that the person is not the parent, the parent with care is approached to establish whether a different alleged non-resident parent can be named.[65] Unless the parent can name an alternate alleged non-resident parent, the case may be closed.

The court can order any party to pay some, or all, of the legal costs of another party – eg, solicitors' fees. Usually, the losing party is ordered to pay the other party's costs.

# 4. Further investigations

The Child Maintenance Service (CMS) may make further enquiries when considering an application. In practice, the CMS usually makes no further investigations if:

- parentage is accepted; *and*
- information is provided to make a calculation; *and*
- any documents requested are provided – eg, a copy of a maintenance agreement, pay slips or a tax calculation notice.

Even if one parent challenges the details provided by the other, the CMS may be reluctant to make any further enquiries unless the parent can provide sufficient evidence to give it reasonable grounds for a revision or supersession to be considered.

The CMS should not request any corroboration of evidence (ie, other evidence to support what the CMS already has), unless the evidence the CMS has is self-contradictory, improbable or contradicted by other evidence.[66]

## Verifying information

The CMS may want to check certain information provided by a parent.

For how the CMS verifies the non-resident parent's gross income, see p68.

**Note:** it is an offence for a person who is required to provide information to fail, without reasonable excuse, to do so, or to provide false information or allow false information to be provided (see p38).

## Asking the Child Maintenance Service to investigate

The CMS does not have a general duty to investigate issues relating to child support applications. However, it may be under a duty to obtain information that is available to it but not to the applicant.[67] The CMS may also be under a duty to investigate if there is a contradiction in the evidence.

In some cases, one of the parties in the child support application may not be satisfied with the way the CMS has investigated the case. If, at any stage, you believe that the CMS ought to make more enquiries, you should ask it to do so. Phone the CMS and explain all the information, ask what enquiries have already been made and suggest further ones. Refer to the CMS's power to request information (see p34) and to use an inspector to conduct investigations (see p51). If the CMS refuses to say what steps have been taken or to make further enquiries, a complaint can be made (see Chapter 11) and judicial review may be possible (see p190).

If an appeal has been made, the First-tier Tribunal can also make enquiries (see Chapter 10). It has more powers than the CMS and it may be easier to persuade it to use them.

A person who is dissatisfied with CMS enquiries can also make her/his own and pass the information to the CMS – eg, a person with care applying for a court order for maintenance may obtain information about the non-resident parent's circumstances.

## Inspectors

The CMS can appoint inspectors to obtain the information it requires.[68] The inspector must have a certificate of appointment, which must be produced when entering premises.[69]

Inspectors can enter premises (except those used only as a home) to make enquiries and to inspect documents. 'Premises' can include vehicles, aircraft, moveable structures and offshore installations. Inspectors cannot enter premises by force. The premises that can be entered include ones where:[70]

- the non-resident parent is, or has been, employed;
- the non-resident parent carries out, or has carried out, a trade;
- there is information held by someone whom the inspector has reasonable grounds for suspecting has information about the non-resident parent acquired in the course of her/his own trade, profession, vocation or business.

An inspector can question any person aged 18 or over found on the premises and request information and documents s/he might reasonably require from:[71]

- an occupier of the premises;
- an employer or employee working there;
- anyone else whose work or business is based there;
- an employee or agent of any of the above.

No one is required to give any evidence or answer any question that might incriminate her/him or her/his spouse or civil partner. Deliberately delaying or obstructing an inspector from carrying out her/his duties is an offence. Failing or refusing to answer a question or to provide the evidence requested is also an offence, unless there is a good reason for not doing so. The maximum fine is currently £1,000.[72]

A solicitor is entitled to claim 'privilege' concerning information about a client's confidential affairs and can refuse to give information. The CMS has also given assurances that the powers of inspectors will not be used for other representatives – eg, an adviser. This does not apply to information required from an employer about an employee.

---

# 5. Change of circumstances

There is no general duty to give information about any change of circumstances to the Child Maintenance Service (CMS).

However, in some circumstances, there is a duty to disclose information to the CMS if the CMS has the right to request the information.

- The non-resident parent must notify the CMS within seven days if s/he changes address.[73] If s/he does not do so, s/he may have committed a criminal offence and a fine (currently up to £1,000) may be imposed.[74] The non-resident parent must also inform the CMS of certain changes when a deduction from earnings order is in force (see p158). In certain circumstances, the CMS may also require the non-resident parent to notify it of increases in her/his gross income (see p77).
- A person with care has a duty to tell the CMS if s/he believes that a calculation has ceased to have effect.[75] This may be because:
  - a relevant person (ie, the person with care, non-resident parent or qualifying child) has died;
  - a relevant person is no longer within CMS jurisdiction – ie, s/he is not habitually resident in the UK (see p16);
  - the non-resident parent is no longer a non-resident parent of the child(ren) named in the calculation – eg, because the child has been adopted;
  - a child no longer counts as a child, or as a qualifying child (see p8); *or*
  - the person with care has stopped being a person with care in relation to the child(ren) named in the calculation.

The person with care must give the reasons for her/his belief in writing, and may be required to give further information to allow a decision to be made.

The person with care is not required to inform the CMS until the change has taken place.

For the consequences of failing to disclose information when required, see p38.

In practice, any party may want to tell the CMS of changes or new information that may affect the amount of child support payable.

# 6. **Disclosure of information**

In the course of its investigations, the Child Maintenance Service (CMS) collects information and evidence about people affected by child support applications. The non-resident parent and person with care (and a child applicant in Scotland) must be given details of how the amount of child support has been worked out (see p126). Some other forms of disclosure are part of the CMS's duties, such as giving information to courts, the First-tier Tribunal, other parts of the Department for Work and Pensions (DWP) and local authorities.

The CMS may disclose information given to it by one party (see p53) to a child support calculation to another party to explain:[76]

- why an application for child support, or for revision or supersession of a decision, has been rejected;

- why an application cannot proceed or why a calculation will not be made;
- why a calculation has been cancelled or ceases to have effect;
- how the amount of child support has been worked out;
- why a decision has been made not to collect child support, or to stop collection;
- why a particular method of enforcement has been used;
- why enforcement methods have not been used or enforcement has ceased;
- why a decision has been made not to accept part-payment for arrears;
- why a decision has been made not to write off arrears in certain circumstances.

*Parties*

For the purposes of the CMS's disclosure of information, the 'parties' are the person who made the application for child support (which, in Scotland, could include a qualifying child aged 12 or over), the person with care, the non-resident parent and a qualifying child.[77] If one of these people has died, and a revision, supersession, appeal or variation request is pending but not decided at the date of death, a representative who was dealing with the request on behalf of the person is also a party.[78]

Any request for the above information must be made in writing to the CMS, giving reasons.[79] However, the CMS can provide the information without a request.

The CMS must only disclose a person's address (or other information which could reasonably be expected to lead to that person being located) if the person concerned has given written permission.[80] (If you are appealing, you should notify the First-tier Tribunal if you do not want your address or other information disclosed – see Chapter 10.[81]) Also, the CMS must not disclose information which could reasonably be expected to lead to the identification of any person other than a person with care, non-resident parent or a qualifying child.[82]

The CMS can disclose any information to the First-tier Tribunal, court and anyone with a right of appeal, if it is for proceedings under the child support or benefits legislation.[83]

In practice, in a child support appeal, CMS papers are included in the CMS submission sent to each party (see p204). The CMS can also disclose information to a court which has made, varied or revived a maintenance order or agreement, if that information is required in relation to those proceedings or other matters arising from them.[84] The CMS can also disclose information to local authorities for their use in administering housing benefit.[85]

In certain circumstances, the CMS can also disclose information about the non-resident parent to a credit reference agency (see p54).

Otherwise, information cannot be given to third parties without the written permission of the person to whom it relates. Any unauthorised disclosure of information is a criminal offence (see p55).

If you want to see a copy of information about you held by the CMS, you can apply in writing. This information must be supplied without delay, and normally within one month of the request at the latest.[86] It should be provided free of charge (but a reasonable fee based on the administrative costs of providing the information may be charged if a request is unfounded or excessive, particularly if it is repetitive). If you have concerns about the collection, retention, accuracy or use of this information, you can contact the Information Commissioner's Office.[87]

## Disclosure to other government departments

The CMS can disclose information to government departments dealing with benefits, including DWP agencies.[88] This includes information obtained using its powers and information disclosed to the CMS voluntarily.

As the DWP has close links with the Home Office, disclosure may create problems for people from abroad and those prohibited from having recourse to public funds. If you have doubts about whether information should be disclosed to the CMS, get advice first from a law centre or independent advice centre dealing with immigration issues (see Appendix 3). You cannot be prosecuted for refusing to give information unless it was requested by the CMS or an inspector (see p51).

CMS staff can exchange information with their counterparts in Northern Ireland and vice versa.

## Disclosure to credit reference agencies

In certain circumstances, the CMS can disclose information about a non-resident parent to credit reference agencies. This information can then be used by the agencies in the credit assessment of individuals. This means that any arrears of child support are likely to have the same effect on a parent's credit assessment as other debts s/he may have.

The parent must consent to the information being passed to the agency, unless a liability order (see p174) is in force against her/him.[89]

The following information can be passed to a credit reference agency:[90]
- the parent's name, last known or notified address and date of birth;
- the CMS reference number for the parent's case;
- the date any liability order in force against the parent was made;
- the amount covered by the liability order;
- the address stated in the liability order, if different from the last known or notified address.

Before passing any information to an agency, the CMS must notify the parent in writing by post to her/his last known or notified address (if s/he can be traced) that it intends to do so. The notification must be sent at least 21 days before the information is given to an agency.[91]

The CMS can also tell a credit reference agency without first notifying the non-resident parent:[92]
- that the amount covered by the liability order has been paid, and the date it was paid;
- that a liability order against the parent has been 'set aside' or quashed.

## Unauthorised disclosure

Unauthorised disclosure of information is a criminal offence. This offence applies to anyone who is, or has been, a child support officer, a DWP employee working for the CMS, a civil servant carrying out a function under the Child Support Acts (eg, a Jobcentre Plus officer helping the CMS make enquiries), First-tier Tribunal staff, various Ombudsmen and their staff, staff at the National Audit Office and anyone who, whether or not a civil servant, is providing services to the DWP.[93] It does not apply to members of the First-tier and Upper Tribunals.

It is not an offence to disclose information if:[94]
- the CMS can do so, or already has done so, under any legal requirement or court order;
- it is in the form of a summary or statistics and it cannot be related to any particular person; *or*
- the person to whom the information relates gives consent or, if that person's affairs are being dealt with under a power of attorney, a receiver under the Mental Health Act, a mental health appointee or a Scottish mental health guardian, the attorney, receiver, guardian or appointee gives consent.

A person who has broken these rules has a defence if s/he can prove that s/he believed s/he was making the disclosure under these rules, or believed that disclosure under these rules had already been made, and had no reason to think otherwise.[95]

On summary conviction, the maximum sentence is six months' imprisonment and/or a fine (in Scotland, the fine is limited to a maximum of £10,000). On conviction on indictment, the maximum sentence is two years' imprisonment and/or a fine.[96]

# Notes

## 1. Information-seeking powers

1 s14 and Sch 2 CSA 1991
2 s12 CSPSSA 2000
3 Reg 4(1) CSI Regs
4 Reg 7(1) CSI Regs
5 ss4(4) and 7(5) CSA 1991; reg 3 CSI Regs
6 Regs 3 and 4 CSI Regs
7 Reg 3(2) CSI Regs
8 Reg 5 CSI Regs
9 Reg 6 CSI Regs
10 See s3 SSA 1998
11 Sch 2 para 1 CSA 1991; Sch 6 para 2 CMOPA 2008
12 s6 and Sch 1 Taxes Management Act 1970; s182 Finance Act 1989
13 Reg 4(2)(b) and (3) CSI Regs
14 Reg 4(2)(c) and (3) CSI Regs
15 Reg 4(2)(d) CSI Regs
16 Reg 4(2)(f) CSI Regs – credit reference agencies are as defined by s145(8) Consumer Credit Act 1974 and Art 89B Financial Services and Markets Act 2000 (Regulated Activities) Order 2001, No.544
17 Reg 4(2)(g) CSI Regs
18 s122D SSAA 1992
19 Reg 4(2)(h)(i) CSI Regs
20 Reg 4(2)(h)(ii) CSI Regs
21 Reg 4(2)(i) CSI Regs
22 Reg 4(j) and (k) CSI Regs
23 Reg 7(1) CSI Regs
24 Reg 7(2) CSI Regs
25 s14A CSA 1991
26 Reg 8 CSI Regs

## 2. Contacting the non-resident parent

27 Regs 7, 11 and 12 CSMC Regs
28 CCS/2288/2005
29 Child Maintenance and Enforcement Commission, *The Child Support Maintenance Calculation Regulations 2012: a technical consultation on the draft regulations*, December 2011

## 3. Parentage investigations

30 R(CS) 13/98
31 CMS leaflet CMSB010GB, *What Happens When Someone Denies They Are the Parent of a Child?*, October 2013
32 CMS leaflet CMSB010GB, *What Happens When Someone Denies They Are the Parent of a Child?*, October 2013
33 CMS leaflet CMSB010GB, *What Happens When Someone Denies They Are the Parent of a Child?*, October 2013
34 s26 CSA 1991
35 Under ss55A or 56 Family Law Act 1986, Art 32 Matrimonial and Family Proceedings (Northern Ireland) Order 1989, No.677(NI4) or s7 LR(PC)(S)A 1986
36 s26(2) CSA 1991, Case E; s5(1) LR(PC)(S)A 1986
37 s26(2) CSA 1991, Cases A1 and A2
38 s26(2) CSA 1991, Case F(a)(i) in 'relevant proceedings' under s12(5) Civil Evidence Act 1968 or affiliation proceedings
39 s26(2) CSA 1991, Case F(a)(i) in 'relevant proceedings' under s8(5) Civil Evidence Act (Northern Ireland) 1971 or affiliation proceedings
40 s26(2) CSA 1991, Case F(a)(ii) in affiliation proceedings
41 s26(2) CSA 1991, Case A3
42 s26(2) CSA 1991, Case B
43 s26(2) CSA 1991, Case B1
44 **E&W** Arts 3 and 4 CSA(JC)O
   **S** Arts 2 and 3 CSA(JC)(S)O
45 CMS leaflet CMSB010GB, *What Happens When Someone Denies They Are the Parent of a Child?*, October 2013
46 CMS leaflet CMSB010GB, *What Happens When Someone Denies They Are the Parent of a Child?*, October 2013
47 CMS leaflet CMSB010GB, *What Happens When Someone Denies They Are the Parent of a Child?*, October 2013
48 s26 CSA 1991, Case A3(b)
49 CMS leaflet CMSB010GB, *What Happens When Someone Denies They Are the Parent of a Child?*, October 2013
50 www.gov.uk/get-dna-test
51 s27A CSA 1991
52 CMS leaflet CMSB010GB, *What Happens When Someone Denies They Are the Parent of a Child?*, October 2013
53 For a current list of accredited agencies, see www.gov.uk/get-dna-test.

54 CMS leaflet CMSB010GB, *What Happens When Someone Denies They Are the Parent of a Child?*, October 2013
55 CMS leaflet CMSB010GB, *What Happens When Someone Denies They Are the Parent of a Child?*, October 2013
56 s27 CSA 1991
57 ss27 and 28 CSA 1991
58 s20 FLRA 1969; *Re H (Paternity: Blood Test)* [1996] 2 FLR 65
59 *W v Official Solicitor* [1972] AC 24
60 s21 FLRA 1969
61 s23 FLRA 1969; *Re A (Paternity: Refusal of Blood Test)* [1994] 2 FLR 463
62 s20(6) FLRA 1969
63 s28(2) CSA 1991; s7 LR(PC)(S)A 1986; r152 AS(CSA) (AOCSCR), inserting Act of Sederunt (Sheriff Court Ordinary Cause Rules), 1993, No.1956 (S.223), Chapter 33.89
64 CMS leaflet CMSB010GB, *What Happens When Someone Denies They Are the Parent of a Child?*, October 2013
65 CMS leaflet CMSB010GB, *What Happens When Someone Denies They Are the Parent of a Child?*, October 2013

4. **Further investigations**
66 *DB v CMEC* [2010] UKUT 356 (AAC)
67 *DB v CMEC* [2010] UKUT 356 (AAC), citing R(SF) 1/04
68 s15(1) CSA 1991
69 s15(8) CSA 1991
70 s15(4), (4A) and (11) CSA 1991
71 s15(5) and (6) CSA 1991
72 s15(7) and (9) CSA 1991

5. **Change of circumstances**
73 Reg 9 CSI Regs
74 s14A CSA 1991
75 Reg 10 CSI Regs

6. **Disclosure of information**
76 Reg 13 CSI Regs; R(CS) 1/00
77 Reg 13(2)(a) and (b) CSI Regs
78 Reg 13(2)(d) CSI Regs
79 Reg 13(3) CSI Regs
80 Reg 13(4) CSI Regs
81 r19(3) TP(FT) Rules
82 Reg 13(4) CSI Regs
83 Reg 12 CSI Regs
84 Reg 12(3) CSI Regs
85 s122C(2)(a) SSAA 1992
86 EU Reg 2016/679, with effect from 25 May 2018
87 https://ico.org.uk
88 s3 SSA 1998
89 s49D CSA 1991

90 Reg 14A(1)(a)-(e) CSI Regs
91 Reg 14A(2) and (3) CSI Regs
92 Reg 14A(1)(f) and (g) and (2) CSI Regs
93 s50 CSA 1991; reg 14 CSI Regs
94 s50 CSA 1991
95 s50(3) CSA 1991
96 s50(4) CSA 1991

# Chapter 4

Calculating the amount of child support

This chapter covers:
1. The rates of child support (below)
2. The non-resident parent's income (p67)
3. Shared care (p79)

---

## 1. The rates of child support

There are four rates of child support:
- nil rate (see p59);
- flat rate (see p60);
- reduced rate (see p61);
- basic rate, including 'basic rate plus' (see p62).

The amount of child support calculated is a weekly amount. In all cases, fractions of a penny are disregarded if they are less than a half, or rounded up to the next penny if a half or over.[1]

If there is more than one non-resident parent, child support is calculated for each separately. This means that a person with care could receive, for example, the flat rate of child support from one non-resident parent and an amount worked out using the basic rate from another. If there is more than one person with care, see below.

**Note:** the child support calculation can be varied in certain circumstances – eg, if the non-resident parent has certain special expenses or additional income. See Chapter 5 for details.

### If there is more than one person with care

If there is more than one person with care, each caring for a different qualifying child in relation to a non-resident parent, the amount of child support may be apportioned between them in relation to the number of qualifying children each person cares for.[2]

Apportionment occurs after child support has been calculated at the appropriate rate, but before any decrease for shared care (see p79).[3]

In basic and reduced rate cases, if an adjustment is made that reduces the non-resident parent's liability to less than £7 (eg, because of shared care or a variation), the amount payable is £7 apportioned between the people with care.[4]

Child support liability is calculated for only one person with care in respect of each qualifying child. If, in practice, another person who is not the non-resident parent provides care for a qualifying child, the Child Maintenance Service (CMS) does not apportion the child support between them. The person with care who receives the child support could agree to pass some of it on to any other person who also provides care for the child. However, this would be an informal agreement and would not be monitored or enforced by the CMS.

## Nil rate

Some non-resident parents do not need to pay any child support. This 'nil rate' applies if the non-resident parent:[5]

- is a child (see p8 for the meaning of 'child');
- is a prisoner (including if serving a prison sentence and detained in hospital);
- is 16 or 17 years old and receiving income support (IS), income-based jobseeker's allowance (JSA) or income-related employment and support allowance (ESA) (or s/he is a member of a couple and her/his partner is receiving one of these benefits for her/him);
- is 16 or 17 years old and receiving universal credit (UC) calculated on the basis that s/he has no earned income (or s/he is a member of a couple and her/his partner is receiving UC calculated on this basis);
- receives an allowance for work-based training for young people. Young people may receive a training allowance or (in Scotland and Wales) an education maintenance allowance;
- is resident in a care home or independent hospital, or being provided with a care home service or/and independent healthcare service, and receives one of the prescribed benefits for the flat rate (see p60) or has all or part of the cost of her/his accommodation met by a local authority;
- has a gross income (including income from any of the prescribed benefits for the flat rate) of less than £7 a week.

*Example 4.1*
Kerry is a parent with care of two children, Mia and Lewis. Her ex-partner, Craig, is in prison. In this case, the nil rate applies. When he comes out of prison, Kerry could ask for a supersession as their circumstances have changed.

## Flat rate

A 'flat rate' of £7 a week applies if the non-resident parent does not qualify for the nil rate and:[6]
- her/his weekly income is £100 or less; *or*
- s/he receives one of the following benefits:[7]
  - Category A, B, C or D retirement pension;
  - state pension;
  - incapacity benefit;
  - contributory ESA;
  - carer's allowance;
  - maternity allowance;
  - severe disablement allowance;
  - industrial injuries benefit;
  - widowed mother's or widowed parent's allowance;
  - widow's pension;
  - contribution-based JSA;
  - a training allowance (other than for work-based learning for young people);
  - war disablement pension;
  - war widow's, war widower's or surviving civil partner's war pension;
  - payments under the Armed Forces Compensation Scheme;
  - a social security benefit paid by a country other than the UK;
  - IS, income-based JSA, income-related ESA, UC calculated on the basis that s/he does not have any earned income, or pension credit (PC) (or her/his partner receives one of these benefits).

The flat rate can be halved if the non-resident parent's partner is also a non-resident parent with a child support application in force, and receives IS, income-based JSA, income-related ESA, UC calculated on the basis that s/he does not have any earned income, or PC. Each pays £3.50.[8] If the non-resident parent is in a polygamous relationship and there is more than one partner who is also a non-resident parent and the non-resident parent or her/his partner receives one of these benefits, each is liable to pay £3.50 a week.

If there is more than one person with care caring for different qualifying children, the flat rate is apportioned between them (see p58).

**Note:** the flat rate is not reduced to take account of any relevant other children (see p64) or relevant non-resident children (see p65).

There are special rules about shared care (see p81).

*Example 4.2*

Craig from Example 4.1 has now come out of prison and gets income-based JSA. Kerry requests a supersession and Craig has a flat rate of £7 child support deducted from his benefit each week.

If Craig moved in with a new partner, Joan, and claimed income-based JSA as a couple, the flat rate of £7 would still apply and Kerry would receive £7 a week. However, if Joan were also a non-resident parent, the flat rate would be halved. In this case, Kerry would receive £3.50 a week.

# Reduced rate

The reduced rate applies if the non-resident parent does not qualify for the flat rate or the nil rate and her/his weekly gross income is less than £200 but more than £100. The flat rate of £7 is added to a percentage of the parent's income between £100 and £200[9] – eg, if gross income is £150, the percentage is applied to £50. The percentage depends on the number of qualifying children (see p8), including any relevant non-resident children (see p65) the non-resident parent has, as well as the number of other children who live with her/him ('relevant other children' – see p64).[10]

*Reduced rate percentages*

| Number of relevant other children | Number of qualifying children (including relevant non-resident children) | | |
|---|---|---|---|
| | One | Two | Three or more |
| None | 17% | 25% | 31% |
| One | 14.1% | 21.2% | 26.4% |
| Two | 13.2% | 19.9% | 24.9% |
| Three or more | 12.4% | 18.9% | 23.8% |

## Step one

Work out the gross weekly income between £100 and £200.

## Step two

Work out the relevant percentage. Apply this percentage to the income worked out in Step one and add this to £7.

## Step three

If different qualifying children are cared for by different people with care, apportion the amount worked out in Step two between them, depending on the number of qualifying children each cares for.

*Example 4.3*

Simon is due to pay child support to Fiona for two qualifying children, Harry and Lily. Simon lives with his new partner, Julie, and their baby, Paul. Paul is a relevant other child. Simon's gross income is £180 a week. The reduced rate of child support applies.

**Step one:** Gross weekly income = £180

Income between £100 and £200 = £80

**Step two:** Relevant percentage for one relevant other child and two qualifying children is 21.2 per cent.

£7 + (21.2% x £80) = £7 + £16.96 = £23.96

Simon is due to pay £23.96 child support a week to Fiona.

If Lily was being cared for by Fiona and Harry stayed with his grandmother, there would still be two qualifying children, each cared for by a different person with care. The child support calculated would need to be apportioned between them.

**Step three:** Each person cares for one qualifying child, so the child support is divided by two.

£23.96 ÷ 2 = £11.98

Simon now pays Fiona £11.98 and the grandmother £11.98.

If the non-resident parent shares the care of any qualifying children, the reduced rate may be decreased by applying the shared care rules (see p82).

## Basic rate

The basic rate applies if none of the other rates (nil, flat or reduced) apply.[11]

If the non-resident parent has a gross weekly income of £200 or more, child support is calculated using the basic rate. If her/his gross weekly income is over £800, the 'basic rate plus' applies.

The basic rate is a percentage of the non-resident parent's gross weekly income, depending on the number of qualifying children (see p8), including the number of any relevant non-resident children (see p65), s/he has.

If the non-resident parent has other children living with her/him (relevant other children – see p64), her/his gross income is reduced before the basic rate is calculated. The basic rate is therefore worked out in two steps.

*Basic rate percentages*[12]

| Number of qualifying children (including relevant non-resident children) | Percentage of gross income up to £800 | Percentage of gross income above £800 |
| --- | --- | --- |
| One | 12% | 9% |
| Two | 16% | 12% |
| Three or more | 19% | 15% |

## Step one

Work out the gross weekly income of the non-resident parent. Reduce this by the appropriate percentage, depending on the number of relevant other children s/he has.

*Basic rate: reduction in gross income for relevant other children*[13]

| Number of relevant other children | Percentage by which gross income is reduced |
|---|---|
| One | 11% |
| Two | 14% |
| Three or more | 16% |

## Step two

Work out the amount of child support as a proportion of the gross income calculated in Step one, depending on the number of qualifying children (including any relevant non-resident children).

- If gross weekly income is £800 a week or less, the basic rate of child support is 12 per cent, 16 per cent or 19 per cent of this gross income.
- If gross income is over £800 a week, the 'basic rate plus' of child support is 12 per cent, 16 per cent or 19 per cent of £800 plus 9 per cent, 12 per cent or 15 per cent of the amount over £800.

*Example 4.4*

Alfie and Susan have separated and their two children, Tracey and Jon, live with Susan. Alfie lives with his new partner and her daughter Donna. Alfie's gross income is £450 a week. Tracey and Jon are the qualifying children, and Donna is a relevant other child.

**Step one:** Alfie's gross weekly income is £450. There is one relevant other child, so this is reduced by 11 per cent.

11% x £450 = £49.50

£450 – £49.50 = £400.50

**Step two:** There are two qualifying children, so child support is 16 per cent of the remaining gross income.

16% x £400.50 = £64.08

Alfie therefore pays £64.08 a week in child support to Susan.

Alfie's gross income is now £980, so the 'basic rate plus' applies.

**Step one:** Alfie's gross weekly income is £980. There is one relevant other child, so this is reduced by 11 per cent.

11% x £980 = £107.80

£980 – £107.80 = £872.20

Step two: This amount is over £800 and there are two qualifying children. So child support is 16 per cent of £800 plus 12 per cent of the 'excess' above £800 – ie, 12 per cent of £72.20.

16% x £800 = £128

12% x £72.20 = £8.66

Alfie therefore now pays £136.66 (£128 + £8.66) a week in child support to Susan.

## Step three

If there is more than one person with care caring for different qualifying children, apportion the amount worked out at Step two between the people with care depending on the number of qualifying children each cares for.

*Example 4.5*

The situation is as in the second part of Example 4.4. If Tracey was being cared for by Susan and Jon lived with his grandmother, the £136.66 child support would be split equally between Susan and the grandmother.

**Step three:** £136.66 is apportioned between two people with care. Each receives £68.33 a week from Alfie.

If the non-resident parent shares the care of any of the qualifying children, the child support calculated may be decreased by applying the shared care rules (see p82).

## Relevant other children

The number of relevant other children affects the calculation of child support. A **'relevant other child'** (or **'relevant child'**) is the term used by the CMS for a child, other than a qualifying child, for whom the non-resident parent or her/his partner receives child benefit.[14] This can include a child who does not live with the parent all the time – eg, because s/he is at boarding school or there is a shared care arrangement for her/him. It can also include a child for whom the non-resident parent or her/his partner would get child benefit, but for the fact that:[15]

- the rules about presence in Great Britain are not met; *or*
- the non-resident parent or her/his partner have elected not to receive child benefit because s/he would be liable to the 'high income child benefit charge' in income tax.

If a relevant other child is cared for by a local authority for some or all of the time, s/he continues to count as a relevant other child if the non-resident parent or her/his partner receives child benefit for her/him.[16]

See CPAG's *Welfare Benefits and Tax Credits Handbook* for full details of the rules on child benefit.

## Relevant non-resident children

The number of relevant non-resident children affects the calculation of child support. **'Relevant non-resident child'** is a term used by the CMS to refer to a child of the non-resident parent for whom an application for child support cannot be made because the non-resident parent is liable to pay maintenance for her/him under a maintenance order (or, in Scotland, registered maintenance agreement), an order of a non-British court or under the legislation of a country outside the UK.[17] This is a child who would be considered a qualifying child if an application for child support could be made for her/him. It includes a child who does not live with the non-resident parent and a child whose care is shared between the non-resident parent and someone else. See p18 for more information about when a court order prevents an application for child support being made.

A child who is not a qualifying child can also count as a relevant non-resident child if the non-resident parent is paying maintenance under another maintenance arrangement (eg, a family-based arrangement) for her/him. The child must be habitually resident in the UK (see p16). There is a wide definition of the other arrangements that can qualify, including verbal agreements. The arrangement must be between the non-resident parent and person with care of the relevant child, and must be for regular payments for the benefit of the child. Payments made to third parties can count, as well as those made to the parent with care.[18]

A relevant non-resident child is counted as a qualifying child in the child support calculation if:[19]
- child support is payable at either the basic rate (including the 'basic rate plus') or reduced rate; *or*
- child support would have been payable at the flat or nil rate, but is payable at the basic rate (including the 'basic rate plus') or reduced rate after applying a variation (see Chapter 5).

The amount of child support calculated is divided by the total number of qualifying children, including any relevant non-resident children. This amount is then multiplied by the number of qualifying children, excluding any relevant non-resident children. This gives the amount of child support the non-resident parent must pay.

If there is more than one person with care, each caring for a different qualifying child, the child support is apportioned between them in relation to the number of qualifying children they care for, including any adjustment for shared care.[20] If the total amount payable by the non-resident parent is less than £7, s/he pays £7 instead, apportioned between the persons with care as appropriate.[21]

Although a relevant non-resident child is counted as a qualifying child when working out the basic and reduced rate of child support, no payment is actually made for her/him. There is also no adjustment of the notional amount for a relevant non-resident child because the non-resident parent shares care or because the child is being looked after by the local authority for part of the time.

*Example 4.6*

James lives with his new partner, Amanda, and her son, Liam. He has three other children. Two (Emma and Joshua) are cared for by Elizabeth; one (Rachel) is cared for by Hilary. James has a court order for child maintenance for Rachel. Hilary cannot apply for child support as the court order is in force. In this case:

Emma and Joshua are qualifying children.

Liam is a relevant other child (even though he is not James's child, James's new partner, Amanda, gets child benefit for him).

Rachel is a relevant non-resident child.

James's gross income is £675 a week. His child support is worked out using the basic rate as follows.

**Step one:** James' gross income is £675. There is one relevant other child, so this is reduced by 11 per cent.

11% x £675 = £74.25

£675 – £74.25 = £600.75

**Step two:** There are two qualifying children and one relevant non-resident child. So child support is 19 per cent of £600.75

19% x £600.75 = £114.14

**Step three:** Divide the child support by the number of qualifying children, including the relevant non-resident child – ie, divide £114.14 by 3 = £38.05.

Multiply £38.05 by the number of qualifying children, excluding the relevant non-resident child – ie, £38.05 x 2 = £76.10.

James is due to pay £76.10 a week child support to Elizabeth.

Hilary receives her usual court order maintenance.

**Note:** if Hilary could apply for child support, she would receive £38.04 (£114.14 – £76.10).

If the situation changes and Emma is now cared for by her grandmother and Joshua is still cared for by Elizabeth, apportionment applies between Elizabeth and the grandmother. As each cares for one qualifying child, each would receive £38.05 a week child support.

## Divided families

If a couple has more than one child together and at least one child is living with each parent, child support liability is still calculated for both parents. However, the amounts are offset so that only the parent with the higher liability makes a balancing payment, while the other parent does not pay anything.[22] The CMS may use the term 'split care' when referring to this situation.

## 2. The non-resident parent's income

The amount of child support payable is based on the non-resident parent's gross weekly income.

'Gross weekly income' is calculated by using either the non-resident parent's 'historic income' (see p68) or 'current income' (see p71) at the 'effective date' of the application (see p127) and converting this into a weekly amount.[23] The rules on the type of income taken into account are complex and are based on how income is treated for income tax purposes. It is not the total income on which tax is due which counts, but the total income on which the parent is 'charged to tax'.[24]

Income from sources other than those described in this section is not counted. Taxable social security benefits are not included, except that incapacity benefit (IB), contributory employment and support allowance (ESA), jobseeker's allowance (JSA) and income support (IS) are included in the historic income figure provided by HM Revenue and Customs (HMRC). Working tax credit is *not* counted as part of the non-resident parent's income.

In some cases, income that is not counted in gross income for the calculation can be taken into account by a variation (see Chapter 5). For example, if a non-resident parent has unearned income from property or investments, a person with care could ask for a variation on the grounds that s/he has additional income. However, in many cases, an application for a variation is only likely to be made if a person with care is aware that the non-resident parent has other sources of income.

**Note:** the government has announced plans to bring notional income from assets, income from capital and foreign income into the calculation of the non-resident parent's income. It also intends to allow unearned income to be included in the initial calculation, rather than only be taken into account after an application for a variation (see p99).[25] No date has yet been set for these changes to take effect.

Contributions to an approved personal or occupational pension scheme (ie, a scheme registered with HMRC) by the non-resident parent in the relevant tax year are deducted when calculating gross weekly income. No other deductions are taken into account.

There is no limit on the amount of pension contributions that can be deducted. If a person with care is aware of the amount of contributions and considers them to be excessive, or that arrangements have been set up deliberately to reduce liability for child support (eg, if the non-resident parent has made a salary sacrifice arrangement in return for increased employer contributions), s/he can apply for a variation on the grounds of diversion of income (see p93).

All the parties (ie, the person with care, the non-resident parent and, in Scotland, any child applicant) are notified of the income figure used. This applies whether the calculation is based on historic income or current income (including if current income is estimated), but does not include a breakdown of the types of income included.[26] See p126 for further details on the notification of decisions.

**Note:** if the Child Maintenance Service (CMS) does not have sufficient information to make a calculation, it may make a default maintenance decision (see p125).

There are special rules for annual reviews of income (see p74), periodic checks if current income is being used (see p76) and for reporting changes to current income (see p77).

## Historic income

In most cases, the child support calculation uses a non-resident parent's 'historic' income. The CMS aims to avoid having to obtain information on income from the parent or her/his employer, and so information on historic income is provided by HMRC using an automated system. This is intended to reduce the possibility of delay, the supply of inaccurate information and demands on employers.

The CMS requests a historic income figure for the latest available tax year from HMRC no more than 30 days before the initial 'effective date' (see p127). The 'latest available tax year' is the most recent tax year for which HMRC has received information on the non-resident parent under either:[27]

- the pay as you earn (PAYE) scheme, for which employers complete end-of-year returns on the taxable earnings of their employees; *or*
- the annual self-assessment returns completed by individual taxpayers on various sources of income.

The latest available tax year must be one of the six tax years before the date the information is sought.[28]

The CMS does not have any discretion to use different income figures[29] – eg, if there is evidence that the non-resident parent has under-reported her/his income on the self-assessment (but see p71 for when 'current' income is used for the calculation instead of 'historic' income).

The CMS does not automatically receive a breakdown of the historic income figure, but may request a breakdown from HMRC if one party queries the figure. It does not normally provide the breakdown to the parties, but may give it to the non-resident parent.

If HMRC supplies a figure that is not from the most recent tax year for which it has received information, this is not a valid historic income figure. The CMS can make a further request to HMRC for an up-to-date historic income figure. It should consider doing so particularly carefully where it is not suitable to use current income, as the automated system can normally only request a historic income figure once each year.

However, if there is good reason to doubt the validity of the figure provided by HMRC, the CMS should make a further request.[30] The First-tier Tribunal considering an appeal may direct the CMS to do so.[31]

The historic income figure takes into account the non-resident parent's taxable income from:[32]

- employment – ie, her/his income from earnings (see p70);
- pensions (see p70);
- the taxable amount of the following social security benefits – IB, contributory ESA, JSA and IS; *and*
- her/his profits from self-employment (see p70).

Self-assessment information is usually available to the CMS by February or March in the year following the end of the tax year on 5 April. Information from PAYE returns is available earlier. If HMRC has information from both the PAYE scheme and a self-assessment for the latest available tax year, information from the self-assessment is used, as it is expected to be more comprehensive.[33]

Contributions to an approved personal or occupational pension scheme (ie, a scheme registered with HMRC) by the non-resident parent in the relevant tax year are deducted by HMRC when providing the historic income figure. If the non-resident parent has made pension contributions during the relevant tax year that have not been deducted under net pay arrangements (eg, payments made directly to a personal pension scheme), s/he can request that the weekly average amount of these is deducted from the gross income figure.[34] The CMS may require her/him to provide further information. Because tax relief is given on pension contributions, actual contributions are less than the gross amount included in the pension plan. The higher gross amount should be deducted from gross income. If a gross amount including higher rate tax relief is being claimed, the CMS is likely to require evidence in the form of an HMRC calculation notice.

The rules on the type of income included are intended to ensure that parents are treated consistently, whether the information held on them by HMRC comes from the PAYE scheme or from self-assessment.

The use of historic income information from HMRC means that taxable payments to those in the following occupations or offices are *not* disregarded (as was previously the case under the '2003 rules'):

- auxiliary coastguards;
- part-time firefighters and lifeboat crew members;
- reserve or territorial force members;
- local authority councillors.

Maintaining consistency, however, means that some types of income captured by self-assessment are not counted as gross weekly income for the calculation, even though HMRC may hold reliable information about them. This includes some taxable social security benefits and some allowances claimed by employees against taxable earnings.[35]

If a parent is both employed and self-employed, it is possible that at the time the calculation is made PAYE details are available for the most recently completed tax year, but self-assessment only for the year before this. Information on employment income is, therefore, likely to reflect the parent's current circumstances more accurately.

## Income from employment

When HMRC provides information on historic income from employment, gross pay is used. **'Gross pay'** is all payments, such as salary, wages, fees, bonuses, commission, tips and overtime, before any income tax or national insurance contributions are deducted. HMRC deducts contributions to an approved personal or occupational pension scheme. Deductions should also be made for expenses that will not be taxed.[36] Payments from an employer to reimburse an employee for legitimate work-related expenses should not be counted in gross pay.[37]

Statutory sick pay, statutory maternity pay, statutory adoption pay, statutory paternity pay and statutory shared parental pay are treated as employment income.

Anything of direct monetary value to the employee that derives from the employment or office is also treated as earnings.[38] There are certain exemptions.[39]

## Income from self-employment

Historic income from self-employment is based on the taxable profits from any 'trade, profession or vocation' in the latest available tax year for which a self-assessment has been completed – ie, the profits in the accounting period that ended in the tax year.[40] For example, if a self-employed parent's accounting year ends in June 2016, the self-assessment for that period will not be returned until January 2018 – 19 months later.[41]

If a business is run on a commercial basis and has made a loss, gross income is nil for that tax year. In certain circumstances, a loss in a previous year can be carried forward and deducted from profits in the next and later tax years. HMRC deducts such losses when determining the historic income figure for self-employment.[42]

## Pension income

Income (before tax) from a personal or occupational pension, or an annuity or other kind of taxable pension income, counts towards gross weekly income.[43]

The full details of pension income that is taxable are complex.[44] Tax-free lump sums paid under an approved personal pension scheme, retirement annuity contract or tax-exempt pension scheme are ignored completely. A lump sum counts if it is for cashing in a small pension, if the fund is too small to pay a pension (within the 'trivial commutation' limit) or if an occupational pension scheme winds up.[45] If a pension is paid because of a work-related illness or disability caused by an injury on duty, only the amount that would have been paid had the parent retired on non-work-related ill-health grounds counts. Any extra amount paid is ignored.[46] Various war disablement pensions are also not counted.[47]

Pension income for these purposes does not include UK social security pensions, even though they are taxable and appear on a self-assessment return.[48] This means that the following are not counted:[49]

- retirement pension;
- graduated retirement benefit;
- industrial death benefit;
- widowed mother's allowance;
- widowed parent's allowance;
- widow's pension.

## Current income

In certain cases, historic income information may not be available or may differ significantly from the non-resident parent's current circumstances. In this case, the calculation is based on the non-resident parent's current income. Unlike for historic income, the source of the current income figure is not limited to HMRC.[50] The CMS approaches the parent to verify her/his employment or self-employment details and, in some cases, may contact her/his employer or accountant for information.

The CMS can seek information on current income if:[51]

- no historic income figure is available – ie, HMRC does not have information for any one of the six tax years before the date of the CMS's request;[52]
- the CMS is unable, for whatever reason, to request or obtain the required information from HMRC – eg, because of problems with the automatic data-sharing system; *or*
- there is at least a 25 per cent difference between the amount of current income and historic income.

If HMRC supplies a historic income figure of 'nil', the CMS accepts this and does not use current income in this case. If the CMS then becomes aware that the non-resident parent has *any* current income, it is automatically treated as at least 25 per cent different from the nil historic income figure and a new calculation decision can be made.[53]

If a person with care believes a non-resident parent with nil historic income has current earnings, s/he can request a revision or supersession (see Chapter 9). The most likely stage at which someone may dispute the accuracy of the historic income figure used and ask for current income to be considered is once an application has been made and information from the non-resident parent starts to be gathered.

'Current income' is the total (calculated or estimated) income from:[54]

- employment;
- self-employment; *and*
- pensions.

Income from the taxable benefits included in historic income (see p68) is not counted in current income. A parent currently receiving one of these benefits usually pays the flat rate (see p60).

Contributions to an approved personal or occupational pension scheme (ie, a scheme registered with HMRC) by the non-resident parent in the relevant tax year are deducted. In many cases, these will already have been deducted by her/his employer when s/he is paid. In this case, the deductions are not included in gross income.[55]

If the non-resident parent has income from employment or self-employment and has made pension contributions during the relevant tax year that have not been deducted by her/his employer (eg, they were made directly to a personal pension scheme), the weekly average amount of these can be deducted from the gross income figure.[56] Because tax relief is given on personal pension contributions, actual contributions are less than the gross amount included in the pension plan. It is the higher gross amount that should be deducted from current income. The CMS does not deduct a higher gross amount to reflect higher rate tax relief, as granting this relief requires a decision by HMRC that it will not yet have been able to make at the time that current income is being assessed.

If any payment is made in a currency other than sterling, charges for converting it to sterling are deducted from the current income figure.[57]

## Estimating current income

The CMS can estimate a parent's current income if the information about it is insufficient or unreliable and:[58]

- the historic income is nil and there is any amount of current income – ie, current income is automatically treated as being 25 per cent different from historic income; *or*
- no historic income information is available, or the CMS is unable, for whatever reason, to request or obtain the required information from HMRC.

The CMS is likely to use this power to encourage non-resident parents to co-operate with providing details of their current income. It can base an estimate on any assumptions about any facts. Assumptions may be based on any information already held about the non-resident parent's circumstances. If the CMS is satisfied that s/he works in a particular occupation, it can assume that s/he has the average weekly income of a person engaged in that occupation in a particular area of the UK.[59] It may use information such as the Office for National Statistics' *Annual Survey of Hours and Earnings*, which gives average earnings for occupations and regions. This can apply to income from employment or self-employment. A parent who works part time or has lower than average wages for any reason should make sure the CMS is aware of this.

If there is no historic income information available, the CMS has not been able to gather information about current income and it does not have enough information to estimate current income, it may make a 'default maintenance decision' (see p125).

## Income from employment

Income from employment is defined for current income purposes in the same way as for historic income (see p70). Gross earnings are taken into account, not including approved pension contributions.

Current income is intended to be assessed in a way that, wherever possible, results in a stable amount of child support liability being set. If the non-resident parent receives any income from a salary, wages or other periodic payments and the CMS considers that this is a settled regular amount likely to continue for the foreseeable future, it converts this into a weekly amount.[60]

If earnings are less frequent, fluctuate or are not a regular settled amount for some other reason, the CMS averages the amounts over an appropriate period before the effective date of the decision and converts this to a weekly amount. Averaging is likely to be used if, for example, the parent is a seasonal worker or has an irregular pattern of hours, shifts or overtime.[61]

Some taxable amounts may be paid at different intervals from regular pay. The total of any bonus or commission payments in the last 12 months that have been paid separately or for a different period than other income is also converted to a weekly amount.[62]

The detailed rules on what income from employment is taxable are complex. Anything of direct monetary value to an employee that derives from her/his employment or office is also treated as earnings, and the amount received in the past 12 months converted into a weekly amount.[63] There are certain exemptions that are not treated as earnings.[64]

## Income from self-employment

Income from self-employment is defined for current income purposes in the same way as for historic income – ie, as the taxable profits from any 'trade, profession or vocation' (see p70).

Profits are determined for the most recently completed tax year or accounting period that a parent would normally report in a self-assessment. If no full tax year or accounting period has been completed, the profits are estimated for the current period. The total profit for the period is converted into a weekly amount.[65] The current income of an established business is normally expected to relate to an annual period equal to that covered by most self-assessments. A shorter period is only expected to be used for a new business. In this case, the CMS tries to identify estimated or projected annual profits – eg, using any completed profit and loss accounts to date and business plans.

It is the profits from the self-employment in which the non-resident parent is engaged on the effective date that are determined. If the CMS accepts that the parent had ceased trading on the effective date, s/he is assessed as having no profits, so her/his current income is nil if s/he has no other source of income. If the parent is a partner in a business, the profits are apportioned according to her/his share.[66]

## Pension income

Pension income is defined for current income purposes in the same way as for historic income (see p70). If current income is being used, the CMS averages pension income over an appropriate period to give a weekly amount.[67]

# Income from outside the UK

Income from outside the UK is included in gross income if it falls into one of the categories of taxable income from employment, self-employment or pensions. The detailed rules on what income is taxable are complex. The following are some types of income that are disregarded:

- social security payments from outside the UK, equivalent to non-taxable UK benefits;[68]
- one-tenth of the amount of any overseas pension or of a pension payable in the UK by the governments of certain other countries;[69]
- tax-free lump-sum payments under an overseas pension scheme;[70]
- income the parent is prevented from transferring to the UK by law or by the government of the country where the income arises or because foreign currency cannot be obtained in that country.[71]

# Annual reviews

The CMS must conduct an annual review of gross weekly income. This is done whether gross income is based on historic income or current income.[72]

The review date is normally on the anniversary of the initial effective date (see p127), but the CMS can use a different date for a particular case or type of case.[73]

If a child support calculation is already in force and a new application is made in relation to the same non-resident parent for a different qualifying child, the review dates for the two cases are aligned. This allows the non-resident parent's income to be assessed at the same time for all cases in which s/he is involved. The first review date for the new case is on the next review date for the calculation already in force.[74] If both parents are non-resident and applications for child support from both have been treated as one application (see p28), the CMS can use different review dates for each non-resident parent.[75]

In order to conduct the review, the CMS requests an updated historic income figure for the latest available tax year from HMRC.[76] It can request this no earlier than 30 days before the review date.[77]

If the gross weekly income shown by the updated figure is different from the historic income figure previously used, the CMS supersedes the calculation decision. The supersession decision takes effect from the review date.[78]

If gross weekly income is based on current income, the current income is compared with the updated historic income figure. If current income is still at least 25 per cent different from the updated historic income, the current income figure is still used. If it is within 25 per cent, the updated historic income figure is used and the calculation is superseded, with effect from the review date.

If a variation to the calculation on the grounds of additional income (see p98) is in force, the CMS may also request updated information on unearned income in the latest available tax year when it asks HMRC for the updated historic income figure. If unearned income has changed, a supersession decision can be made. This takes effect from the review date.[79]

When the CMS gets the updated historic income figure, it writes to the person with care and non-resident parent (and child applicant in Scotland) giving details of the income figure to be used for the coming year. This includes a breakdown of the calculation, including details such as qualifying children, relevant other children, other maintenance arrangements taken into account and shared care. This notification is not a formal decision that can be challenged, but a notification that the calculation is expected to be based on this information. The parties have 30 days to notify the CMS of any changes and provide any additional information or evidence.[80]

The formal decision on the child support calculation for the coming year is then issued to the parties on the effective date of the annual review. This formal decision can be challenged by the parties.

Any changes reported by any of the parties during this 30-day period may also result in a supersession of the current child support calculation from the date the change is reported.

* * *

### Example 4.7

The situation is as in the first part of Example 4.4 (see p63). Alfie is paying £64.08 a week child support to Susan. This is based on historic income information, showing his gross weekly income to be £450. The annual review date is 8 March.

On 6 February (30 days before the annual review), the CMS receives updated historic income information, showing a gross weekly income of £500, and notifies Alfie and Susan. The CMS receives evidence from Alfie on 12 February, showing that he has changed his working pattern and that his current gross weekly income is now £320.

This current income figure varies by more than 25 per cent from the updated historic income figure of £500, so Alfie's new child support liability from 8 March is based on the current income figure of £320 gross weekly income.

**Step one:** Alfie's gross weekly income is £320. There is one relevant other child, which means this is reduced by 11 per cent.

11% x £320 = £35.20

£320 – £35.20 = £284.80

**Step two:** There are two qualifying children, so child support is 16 per cent of the remaining gross income.

16% x £284.80 = £45.57

Alfie will, therefore, pay £45.57 a week in child support to Susan from the review date. The CMS also compares the new current income figure of £320 with the historic income figure used in Alfie's existing child support liability (£450). This is also more than 25 per cent different, so there are grounds for a supersession of the existing liability (see p198). Alfie's liability from the date he reported the change (12 February) until the review date (8 March) is also changed to £45.57 a week.

## Periodic checks of current income

The CMS can undertake a 'periodic check' of a parent's current income if:[81]
- her/his gross weekly income has been based on current income; *and*
- no supersession decision changing the amount has been made for at least 11 months.

A periodic check is likely to happen if the current income figure has not been updated at the annual review and is still at least 25 per cent different from the updated historic income figure obtained at the review.

This periodic check is separate from the annual review process and is not normally done at the same time. If current income is used to determine gross weekly income, in some cases this may only have been in place for a short time at the annual review date. Once it has been in place for 11 months, a periodic current income check takes place.

If current income has previously been used, but the annual review results in historic income now being used, a periodic check of current income is not undertaken. Therefore, if a periodic check is due to take place around the same time as the annual review, the annual review is done first.

The non-resident parent must provide updated evidence of her/his current income for the periodic check.[82] Any updated evidence on current income is compared against the updated historic income figure for the latest available tax year that was provided at the most recent annual review. Any information provided by a person with care can also be considered.

If the person with care requests a supersession while the periodic check is being conducted and provides any relevant information, this is considered to be part of the periodic check.[83]

If the evidence provided by the non-resident parent is sufficient to make a new decision on current income, a supersession of the calculation decision is made.[84] If the evidence shows that the up-to-date current income figure varies by at least 25 per cent from the most recently updated historic income figure, the calculation continues to be based on the current income. If the current income is no longer at least 25 per cent different, a supersession decision is made with gross weekly income based on the updated historic income figure. If the non-resident parent fails to provide evidence for the periodic check, the CMS may decide to supersede the calculation decision and use the updated historic income figure for gross weekly income.[85]

The effective date of a supersession decision arising from a periodic check of current income is the day the decision is made.[86] This is usually expected to be 30 days after the CMS writes to the non-resident parent to request her/his updated income details.[87]

If there has been a change in current income that should have been reported by the non-resident parent (ie, a change of 25 per cent or more that s/he should reasonably have understood to be likely to lead to increased liability for child support – see below), the effective date for the supersession decision is the date the income changed.[88]

## Change of circumstances

The CMS intends calculations to remain in place for a reasonable period. In many cases, a calculation based on historic income is likely to remain in force for the year ahead.

If gross weekly income is based on current income, a change of circumstances does not result in a supersession decision unless a parent's current income has changed by at least 25 per cent.[89] Calculations are not adjusted for smaller or short-term changes in income – eg, due to temporary sickness, temporary promotion and seasonal work.

If current income has changed by at least 25 per cent, a supersession decision is made, even if the change means that current income is now less than 25 per cent different from the historic income figure for the latest available tax year.[90]

*Example 4.8*
The situation is as in the first part of Example 4.4 (see p63). Alfie is paying £64.08 a week child support to Susan. This is based on current income information, showing his gross weekly income to be £450. Alfie's current income was used at the time the calculation was made as it was more than 25 per cent different from the historic income data provided by HMRC, which showed his gross weekly income to be £300.

> After the calculation has been in force for a few months, Alfie provides the CMS with new evidence, showing that he has changed his working pattern and his current gross weekly income is now £320.
>
> This new current income figure is more than 25 per cent different from the current income figure used to make the calculation decision. The CMS makes a supersession decision and calculates his child support liability based on a gross weekly income of £320. This takes effect from the date it received the new evidence. This can be done even though £320 is less than 25 per cent different from the most recent historic income figure.

Even if current income has not changed by 25 per cent, a supersession decision can still be made if:[91]

- the supersession results from changes that are considered by the CMS at an annual review or periodic check; *or*
- the supersession is made on the grounds that the original decision was based on an error of law; *or*
- the CMS supersedes a calculation that was based on an estimate of current income.

Certain changes to historic income (eg, if the historic income information is changed by HMRC, or if the non-resident parent amends a self-assessment) are grounds for the calculation to be revised.[92] However, HMRC does not routinely inform the CMS of minor changes, and so a revision is only likely to be done if the non-resident parent or person with care queries the accuracy of the historic income figure.

For full details of revisions and supersessions of decisions, see Chapter 9.

## Reporting changes in income

Parents are not required to report changes in their circumstances on a routine basis, except in specific instances – eg, if a qualifying child dies. See p51 for the changes that must be reported. However, there are specific duties on non-resident parents to report certain changes in their income.

If a parent's gross weekly income is based on her/his current income, s/he may be informed by the CMS that s/he must report relevant changes of circumstances. S/he is informed of this in the written notification of the child support calculation decision. S/he must report any such change in writing within 14 days of its occurring. The CMS may specify a longer period.[93] Failure to provide the required information may be an offence (see p38).[94]

If the non-resident parent is paying child support at the basic rate (including 'basic rate plus'), reduced rate or flat rate and gross weekly income is based on her/his current income from employment, s/he must tell the CMS if s/he:[95]

- starts a new job; *or*
- receives a new rate of pay for her/his existing job; *or*
- changes her/his working pattern in her/his existing job.

These changes must be reported if the parent could reasonably be expected to know that they may lead to an increased amount of child support being due. This duty does not apply to those who are self-employed.

Fluctuations in wages from week to week or month to month may not necessarily need to be reported. However, the parent must tell the CMS if her/his wages increase so that over a longer period (ie, five payments if paid weekly, three if paid fortnightly, and two if paid four-weekly or monthly) the average weekly amount is at least 25 per cent more than the gross weekly income that was taken into account in the calculation.[96]

If the non-resident parent is liable for the nil rate and gross weekly income is based on current income, s/he must tell the CMS if her/his gross weekly income increases to £7 or more. This duty applies to income from employment, self-employment and pensions (including income from any of the benefits that qualify for the flat rate).[97]

If gross weekly income is based on historic income, there is no duty on the non-resident parent to notify the CMS if her/his current income becomes (at some point during the year after the calculation decision is made) more than 25 per cent different from the most recent historic income figure. However, if this does happen, the person with care or the non-resident parent could apply for the calculation to be superseded. If the person with care alleges that the current income is at least 25 per cent more than the historic income figure used in the calculation, the CMS is only likely to investigate this if s/he provides information that gives reasonable grounds to do so.

# 3. **Shared care**

A number of people may be involved in caring for a qualifying child. The term **'shared care'** is used in this *Handbook* to describe a situation where there is more than one person looking after a particular child and those people live in different households. If the people providing care live in the same household (see p12), this is not shared care.[98]

If parents share the care of a qualifying child equally, there is no liability for child support (see p14).[99] However, if one parent provides day-to-day care for a child *to a lesser extent* than the other parent (or person with care), s/he may be treated as a non-resident parent and be liable to pay child support (see p14).

If a parent who is (or who is treated as) non-resident provides sufficient care (see p80) for a qualifying child, the amount of child support s/he has to pay may be reduced to reflect the care s/he provides.

If a qualifying child is looked after by a local authority for part of the time, see p87.[100]

**Note:** 'shared care' is different from the situation where different children of the same family have different homes. If the children of a family are divided between two households (eg, if one child lives with one parent and another child with the other parent), two separate child support calculations are carried out. In one, the first parent is the parent with care and the second parent is the non-resident parent. In the second, the roles are reversed. This situation is referred to as 'divided families' in this *Handbook*. The Child Maintenance Service (CMS) may refer to this as **'split care'** (see p66).

## If a non-resident parent shares care

In order for the shared care to affect the child support calculation, a non-resident parent must look after, or be expected to look after, a qualifying child for at least 52 nights a year (ie, one night a week) on average. The care must be provided overnight, and the non-resident parent and the child must stay at the same address.[101] The care could be provided away from the non-resident parent's normal home – eg, while on holiday or at a relative's home. The non-resident parent could also look after the child overnight in the person with care's home while the person with care is away from home during the relevant nights.[102]

The CMS determines the number of nights that count for shared care, based on the number of nights the non-resident parent is expected to provide overnight care for the qualifying child(ren) during the 12 months starting with the effective date of the calculation.[103]

The CMS can use a shorter period than this if appropriate – eg, if both parents have agreed a pattern of shared care for a shorter period.[104] If a shorter period is used, the number of nights of care in that period must be in the same ratio as 52 nights is to 12 months.

In determining the number of nights of shared care, the CMS looks at all the evidence. Verbal or written evidence may be accepted. Normally, this information is obtained at the time of the child support application – ie, from telephone contact with the person with care and non-resident parent or from written material provided by them. The CMS must consider:[105]

- the terms of any agreement between the person with care and the non-resident parent, or the terms of any court order providing for contact between the non-resident parent and the qualifying child;
- if there is no such agreement or order, any pattern of care that has been established over the previous 12 months (or a shorter period that the CMS thinks is appropriate to use).

Contact arrangements ordered by a court or agreed in writing are only evidence and not decisive proof of the care situation.[106] If the evidence of the person with care and non-resident parent conflicts, further evidence may be required to resolve the issue. Parents should keep a note of the nights the child spends with them and, in case of a dispute, be willing to supply further evidence – eg, a diary. The CMS (and, in any subsequent appeal, the First-tier Tribunal) must then determine the number of nights spent in each person's care over the period.[107]

The CMS does not review whether agreed shared care arrangements are being kept to. If it is reported that an agreement about shared care is not being complied with, the CMS may seek further evidence from the parties to allow the calculation to be revised.

If the CMS accepts that the person with care and non-resident parent have agreed to share care, but there is not enough evidence to determine the number of nights of shared care, the CMS can assume that the non-resident parent provides care for one night per week. This assumption can be made if the parties provide conflicting evidence and the number of nights of shared care cannot be determined, even if both parties agree that shared care is provided on more than one night per week. The assumption is applied until a supersession is requested and there is sufficient evidence to determine the actual number of nights of shared care.[108]

If the qualifying child is a boarder at a boarding school or a hospital patient, any night spent there counts as a night with the person who would normally have been looking after the child on that night (see p86).[109]

**Note:** if a non-resident parent is providing some care but not as much as 52 nights a year on average, the child support calculation is not adjusted to take account of the level of care s/he provides, and s/he is expected to pay the same amount of child support as if s/he were not looking after the child at all. This means, for example, that a parent who provides some regular care for her/his children may pay the same amount of child support as one who does not. However, a non-resident parent in this situation can apply for the calculation to be varied on the grounds that the contact costs are 'special expenses'. A variation for contact costs may also be considered even if the contact *is* also enough to affect the calculation. See Chapter 5 for details on variations.

### The effect of shared care on the flat rate

If a non-resident parent has been assessed as liable for the flat rate of child support because her/his gross weekly income is less than £100, this is not adjusted to take into account any care s/he provides. However, the amount of child support due is reduced to nil if a non-resident parent:[110]

- is liable to pay the flat rate because s/he is in receipt of a relevant benefit (see p60) or s/he or her/his partner receives income support, income-based jobseeker's allowance, income-related employment and support allowance (ESA), universal credit calculated on the basis that the parent does not have any earned income, or pension credit (including if a reduced flat rate of £3.50 applies); *and*
- cares for the qualifying child for at least 52 nights a year.

The flat rate of £7 is apportioned in relation to the number of qualifying children before any adjustment for shared care is made (see p58). This may mean that a non-resident parent's liability reduces to nil for one person with care because of shared care. However, s/he is still liable for the remaining amounts to the other person(s) with care, in which case s/he pays an amount which is less than £7.

**Note:** apportioning and rounding may result in adjustments of a penny in some calculations done by the CMS.

*Example 4.9*

Alistair is the non-resident parent of Ben, who lives with his older brother Neil, and Katie, who lives with her mother, Rachel. Alistair looks after Katie one or two nights a week. Both Neil and Rachel apply for child support. Alistair receives income-related ESA.

**Step one:** Alistair is due to pay child support at the flat rate of £7, as he receives income-related ESA.

**Step two:** Apportion the flat rate of £7 between the people with care in relation to the qualifying children each cares for – ie, the amount is halved.
To Neil for Ben = £3.50
To Rachel for Katie = £3.50

**Step three:** Alistair cares for Katie over 52 nights a year, so the amount due to Rachel reduces to nil.
Alistair remains liable to pay £3.50 in child support to Neil for Ben.

## The effect of shared care on the basic and reduced rate

If a non-resident parent shares the care of a qualifying child for 52 or more nights a year, the amount of child support s/he is due to pay at the basic rate (including 'basic rate plus') or reduced rate is reduced by an appropriate fraction, depending on the number of nights of shared care.[111] If there is more than one qualifying child, see below.

| Number of nights | Fraction to subtract |
| --- | --- |
| 52 to 103 | One-seventh |
| 104 to 155 | Two-sevenths |
| 156 to 174 | Three-sevenths |
| 175 or more | One-half |

If a non-resident parent shares the care of a qualifying child for a sufficient number of nights for the one-half fraction to apply, an additional £7 decrease in her/his child support liability is applied in respect of that child.[112] This is known as **'abatement'** and is applied for each child for whom at least 175 nights of shared care applies.

If the decrease results in a non-resident parent being liable to pay a person with care less than £7, s/he pays the flat rate of £7 instead.[113] This includes the situation where the total amount of child support due to all the people with care is decreased to less than £7. In this case, the £7 is apportioned between them in relation to the number of qualifying children.

*Example 4.10*

Alex shares the care of Mark with the person with care, Diane. He looks after Mark on average two nights at the weekend and a couple of weeks in the school holidays. Although Alex provides day-to-day care of Mark, he is treated as a non-resident parent as he does so to a lesser extent than Diane. Alex's gross weekly income is £480.

Step one: Basic rate of child support = 12% x £480 = £57.60

Step two: **Apply decrease for shared care**

Alex shares care in the 104–155 band (two-sevenths).

£57.60 child support must be decreased by two-sevenths – ie, £57.60 – £16.46 = £41.14

Alex pays Diane £41.14 a week.

**Note:** if Alex has costs for keeping in contact with Mark, he may also be able to apply for a variation (see p93).

Alex increases the amount of time he cares for Mark to three nights one week and four nights the next. In this case, Alex shares care for over 175 nights and the one-half fraction is applied. Alex's child support calculated under the basic rate remains £57.60.

Step two: £57.60 decreased by one-half and a further £7 subtracted – ie, £28.80 – £7 = £21.80

Because of the increase in shared care, Alex pays £21.80 to Diane.

Alex's circumstances change again and his gross weekly income is now £160.

Step one: Reduced rate of child support = £7 + (17% x £60) = £7 + £10.20 = £17.20

Step two: **Apply decrease for shared care**

The fraction to apply remains at one-half, with a further £7 subtracted.

(50% x £17.20) – £7 = £8.60 – £7 = £1.60

Step three: Child support due is below £7, so Alex pays £7 a week to Diane.

**Note:** if the increased amount of time Alex spends caring for Mark is accepted as meaning that care is shared equally with Diane, the child support calculation may be cancelled (see p14).

**If there is more than one qualifying child**

If a person with care and non-resident parent have more than one qualifying child, the fractions that apply for shared care for each qualifying child are added together, then divided by the number of qualifying children.[114] This applies where care is shared for some, but not all, of the qualifying children or if there are shared care arrangements for each qualifying child.

### Example 4.11

Pat is the non-resident parent of Lea and Dylan. Both are cared for by their grandmother, Jean. Lea does not like staying with Pat and only does so occasionally. However, Dylan stays with him on Friday and Saturday nights. Both children stay with him for a few days at Christmas and during the school holidays. Pat's gross weekly income is £420.

| | |
|---|---|
| **Step one:** | Basic rate of child support for two children = 16% x £420 = £67.20 |
| **Step two:** | **Apply decrease for shared care** |
| | Lea does not stay with Pat for sufficient days for it to count as shared care. Dylan is in the 104–155 band (two-sevenths). |
| | The fractions which apply are added together and divided by two, as there are two qualifying children cared for by Jean. |
| | $(0 + 2/7) \div 2 = 2/14$ |
| | Pat's child support is decreased by 2/14 of £67.20 = £9.60 |

Because of the shared care, Pat must pay £57.60 (£67.20 – £9.60) to Jean.

**Note:** if Pat has costs for keeping in contact with Lea, he may also be able to apply for a variation (see p93).

Lea increases the amount of time she spends with her father and now this counts as shared care.

| | |
|---|---|
| **Step two:** | Lea is in the 52–103 band (one-seventh). |
| | Dylan is in the 104–155 band (two-sevenths). |
| | The fractions are added together and divided by two – ie, $3/7 \div 2 = 3/14$ |
| | The child support due is, therefore, decreased by 3/14 because of shared care. |
| | Pat's child support is decreased by 3/14 of £67.20 = £14.40 |

Because of shared care, Pat must pay £52.80 (£67.20 – £14.40) to Jean.

Dylan stays with his father more often and increases the amount of care, so that:

| | |
|---|---|
| **Step two:** | Lea is in the 52–103 band (one-seventh). |
| | Dylan is in the 175 or more band (one-half). |
| | The decrease is $(1/7 + 1/2) \div 2 = 9/28$ |
| | $9/28 \times £67.20 = £21.60$ |
| | £67.20 – £21.60 = £45.60. However, because care for Dylan is in the one-half band, the further £7 reduction applies and the amount of child support due is decreased by a further £7. |

Pat now pays Jean £38.60 (£45.60 – £7).

**Note:** if the increased amount of time Pat spends caring for Dylan is accepted as meaning that care is shared equally with Jean, no child support may be payable for Dylan (see p14).

### If care is shared for more than one child with different persons with care

A non-resident parent may be liable to pay child support to more than one person with care (eg, if a father has two children who live with two different mothers) and may share the care of the children with them.

Child support liability is calculated for only one person with care in respect of each qualifying child. The child support due is first apportioned between the persons with care, in proportion to the number of qualifying children each cares for. The amount payable to each is then adjusted to take account of any shared care the non-resident parent provides for the child(ren).

If another person who is not the non-resident parent provides care for a qualifying child, the CMS does not apportion the child support liability between them. The person with care could agree to pass on some of the child support – eg, an amount reflecting the number of days a week the other person has care of the child. However, this would be an informal arrangement and will not be monitored or enforced by the CMS.

---

*Example 4.12*

Ewan is the non-resident parent of two children – Holly, whose parent with care is Ellen, and Jamie, whose parent with care is Laura. Ewan looks after Holly when Ellen is on night shifts, which is every other week apart from holidays, and takes her camping with him on the odd weekend. Jamie and Laura live further away, so Ewan only sees Jamie for a long weekend once a month and two weeks in the summer holidays. Ewan's gross weekly income is £387.50.

**Step one:**    The basic rate of child support applies for two qualifying children.

16% x £387.50 = £62

The child support due is apportioned between each person with care.

Ellen and Laura each care for one qualifying child, so the child support is halved between them.

To Ellen for Holly = £31

To Laura for Jamie = £31

**Step two:**    **Apply decrease for shared care**

*Child support paid to Ellen for Holly*

Holly is in the 156–174 band (three-sevenths).

3/7 x £31 = £13.29

£31 – £13.29 = £17.71

*Child support paid to Laura for Jamie*

Jamie is in the 52–103 band (one-seventh).

1/7 x £31 = £4.43

£31 – £4.43 = £26.57

**Step three:**    The total child support due is £17.71 (to Ellen) + £26.57 (to Laura) = £44.28

---

## A qualifying child is in hospital or at boarding school

If a qualifying child is in hospital or at boarding school, any night spent there counts as a night with the person who would normally provide care at that time.[115] This includes nights normally spent with a non-resident parent,[116] person with care or local authority.[117]

These nights count in determining whether care of the child is shared and when establishing who is a person with care (see p10) or which parent is to be treated as non-resident (see p14).

---

*Example 4.13*

Nick, who has been living with his mother during the week and spending Friday nights with his father, goes to boarding school. The time as a boarder continues to be treated as if he were living with his mother. Even if the care arrangement changes, so that Nick spends alternate weekends with his father, the nights at school still count as having been spent with his mother.

---

If the parents agree, or the periods involved are infrequent, the case may be straightforward. However, if the arrangements break down, a normal pattern cannot be established or the parents disagree, the CMS must make a decision on shared care.

---

*Example 4.14*

Ella is a qualifying child cared for most of the time by her mother, Sarah, although her father, Stuart, looks after her on Wednesday and Saturday nights. Over the past year Ella has undergone treatment for cancer, which has resulted in her spending periods in hospital. Because of this, Stuart has only looked after Ella for 42 nights in the year. On 16 of the remaining nights that Ella should have stayed with him, she was in hospital. On the other nights that Ella should have stayed with Stuart, she was unwell and wanted to stay with Sarah. The CMS must decide whether to consider Ella as staying with Stuart for 58 nights or accept that the intention was for her to stay with Stuart on 104 nights in the year. Both parents have the right to challenge the CMS's decision.

---

If a night spent in hospital or at boarding school would not otherwise have been a night spent with a person with care, a non-resident parent who shares care or a local authority who has part-time care, the child is treated as being in the principal provider's care for that night. For example, if a babysitter looks after a child one night a week, then the child goes into hospital, the babysitter is not a person with care, non-resident parent or local authority. Therefore, that night is treated as one normally spent with the principal provider of day-to-day care.

## A local authority provides part-time care

If a local authority has part-time care of a qualifying child for 52 nights or more in the 12-month period ending with the effective date of the calculation decision (see p127), the child support to be paid by the non-resident parent may be decreased.[118] This applies if:

- a non-resident parent is liable to pay the basic rate (including 'basic rate plus') or reduced rate, (including if a variation has been made which results in her/him paying child support at either of these rates;[119] *and*
- a qualifying child is cared for by a local authority at least one night a week on average, but not more than five (see below).

Part-time local authority care has no effect on the flat rate of child support.

A local authority cannot be a person with care.[120] Therefore, if a child is being looked after by a local authority for more than five nights a week, no child support is payable by the non-resident parent because there is no one who can be regarded as caring for the child for a sufficient amount of time to be classed as a person with care. If a child is at a boarding school, even if this is publicly funded education provision, s/he does not count as being looked after by the local authority.[121]

The CMS may use a period other than the 12 months ending with the effective date if it considers it to be more representative of the current arrangements. A future period may also be considered if the qualifying child is to go into local authority care on or after the effective date.[122] If an alternative period is used, the number of nights of care must be in the same ratio as 52 nights to 12 months.[123] (Nights spent in hospital or at boarding school that normally would have been spent in care are included – see p86.)

The child support calculation is only affected if a qualifying child is being looked after by a local authority. If a relevant other child (see p64) is being looked after by a local authority (either full or part time), the calculation is not affected, provided the non-resident parent or her/his partner continues to receive child benefit for her/him (or has elected not to receive child benefit because s/he would be liable for the 'high income child benefit charge' in income tax).[124]

### The decrease for part-time local authority care

The basic or reduced rate of child support is decreased in relation to the number of nights the qualifying child spends in local authority care.[125] This calculation may be carried out either on its own if a non-resident parent does not share care, or alongside one carried out because a non-resident parent shares care (see p80).

*The effect of part-time local authority care*

| Number of nights | Fraction to subtract |
|---|---|
| 52 to 103 | One-seventh |
| 104 to 155 | Two-sevenths |
| 156 to 207 | Three-sevenths |
| 208 to 259 | Four-sevenths |
| 260 to 262 | Five-sevenths |

If a person with care and non-resident parent have more than one qualifying child, the fractions that apply for each qualifying child in local authority care are added together and divided by the number of qualifying children for whom child support is calculated.[126] This applies if one child or all the children are being looked after by the local authority.

If the decrease because of part-time local authority care would reduce the amount of child support to less than £7, the amount due is £7.

*Example 4.15*

Jake is the non-resident parent of Michael and Leanne. Michael has just been placed under local authority supervision, which means that over the next six months he will spend four nights a week in a residential unit and the rest of the time with his mother, Naomi. Jake has a gross weekly income of £350 and currently pays child support of £56 (basic rate). This must now be superseded because of the local authority care. The CMS supersedes the decision, considering the ratio in the six-month period.

**Step one:** The basic rate of child support applies.

16% x £350 = £56

**Step two:** **Apply the decrease because of part-time local authority care**

Local authority care for Michael is in the 208–259 band (four-sevenths).

The fractions which apply are added together and divided by the number of qualifying children – ie, (0 + 4/7) ÷ 2 = 4/14

Jake's child support is decreased by 4/14 of £56 = £16

Jake now pays Naomi £40 (£56 – £16).

If Leanne were also in care for two nights a week:

**Step one:** Same as above.

**Step two:** Local authority care for Leanne is in the 104–155 band (two-sevenths).

Local authority care for Michael is in the 208–259 band (four-sevenths).

The fractions are added together and divided by two:

(2/7 + 4/7 ) = 6/7 ÷ 2 = 6/14

Jake's child support decreases by 6/14 of £56 = £24

Jake now pays Naomi £32 (£56 – £24).

## A non-resident parent shares care and the local authority has part-time care

If a non-resident parent shares the care of a qualifying child and a local authority also has part-time care of a qualifying child in relation to the same person with care, the appropriate fractions are worked out under each provision and are added together.[127] The non-resident parent's child support liability is then decreased by this fraction.

If this decrease would result in a non-resident parent being due to pay less than £7 , s/he pays £7.[128]

This calculation is carried out at Step two.

*Example 4.16*

The situation is as in Example 4.15, except that Leanne spends one night a week with Jake, but Michael does not.

**Step two:**      Jake cares for Leanne in the 52–103 band (one-seventh).

The fractions which apply are added together and divided by the number of qualifying children:

$(0 + 1/7) \div 2 = 1/14$

Jake's child support liability because of shared care is reduced by 1/14.

Because Michael is in local authority care, the child support due is reduced by 4/14.

$1/14 + 4/14 = 5/14$

Jake's child support liability is reduced by £20 (ie, 5/14 x £56).

Jake now pays Naomi £36 (£56 – £20).

If Leanne is also in care two nights a week, but still spends one night a week with Jake:

**Step two:**      Jake's child support liability because of shared care is reduced by 1/14 (as above).

Local authority care for Michael and Leanne reduces Jake's child support liability by 6/14 (see the second part of Example 4.15).

$1/14 + 6/14 = 7/14 = 1/2$

Jake's child support liability is reduced by £28 (1/2 x £56).

Jake now pays Naomi £28 (£56 – £28).

# Notes

## 1. The rates of child support
1 Reg 6 CSMC Regs
2 Sch 1 para 6 CSA 1991
3 Sch 1 para 1(2) CSA 1991
4 Sch 1 para 7(7) CSA 1991
5 Sch 1 para 5(b) CSA 1991; reg 45 CSMC Regs
6 Sch 1 para 4 CSA 1991
7 Sch 1 para 4(1)(b) CSA 1991; reg 44(1) and (2) CSMC Regs
8 Sch 1 para 4(2) CSA 1991; reg 44(3) CSMC Regs
9 Sch 1 para 3 CSA 1991
10 Reg 43 CSMC Regs
11 Sch 1 para 1(1) CSA 1991
12 Sch 1 para 2 CSA 1991; reg 2 CSM(CBR) Regs
13 Sch 1 para 2 CSA 1991; reg 2 CSM(CBR) Regs
14 Sch 1 para 10C CSA 1991
15 Sch 1 para 10C(2)(b) CSA 1991; reg 77 CSMC Regs
16 Reg 54 CSMC Regs
17 Reg 52 CSMC Regs
18 Sch 1 para 5A(6)(b) CSA 1991; reg 48 CSMC Regs
19 Sch 1 para 5A CSA 1991; reg 52 CSMC Regs
20 Sch 1 para 6 CSA 1991
21 Sch 1 paras 5A(2) and 7(7) CSA 1991
22 Reg 5 CS(MPA) Regs

## 2. The non-resident parent's income
23 Reg 34(1) CSMC Regs
24 *FQ v SWWP and MM (CSM)* [2016] UKUT 446 (AAC), reported as [2017] AACR 24
25 DWP, *Child Maintenance: a new compliance and arrears strategy – public consultation*, December 2017
26 Reg 25(1)(b) CSMC Regs
27 Reg 4(1) CSMC Regs
28 Reg 4(1) CSMC Regs
29 *IW v SSWP and DW (CSM)* [2016] UKUT 312 (AAC)
30 *SB v SSWP and TB (CSM)* [2016] UKUT 84 (AAC); *IW v SSWP and DW (CSM)* [2016] UKUT 312 (AAC)
31 *AR v SSWP and LR (CSM)* [2017] UKUT 69 (AAC), reported as [2017] AACR 23
32 Reg 36(1) CSMC Regs

33 Reg 36(5) CSMC Regs
34 Reg 35(3) CSMC Regs
35 Reg 36(1)(c) CSMC Regs
36 Reg 36(1) CSMC Regs; in *SH v SSWP, CH and HMRC (CSM)* [2018] UKUT 157 (AAC) it was decided that reg 36 is internally contradictory and para (2)(b) should be disregarded.
37 *AR v SSWP and LR (CSM)* [2017] UKUT 69 (AAC), reported as [2017] AACR 23
38 Part 3 IT(EP)A 2003
39 Part 4 IT(EP)A 2003
40 Reg 36(1)(d) CSMC Regs; s5 IT(TOI)A 2005
41 s198 IT(TOI)A 2005
42 Reg 36(4) CSMC Regs
43 Reg 36(1)(b) CSMC Regs
44 Part 9 IT(EP)A 2003
45 s637 IT(EP)A 2003
46 s644 IT(EP)A 2003
47 ss638-41 IT(EP)A 2003
48 Reg 36(3) CSMC Regs
49 s577(1) IT(EP)A 2003
50 *IW v SSWP and DW (CSM)* [2016] UKUT 312 (AAC)
51 Reg 34(2) CSMC Regs
52 Reg 4(2) CSMC Regs
53 Reg 34(2A) CSMC Regs
54 Reg 37(1) CSMC Regs
55 Reg 38(5) CSMC Regs
56 Reg 40 CSMC Regs
57 Reg 37(2) CSMC Regs
58 Reg 42(1) CSMC Regs
59 Reg 42(2) CSMC Regs
60 Reg 38(2)(a) CSMC Regs
61 Reg 38(2)(b) CSMC Regs
62 Reg 38(3) CSMC Regs
63 Part 3 IT(EP)A 2003; reg 38(4) CSMC Regs
64 Part 4 IT(EP)A 2003
65 Reg 39(2), (3) and (4) CSMC Regs
66 Reg 39(1), (5) and (6) CSMC Regs
67 Reg 41 CSMC Regs
68 s681 IT(EP)A 2003
69 ss567 and 615 IT(EP)A 2003
70 s637 IT(EP)A 2003
71 s575(2)(b) IT(EP)A 2003
72 Reg 19(1) CSMC Regs
73 Reg 19(2) CSMC Regs
74 Reg 19(3) CSMC Regs

75 Reg 19(4) CSMC Regs
76 Reg 20(1) CSMC Regs
77 Reg 35(2)(b) CSMC Regs
78 Reg 20(2) CSMC Regs
79 Reg 21(2) CSMC Regs
80 Child Maintenance and Enforcement Commission, *The Child Support Maintenance Calculation Regulations 2012: a technical consultation on the draft regulations,* December 2011
81 Reg 22(1) CSMC Regs
82 Reg 22(1) CSMC Regs
83 Child Maintenance and Enforcement Commission, *The Child Support Maintenance Calculation Regulations 2012: a technical consultation on the draft regulations,* December 2011
84 Reg 22(3) CSMC Regs
85 Reg 22(2) CSMC Regs
86 Reg 22(4) CSMC Regs
87 Child Maintenance and Enforcement Commission, *The Child Support Maintenance Calculation Regulations 2012: a technical consultation on the draft regulations,* December 2011
88 Reg 22(5) CSMC Regs
89 Reg 23(1) and (2) CSMC Regs
90 Reg 23(4) CSMC Regs
91 Reg 23(3) CSMC Regs
92 Reg 14(1)(f) CSMC Regs; *FQ v SSWP and MM (CSM)* [2016] UKUT 446 (AAC), reported as [2017] AACR 24
93 Reg 9A(1), (4) and (5) CSI Regs
94 s14A(3A) CSA 1991
95 Reg 9A(2) and (6)(a) CSI Regs
96 Reg 9A(2) and (6)(b) CSI Regs
97 Reg 9A(3), (9) and (10) CSI Regs

**3. Shared care**
98 Reg 50(1)(b) CSMC Regs
99 Reg 50(2) CSMC Regs
100 Regs 46, 47 and 50-55 CSMC Regs
101 Sch 1 para 7(4) CSA 1991; reg 46(5)(a) CSMC Regs
102 R(CS) 7/08
103 Reg 46(2) CSMC Regs
104 Reg 46(3) CSMC Regs
105 Reg 46(4) CSMC Regs
106 CCS/2885/2005; *JH v SSWP and LH (CSM)* [2016] UKUT 440 (AAC)
107 CCS/11728/1996
108 Sch 1 para 9(2) CSA 1991; reg 47 CSMC Regs
109 Reg 55 CSMC Regs
110 Sch 1 para 8 CSA 1991
111 Sch 1 para 7 CSA 1991
112 Sch 1 para 7(6) CSA 1991
113 Sch 1 para 7(7) CSA 1991
114 Sch 1 para 7(5) CSA 1991
115 Reg 55 CSMC Regs
116 Reg 46(5)(c) CSMC Regs
117 Reg 53(11) CSMC Regs
118 Reg 53(2) and (4) CSMC Regs
119 Reg 53(1) CSMC Regs
120 Reg 78(1)(a) CSMC Regs
121 R(CS) 1/04; R(CS) 2/04
122 Reg 53(2)(c) CSMC Regs
123 Reg 53(5) CSMC Regs
124 Reg 54 CSMC Regs
125 Reg 53(6) CSMC Regs
126 Reg 53(7) CSMC Regs
127 Reg 53(8) CSMC Regs
128 Reg 53(9) CSMC Regs

# Chapter 5

. . . . . . . . . . . . . . . . . . . . . . . . . . . . . . . . . . . . . . . . . . . . . . . . . . . . . . .

# Variations

**This chapter covers:**

## 1. What is a variation

In certain circumstances, it is possible to apply for a child support calculation made according to the rules explained in Chapter 4 to be varied. A variation allows situations that are not taken into account by the usual calculation to be considered by the Child Maintenance Service (CMS).

A variation can only be made on a ground specified in the legislation and only if it would be 'just and equitable' to do so (see p93).

It is possible to apply for a calculation to be varied either before it is made or once it is in force.[1]

If an application for a variation is successful, it may result in a child support calculation being made or, if a calculation already exists, its being revised or superseded with the variation incorporated.

If a default maintenance decision (see p125) is in force, an application for it to be varied may contain sufficient information for it to be revised and replaced with a calculation.

Variations are one of the areas of child support law in which disputes frequently arise. There is much caselaw on the issues, and it is best to get advice if you are unsure. Many of the principles established in caselaw were decided on the rules for '2003 rules' cases, but they also apply to variations in '2012 rules' cases.

## 2. Grounds for a variation

A variation can be made for:
- special expenses (see below);
- additional income (see p98).

### Special expenses

A non-resident parent can apply for a variation to have her/his child support liability reduced on the grounds that s/he has the following special expenses:[2]
- costs of maintaining contact with the qualifying child(ren) (see below);
- costs of a long-term illness or disability of a 'relevant other child' (ie, a child who lives with her/him) – see p95;
- previous debts, incurred before the couple separated (see p96);
- boarding school fees paid for a qualifying child(ren) (see p97);
- costs of repaying a mortgage on the home of the person with care and qualifying child (see p98).

Except for costs associated with an illness or disability of a relevant other child, special expenses can only be considered if they are over a certain amount. This threshold is £10, regardless of the income of the non-resident parent. If expenses are being considered in more than one category, the threshold applies separately to each. If the expenses in any category are less than £10 a week, a variation is not allowed on that ground. If the expenses in any category are £10 or more a week, the whole amount is counted in full (not just the excess over £10).[3]

The Child Maintenance Service (CMS) can also substitute a lower amount for any special expenses it considers are unreasonably high or have been unreasonably incurred. This may be below the threshold amount or nil. In the case of contact costs, any reduced amount must not be so low that it makes it impossible for the non-resident parent to maintain contact with the child at the level of frequency stated in any court order, provided that contact is actually taking place.[4]

A variation for special expenses reduces the gross weekly income of the non-resident parent that is taken into account in the child support calculation.[5]

### Contact costs

A variation can be considered if the non-resident parent incurs costs, or is reasonably expected to incur costs, in relation to her/his contact with the qualifying child.[6] The costs can be for the non-resident parent or the child. The cost of a travelling companion can also be included – eg, because of disability or long-term illness (of the non-resident parent or the child) or the child's young age. Costs of contact with another child (eg, a child who might have been a qualifying child but for the fact that s/he does not live in the UK) do not count.[7]

Expenses for contact costs may be considered even if they arise for contact that is also being counted as part of a shared care arrangement.

The following count as contact costs:[8]

- public transport fares;
- fuel for a private car;
- taxi fares, but only if the illness or disability of the non-resident parent or qualifying child makes it impractical to use another form of transport;
- car hire, if the cost of the journey would be less than by public transport or taxis, or a combination of both;
- accommodation costs for the parent or the child for overnight stays, if a return journey on the same day is impractical, or the pattern of care includes contact over two or more days;
- minor incidental costs associated with travelling, such as road or bridge tolls or fees. This may include parking fees and ticket reservation fees if it was necessary to incur these to maintain contact with the child. Other costs necessary to maintain contact with the child, such as fees for a contact centre if a court required contact to be supervised, do not count.[9]

The costs are based on an established pattern of visits, if one exists.[10] If there is no current established pattern, a previous one may be referred to if contact is to begin again. Alternatively, an intended pattern, agreed between the non-resident parent and person with care, may also be used. The pattern set out in a court order may also be used. When contact is set out in a court order, it may only specify an upper limit on visits.

The costs are calculated as an average weekly amount. This is based on a 12-month, or shorter, period that ends immediately before the day the variation would take effect.[11] If it is based on a pattern of contact that has ended before the date of the variation application, the CMS considers the costs incurred between the effective date of the variation and the date on which it would cease – ie, the date on which the circumstances giving rise to the variation end.[12] In other cases, it can be based on anticipated costs.

To determine whether the cost for fuel is reasonable, the CMS may compare the amount claimed with an average figure.

If a non-resident parent returns from abroad and contact is only one reason for the trip, the CMS may limit costs to those of travel from her/his home in the UK.

Overnight costs only include reasonable accommodation costs if an overnight stay is necessary. They do not cover the cost of meals and sundries.

Changes in contact may mean the variation is also changed. If contact stops, even through no fault of the non-resident parent, the calculation may be superseded to reflect this.

*Example 5.1*

Bronwen has gross weekly income of £628 and pays the basic rate of child support of £100.48 a week to Ivan for Ursula and Gretchen. She claims a special expenses cost for contact with her children, amounting to £2,100 over a six-month period since the girls attend boarding school. This includes travel from Northern Ireland by ferry, petrol and overnight stays in hotels, amounting to 12 nights over the six-month period.

The amounts included are considered reasonable in the circumstances and the weekly amount is calculated:

£2,100 ÷ 26 = £80.77 a week on average.

This is above the threshold of £10. Therefore, a variation of £80.77 for contact costs may be considered, and Bronwen's gross income reduced by this amount.

Bronwen's gross weekly income is now treated as being £547.23 (£628 – £80.77). The amount of child support due is now £87.56 a week (£547.23 x 16%, as the basic rate applies and there are two qualifying children).

## Costs of a relevant other child's long-term illness or disability

A variation can be considered if the non-resident parent incurs costs for a long-term illness or disability of a relevant other child (see p64).[13]

A long-term illness is one that exists at the date of the variation application or from the date the variation would take effect. It must be likely to last for at least a further 52 weeks or be terminal.[14] A child is considered disabled if:[15]

- the care component of disability living allowance (DLA), the daily living component of personal independence payment (PIP) or armed forces independence payment is paid for her/him;
- s/he would receive DLA care component or PIP daily living component but for the fact that s/he is in hospital; *or*
- s/he is registered blind.

**Note:** receipt of the mobility component of DLA or PIP does not count for this purpose.

The reasonable additional costs of any of the following count:[16]

- personal care, attendance or communication needs;
- mobility;
- domestic help;
- medical aids that cannot be provided on the NHS;
- heating, clothing and laundry;
- food essential for a diet recommended by a medical practitioner;
- adaptations to the non-resident parent's home;
- day care, respite care or rehabilitation.

If an aid or appliance can be provided on the NHS, a variation is not normally agreed, even if the item is not available because of a lack of funds at a particular time. However, a variation may be considered if there is likely to be a serious delay in supplying an item which would prevent the child's condition from seriously deteriorating. The CMS may also consider the cost of the aid and whether it can be obtained at a cheaper price.

Any financial help towards these costs from any source, paid to the non-resident parent or a member of her/his household, is deducted if it relates to the expense claimed.[17] Any DLA care component, PIP daily living component or armed forces independence payment being paid for the relevant other child is also deducted from the costs. If DLA, PIP or armed forces independence payment has been applied for, but is not yet in payment, it can be included if it covers the date the variation starts.

## Debts of the relationship

A variation can be considered if the non-resident parent is repaying debts incurred before s/he became a non-resident parent (see p12) of the qualifying child. These costs can count as special expenses, provided the debt arose when that parent and the person with care were a couple.[18] The loan must have been taken out for the benefit of at least one of the following:[19]

- the non-resident parent and person with care, jointly;
- the person with care alone, if the non-resident parent is liable for the repayments;
- a person who is not a child, but at the time the loan was taken:
  - was a child;
  - lived with the non-resident parent and person with care; *and*
  - was the child of the non-resident parent, person with care or both of them;
- the qualifying child;
- any child other than the qualifying child who at the time the debt was incurred:
  - lived with the non-resident parent and person with care; *and*
  - is a child of the person with care.

Loans only count if they are from a qualifying lender, or from a non-resident parent's current or former employer.[20] Qualifying lenders include banks, building societies or other registered lenders – eg, hire purchase.[21]

The following do *not* count as debts for this purpose:[22]

- debts incurred to buy something which the non-resident parent kept for her/his own use after the relationship ended;[23]
- a debt for which the person who applied for the variation took responsibility under a court order or a financial settlement with her/his ex-partner;

- a debt for which a variation has previously been agreed, but which has not been repaid in the period for which the variation has been applied to the child support calculation;
- debts of a business or trade;
- secured mortgage repayments, except for amounts to buy, repair or improve the home of the person with care and qualifying child;
- endowment or insurance premiums, except those to buy, repair or improve the home of the person with care and qualifying child;
- gambling debts;
- legal costs of the separation, divorce or dissolution of the civil partnership;
- credit card repayments;
- overdrafts, unless taken out for a specified amount repayable over a specified period;
- fines imposed on the non-resident parent;
- any debt incurred to repay one of the above;
- any other debt the CMS considers reasonable to exclude.

Payments on a loan taken out to pay off any negative equity on the former joint home once it has been sold do not count as debts, as the person with care no longer lives there.

A loan taken out to repay a previous debt which would have counted may be included. This means that a debt incurred *after* a person has become a non-resident parent may be grounds for a variation.[24] This can apply whether paying off the previous debt is the sole purpose, or only part of the purpose, of incurring the new debt.[25]

A variation is normally based on the original debt repayment period; any rescheduling of the debt is usually ignored. However, if the person who applied for the variation has been unemployed or ill and the creditors have agreed to extend the repayment period, the CMS can take the extended period into account.

## Boarding school fees

A variation can be considered if the non-resident parent incurs, or reasonably expects to incur, costs for the maintenance element of boarding school fees for the qualifying child.[26] Only term-time costs for non-advanced education at a recognised educational establishment can be included.[27]

If the maintenance element cannot be distinguished from other school fees, the CMS can decide what to include, but this amount should not be more than 35 per cent of the total fees.[28]

If the non-resident parent receives financial help to pay the fees, or pays part of the fees with someone else, a proportion of the costs are included. This is calculated in the same ratio as the maintenance element to overall fees.[29]

In all cases, a variation for boarding school fees must not reduce the amount of income used to calculate child support by more than 50 per cent.[30]

---

*Example 5.2*

The situation is as in Example 5.1. Bronwen claims special expenses for her contribution to the costs of Ursula and Gretchen's boarding school. She pays the school £1,500 a term – ie, £4,500 a year. Ivan pays the rest of the fees – ie, £4,500 a year. Bronwen's gross weekly income is £628.

The fees for each child each term are £1,500 and the maintenance element is £500 a term. Bronwen's contribution to the maintenance element of the fees is £250 a child each term – ie, £500. Over the three terms this amounts to £1,500, which is converted into a weekly figure (£1,500 ÷ 365 x 7 = £28.77). This is above the threshold of £10, so a variation for a contribution to boarding school fees of £28.77 may be considered. **Note:** if this is accepted, it does not reduce her gross income by more than 50 per cent.

---

### Payments for mortgages, loans and insurance policies

A variation can be considered if the non-resident parent makes payments to a mortgage lender, insurance company or person with care for a mortgage or loan if:[31]

- it was taken out to buy, or carry out repairs/improvements to, the property by someone other than the non-resident parent; *and*
- the payments are not made because of a debt or other legal liability of the non-resident parent for the period in which the variation is applied; *and*
- the property was the person with care's and non-resident parent's home when they were a couple, and it is still the home of the person with care and qualifying child; *and*
- the non-resident parent has no legal or financial rights in the property – eg, a charge or equitable interest.

Payments may also be considered for an insurance or endowment policy taken out to discharge a mortgage or loan as above, except if the non-resident parent is entitled to any part of the proceeds when the policy matures.[32]

See also p141 for information on when payments made by a non-resident parent to a third party may be offset against child support owed.

### Additional income

A variation can be considered on the grounds that the non-resident parent has certain additional income that has not been taken into account when calculating her/his child support liability. A variation results in such income being added to her/his gross weekly income used for the calculation, increasing the amount of child support due.

A variation can be considered if the non-resident parent:

- has unearned income – ie, income that has not been counted in gross weekly income (see below);
- is on the nil or flat rate in certain circumstances, but has gross weekly income of more than £100 (see p102);
- has 'diverted' income (p103).

## Unearned income

A variation can be considered if the non-resident parent has taxable unearned income of £2,500 or more a year.[33] Not all taxable income counts. '**Unearned income**' for this purpose is income that is subject to UK income tax from:[34]

- land or property (see p100);
- savings and investments (see p101);
- other miscellaneous sources (see p102).

**Note:** the definitions of the different types of income that are classed as unearned for this purpose are complex and rely on how the sources of the income are treated for income tax purposes. This chapter includes only a summary of some of the main types.

Information on unearned income is collected by HM Revenue and Customs (HMRC) through self-assessment tax returns, and details of the amount in the latest available tax year are provided by HMRC to the CMS. The CMS only requests this following an application for a variation. **Note:** the government has announced plans to allow unearned income to be included in the initial calculation, rather than only be taken into account after an application for a variation.[35] No date has yet been set for this change to take effect.

The CMS can decide the amount of unearned income based on the most recent tax year if:[36]

- the latest available tax year is not the most recent tax year; *or*
- the information for the latest available tax year does not include a self-assessment; *or*
- the CMS is unable, for whatever reason, to request or obtain the information from HMRC – eg, because there has been a failure in the automatic data-sharing system.

The CMS should only do this if it is satisfied that there is sufficient evidence to do so. It should base its decision on information that would need to be provided on a tax self-assessment form.

The CMS bases the variation decision on actual unearned income figures for a complete tax year, rather than notional amounts based on the non-resident parent's assets and lifestyle. The use of HMRC figures also means that the CMS does not rely on the person with care to provide evidence of the non-resident parent's financial circumstances.

There are no grounds for a variation on the basis of the value of assets themselves if they do not produce income. Also, the fact that assets have been sold for a capital gain that would be taxable is not a ground for a variation. **Note:** the government has announced plans to bring notional income from assets into the initial calculation of the non-resident parent's income (see p67).[37] No date has yet been set for this to come into effect.

If the CMS agrees to make a variation on this ground, the unearned income is converted into a weekly amount and added to the existing gross weekly income.[38] If the non-resident parent has paid approved pension contributions that have not otherwise been taken into account in the child support calculation, the average weekly amount of these contributions is deducted from the unearned income amount. The pension contributions must have been made in the same tax year to which the unearned income relates.[39]

### Income from land or property

Any taxable income from the use of property or land in the UK or elsewhere counts as additional income. The capital value of property or land is ignored.

In most cases, property income is the rent from tenants or licensees from furnished or unfurnished commercial and domestic premises, and from any bare land. Certain other payments also count, including:[40]

- ground rent and feu duties;
- if property is let furnished, any payment by the tenant for the use of the furniture;
- premiums and other similar lump sums received for granting certain leases;
- income from caravans or houseboats where these are not moved around various locations;
- service charges from tenants for certain services normally provided by a landlord – eg, cleaning of communal areas, fuel and heating, and arranging repairs;
- deposits/bonds from tenants.

Any expenses incurred wholly and exclusively for the purpose of the property business and that are not of a capital nature (such as the cost of furniture, appliances and improvements to the property) are first deducted from the taxable income.[41] Some of the main categories of allowable expenses include:[42]

- council tax, business rates and water charges, if the agreement specifies that these are the responsibility of the landlord;
- the cost of maintenance and repairs (but not improvements);
- in some cases, the cost of certain energy efficiency measures installed before 6 April 2015;
- for fully furnished properties, certain costs for the wear and tear or renewal of furnishings;

- insurance premiums for contents, building and loss of rent;
- interest on a mortgage or loan taken out to purchase the property;
- the cost of providing services, including the wages of gardeners and cleaners;
- letting agent fees, and certain legal and accountancy fees;
- rent, ground rent and service charges;
- other direct costs – eg, phone calls, stationery and advertising for new tenants.

If only part of a property is let and part is occupied by the non-resident parent, a suitable proportion of the charges can be deducted. Any loss on a property business can usually be set against the property business profits of the following year.[43]

Rent and other receipts from properties outside the UK are treated in the same way. Losses on overseas property cannot be offset against profits on UK property, and vice versa.

If a non-resident parent rents out a room in her/his home under the 'rent-a-room' scheme, the first £7,500 (for the tax year 2018/19) income a year is not taxable. When calculating the income in this case, expenses cannot be deducted.[44]

Income from property rented as a business (eg, running a hotel, B&B or guest house), or from services not normally offered by a landlord (such as meals, laundry or room cleaning), usually counts as income from self-employment (see p67). Rental income from tied houses and caravan sites, and income from other land-related activity, such as farming and market gardening, are also treated as income from self-employment.[45]

**Income from savings and investments**
Any taxable income from savings and investments counts as additional income. The capital value of any savings or investments is ignored.

The main types of income that count are:[46]

- interest on invested money, including outside the UK – eg, interest on savings in a bank or building society (including income from selling a right to receive interest);
- dividends and other distributions from UK companies (including the tax credit payable with the dividend), and foreign dividends;
- discounts from securities – ie, the profit from trading in securities such as government stocks and bonds;
- income from government stocks and bonds;
- taxable payments from a life assurance policy, life annuity contract or capital redemption policy;
- payments from a trust;
- payments from the estate of someone who has died;
- interest arising from a debt;
- artificial transactions in futures and options.

Certain types of income are exempt from tax and therefore disregarded. These include:[47]

- interest, dividends or bonuses from an individual investment plan, such as an ISA;
- income from certified save as you earn schemes;
- interest under an employee share scheme;
- income from national savings certificates and tax reserve certificates;
- venture capital trust dividends;
- tax-exempt annual payments made by an individual in the UK not for commercial reasons – eg, from a covenant;
- periodic or annuity payments of personal injury damages;
- annuity payments from a Criminal Injuries Compensation Scheme award;
- gains from dealing in certain commodities, financial futures and options;
- the capital element of purchased life annuities;
- tax-free health and employment insurance or immediate-needs annuity payments.

**Miscellaneous income**

Any taxable income from other miscellaneous sources may count as additional income. This can include, for example, casual income from one-off jobs, royalties and other income from intellectual property such as sales of patent rights, and other recurring income not included in the other categories above.[48]

Certain types of income that are exempt from tax are not counted, including:[49]

- income from an educational bursary or scholarship;
- payments to adopters;
- certain foreign maintenance payments;
- certain compensation payments to World War Two victims;
- income from domestic electricity microgeneration;
- winnings from premium bonds, lotteries and gambling.

## Income of a non-resident parent liable for the nil or flat rate

In certain circumstances, if a non-resident parent has been assessed as liable for the nil rate (see p59) or flat rate (see p60) of child support and has income which would otherwise be taken into account in a child support calculation, a variation can be considered.

A variation on this ground is possible if the non-resident parent has gross weekly income of more than £100 that would normally be taken into account were it not for the fact that the parent is liable for:[50]

- the nil rate because s/he is:
  - a child; or
  - a prisoner; or
  - receiving an allowance for work-based training for young people; or

- resident in a care home or independent hospital, or is being provided with a care home service and/or independent healthcare service and receiving one of the qualifying benefits for the flat rate (see p60), or has the whole or part of the cost of her/his accommodation met by a local authority; *or*
- the flat rate because s/he receives a qualifying benefit (see p60).

If the CMS agrees to make a variation on this ground, the non-resident parent is treated as having the whole amount of the income for the purpose of calculating a new child support liability. Child support is calculated on this income at the reduced rate, basic rate or basic rate plus as appropriate. The liability calculated in this way is then added to the nil or flat rate.[51]

If a variation has been agreed on this ground, information about the additional income is sought and treated in the same way as for gross weekly income used in the child support calculation. Historic income information from HMRC for the latest available tax year is normally used. If current income is at least 25 per cent different from the historic income, current income can be used for the variation. If current income is used, the non-resident parent must notify the CMS if it changes by 25 per cent or more (see p78).

## Diverted income

A variation can be considered if:[52]
- the non-resident parent can control, whether directly or indirectly, the amount of income that s/he receives or that is taken into account as her/his gross income; *and*
- the CMS is satisfied that s/he has unreasonably reduced the amount of income that s/he would have received (and which would have been taken into account in the child support calculation or under a variation) by 'diverting' it to someone else or for some other purpose. The diversion does not have to have been arranged specifically to avoid child support responsibilities. The CMS (or First-tier Tribunal) has a broad discretion to judge what is unreasonable in the circumstances.[53]

This applies to income that would count as gross weekly income and as unearned income.

The non-resident parent may have diverted income:
- to a third party – eg, a new partner or close family member;
- to a business (eg, if s/he takes a lower income[54]) or to a pension scheme from which the non-resident parent will benefit later. In this situation, it must be reasonable to make a variation;
- towards other purposes – eg, if s/he uses company assets for private use or business funds for day-to-day expenditure.

Diverting earnings from a form that counts as income to one that results in their being excluded in the calculation can be classed as diverting income.[55]

---

*Example 5.3*

Marcus runs his own import/export business, employing his new partner, Shamira, and his brother. His brother is paid £800 a week and he and Shamira each receive £400. His ex-wife, Helene, gets basic rate child support of £64 for their two children. Helene applies for a variation because she thinks Marcus is diverting income via the company, especially as Shamira does not seem to do any work.

Shamira's salary could be a token payment, and Marcus takes less from the business than he pays his brother. The CMS considers that, on balance, there could be diversion of income via the company and Shamira's wages. Given its contentious nature, the case is referred to the First-tier Tribunal.

---

Deciding whether a parent has the ability to control the income s/he receives or whether a reduction in income received is unreasonable can be difficult. Many cases may require detailed investigation of the circumstances – eg, if a parent is a director, employee or shareholder of a small business. The way that money is held and distributed in the business is important, particularly whether this follows recognised business and accounting practices and/or is done for justified business reasons.[56] What counts is whether the parent has the ability to control the income in practice (eg, if it is clear that other shareholders involved in a business will agree to her/his proposed distribution of funds) and whether or not this could be legally enforced.[57]

The full weekly equivalent amount of any diverted income is added to gross weekly income to calculate the new amount of child support.[58]

## Changes in additional income

Variations on unearned income grounds are based on information provided by HMRC, and are considered by the CMS at the annual review (see p74).

The CMS seeks updated information from HMRC as part of the annual review process and can make a supersession decision on the basis of that information. The supersession decision takes effect from the review date.[59]

If the CMS accepts that the non-resident parent had unearned income in a past tax year but no longer has unearned income in the current tax year (eg, if s/he has sold a property that generated income), it can treat the parent as having no unearned income.[60]

A calculation decision that includes a variation on the ground that the non-resident parent has gross weekly income of more than £100 based on current income can be superseded before the annual review date if her/his current income changes by at least 25 per cent.

There is no obligation on parents who have unearned income included in their gross weekly income to report changes in this.

A variation based on diverted income is not reviewed routinely, as it is not based on information provided by HMRC. A person with care, non-resident parent or child applicant in Scotland can apply for a supersession at any time if the circumstances relating to the diversion change.

# 3. Applying for a variation

A person with care, non-resident parent or a child applicant in Scotland can all apply for a variation.[61] An authorised representative can also apply. In certain circumstances, the Child Maintenance Service (CMS) has discretion to reinstate a previous variation without an application having been made (see p116).

An application for a variation can be made either verbally or in writing.[62] This means an applicant may give details over the phone, although the CMS may ask for a written application – eg, because complicated special expenses are being considered.

The application must state the grounds on which it is made.[63] If it does not, or at least give a reason, it is not accepted as properly made.

*Example 5.4*
1. Joe applies for a variation because he believes his child support is too high. The CMS does not accept it as a properly made application.
2. Joe applies for a variation because he believes his child support is too high and he cannot afford it because of the high cost of pet food. The CMS accepts the application as properly made, but then rejects it as it is not on one of the specified grounds.
3. Joe applies for a variation because he believes his child support is too high because he cannot now afford the kennel costs he incurs when he travels to see his children. The CMS accepts the application as properly made and it is given a preliminary consideration (see p106). It rejects the application as kennel costs are not one of the specified grounds. Had Joe referred to his other contact costs (eg, his travel costs), his application would probably have proceeded.

An application for a variation can be made before a child support calculation decision has been made.[64] If a calculation is already in force and a new application is made by the same person, the CMS may (but does not have to) treat it as a request for a variation, depending on the circumstances and the information contained in it,[65] even if the application did not expressly ask for a variation.[66] An appeal can also be treated as an application for a variation if it would be more advantageous to the person appealing. The CMS must bear in mind, however, that what is advantageous to the appellant may not be to another party to the calculation.[67]

If an application for a variation is made, but there is insufficient information to decide whether to proceed, the CMS may request further information. This should be provided within 14 days, or a longer period if it is reasonable in the circumstances – eg, if the applicant is in hospital.[68] If the time limit is exceeded without good cause, the effective date of the variation may be affected. If the information is not provided, the CMS has the discretion either to reject the application or to proceed.[69]

There is no specific provision to allow an application for a variation to be amended or withdrawn. In practice, an application could be withdrawn verbally or in writing at any time before a decision is made on it. If a change relates to a period after the effective date of an application, a separate new application for a variation could be made and a separate decision would be made for the period covered by each circumstance.

Two or more applications for a variation may be considered at the same time. In addition, if appropriate, an application made on one ground may be treated as an application on a different ground.[70]

## 4. What happens after an application is made

Once an application has been made, the procedure is as follows.
- The Child Maintenance Service (CMS) considers the application (see below).
- Unless the application is rejected, the other parties are notified and asked to make representations. This is known as 'contesting' (see p107).
- The CMS may make an interim maintenance decision (see p109) or impose a regular payment condition on the non-resident parent (see p109).
- The CMS decides whether or not to vary the amount of child support payable (see p110).

The CMS may also pass a case to the First-tier Tribunal for a determination (see p110).

The application may not proceed in the above way if the CMS refuses to consider it further – eg, because:[71]
- one of the grounds for rejection is established (see p107);
- it is withdrawn; *or*
- the regular payment condition (see p109) has not been met.

### Considering the application

Once an application is properly made, the CMS considers whether it should go ahead (a 'preliminary consideration').[72] At this point, the CMS may reject the application for a variation and decide to:

- revise or supersede the child support calculation, or to refuse to revise or supersede it; *or*
- make the calculation, or make a default maintenance decision (see p125).

### Grounds for rejecting an application

The CMS may reject an application for a variation after a preliminary consideration if:[73]

- there are no grounds for a variation;
- it has insufficient information to decide the child support application and so a default maintenance decision is likely to be made;
- the applicant does not state a ground or provide sufficient information to allow a ground to be identified;
- the requirements of the stated ground are not met, or no information has been given that supports the ground or that is sufficient to allow further enquiries to be made;
- a default maintenance decision is in force;
- the non-resident parent is liable to pay the nil or flat rate because s/he, or her/his partner, receives one of the qualifying benefits (see p60);
- a variation was sought on the grounds that the non-resident parent has additional income, but gross weekly income is already at least the capped amount of £3,000; *or*
- the non-resident parent has made the application for a variation on special expenses grounds and:
  - the amount of the expenses is below the threshold (see p93);
  - s/he is already paying £7 or less child support a week;
  - after deducting special expenses, her/his gross weekly income is still above the capped amount of £3,000; *or*
  - gross weekly income has been estimated because insufficient information was available.

### Contesting the application

If it has not rejected an application, the CMS usually then notifies the other relevant parties. This may be done by phone or in writing and must include the grounds on which the application has been made and provide any information or evidence the applicant has given to support it or which has been obtained by the CMS, except information that must not be disclosed (see p108).[74]

The CMS may invite the other parties to the child support calculation to make representations within 14 days about anything to do with the application. The 14-day time limit may be extended, if the CMS is satisfied that it is reasonable.[75]

The CMS does not need to notify the other parties if:[76]

- it is satisfied that, on the available information, the application for a variation would not be agreed to;

- the application is on the grounds of unearned income, the latest available tax year information from HM Revenue and Customs (HMRC) does not show unearned income above the threshold and the CMS does not have further information that justifies making further enquiries; *or*
- a previously agreed variation can be reinstated without an application (see p116).

The CMS tends to inform the other parties in writing. If an application has been made by phone, the evidence may be a transcript of the call.

The other parties may respond by phone or in writing, although the CMS may require it in writing. If no contesting information is provided, the CMS may make a decision on the application as it stands.[77]

Any information provided by another party, other than that which may not be disclosed (see below), may be forwarded to the applicant if the CMS considers this reasonable. The applicant is given 14 days to comment on the evidence or information supplied by the other party. This 14-day time limit may also be extended if the CMS is satisfied that it is reasonable. The application must not be decided until this period is over.[78]

It is possible that the applicant may supply further information outside the 14-day time limit and the CMS may already have decided in the meantime to proceed with the application and notify the other parties. In this case, the further information is likely to be passed to the other parties and a further 14 days from the date of this notification (or longer if the CMS is satisfied that it is reasonable) allowed for representations.

## Information that must not be disclosed

In addition to the general rules on disclosing information (see p52), there are additional rules for variations. Supporting evidence or information from one party is not notified to another party if it contains:[79]

- details of an illness or disability of a relevant other child if the non-resident parent has requested that this not be disclosed and the CMS agrees;
- medical evidence that has not been disclosed to the applicant or a relevant person (ie, person with care, non-resident parent or child applicant in Scotland) and which would be harmful to her/him;
- the address of a relevant person or qualifying child, or information that could lead to that individual or child being located, and there is a risk of harm or undue distress to that person or child or any other child(ren) living with that person.

If you request that information is not disclosed, this is discussed with you. It may be possible to make an amended application which does not include the relevant details. If you refuse to disclose information that is relevant for the other party to contest the application, your application could be rejected. However, there may be a good reason for non-disclosure, and each case should be considered on its own merits.

## Interim maintenance decision

If an application for a variation is made before the child support calculation decision has been made, the CMS may make an interim maintenance decision.[80] The amount of the interim maintenance is the child support calculated in the normal way, ignoring the variation. This is to allow the application for a variation to be considered.

An interim maintenance decision can be challenged in the usual way. However, when a calculation is made which replaces this, any appeal against the interim decision may lapse.[81] If the interim maintenance decision is superseded, the usual rule tolerating a 25 per cent change in current income (see p77) does not apply.

## Regular payment condition

If a non-resident parent has applied for a variation, the CMS may impose a regular payment condition on her/him if s/he has:[82]
- a poor payment record or arrears;
- failed to make payments while the variation application was being contested and considered; *or*
- special expenses that make it difficult for her/him to meet her/his child support liability.

The amount due under a regular payment condition is either:[83]
- the child support calculated, including that set under an interim maintenance decision; *or*
- the amount that would be due if the variation were agreed.

This means that if the CMS believes that the variation application will be successful, it may set a regular payment condition that adjusts the child support calculated to reflect the variation, reducing the financial burden on the parent. However, if it believes that the application will be unsuccessful and a regular payment condition is imposed, it is set at the calculation rate.

A regular payment condition does not affect the amount of child support the non-resident parent is liable to pay. Therefore, if the set amount is lower than the amount due, there will be arrears if the variation application fails.

The regular payment condition is set independently of any other arrears arrangement the parent may have. It ends either when the CMS makes a final decision on the calculation (whether or not the variation is agreed) or when the variation application is withdrawn.[84]

When a regular payment condition is imposed, the non-resident parent, person with care and/or qualifying child applicant in Scotland are sent written notification.[85] This makes it clear that if the condition is not met, the application for a variation may lapse.[86]

If a non-resident parent does not meet the regular payment condition within one month of this notification, written notification of this is sent to all the relevant parties.[87] If the regular payment condition has not been met, the CMS may refuse to consider the application for a variation.[88] A refusal to consider the application cannot be appealed.

## Referral to the First-tier Tribunal

Once the application has passed the preliminary consideration and contest stage, it may be passed to the First-tier Tribunal for a determination on whether or not to agree to the variation.[89] This normally only occurs if a novel or particularly contentious issue is being considered.

If a referral is made, it can only be withdrawn by the CMS. The tribunal can proceed, even if the parties come to an agreement.[90] It is also possible for an applicant to add a further ground of variation to an application before it is decided by the tribunal.[91] The tribunal applies the same rules as the CMS and decides that the variation should be either agreed to or refused.[92] In doing so, it must make a revision or supersession decision, but passes it back to the CMS to make the child support calculation.[93] This decision by the CMS (ie, to revise or supersede, or to refuse to revise or supersede, the child support calculation) may then be challenged in the normal way (see Chapters 9 and 10).

## 5. **Decisions**

The Child Maintenance Service (CMS) has some discretion when deciding whether to vary the child support calculation. It must bear in mind the general principles of child support law – ie, that:[94]
- a parent is responsible for maintaining her/his children when s/he can afford to do so;
- a parent is responsible for maintaining all her/his children equally;
- the welfare of any child affected by an application for a variation must be taken into account (see p122).

In addition, the CMS must be satisfied that:[95]
- the grounds are met; *and*
- it is just and equitable to agree to the variation (see p111).

The CMS must take into account any representations made by any of the relevant parties to the application.[96]

If the variation application is made by the person with care and the CMS considers that further information would affect its decision, the onus is on the CMS to investigate. There is no onus on the person with care to prove that a variation is justified. The CMS must consider any information that is available to it (eg, information that it can obtain from HM Revenue and Customs), and must take appropriate steps to obtain any such further information.[97]

The CMS must not agree to make a variation if:[98]

- it has insufficient information to make a child support calculation and so would make a default maintenance decision (see p125); *or*
- any of the circumstances apply that would lead to a variation application being rejected after a preliminary consideration (see p106).

A variation is applied by revising or superseding the child support calculation decision. Whether the decision is revised or superseded depends on when the variation application is made. If the grounds for the variation existed at the time the original calculation decision was made, the decision may be revised. If the grounds result from a change of circumstances, the decision may be superseded.

If the CMS agrees to a variation, it can:[99]

- revise or supersede the calculation/replace the interim maintenance decision (see p109); *or*
- make a calculation (this may replace an interim maintenance decision) or default maintenance decision (see p125).

In some cases, a variation may be agreed which makes no difference to the amount of child support calculated. A revision or supersession is still carried out, as each decision gives further appeal rights.

Once a variation is made, it will be considered each time there is a revision or supersession of the calculation under the usual revision/supersession rules (see Chapter 9). Some changes in circumstances may mean that the variation ceases to have effect, in which case the calculation may be suspended or cancelled in order to remove the variation element. In certain cases, if there is a further change in circumstances, the variation may be reinstated by the CMS without an application (see p116). In other cases, a new request for a variation may need to be made.

## Just and equitable

Even though the grounds are met, a variation is only agreed if it is 'just and equitable' to do so.[100]

There are no specific factors that the CMS must take into account in deciding whether it is just and equitable to make a variation. However, examples of factors that are likely to be considered include:

- the welfare of any child likely to be affected if the variation is agreed (see p122);

- whether agreeing to a variation would lead the non-resident parent or parent with care to give up employment;
- if the applicant is the non-resident parent, whether there is any liability to pay child maintenance under a court order or agreement before the effective date of the child support calculation;
- if the non-resident parent has applied for a special expenses variation, whether s/he could make financial arrangements to cover those expenses or could pay for them from money currently spent on non-essentials.

This decision is, however, discretionary and the CMS must make it based on the individual circumstances of the case.

The following must not be taken into account:[101]
- whether or not the child's conception was planned;
- who was responsible for the breakdown of the relationship between the non-resident parent and the person with care;
- whether the non-resident parent or person with care is in a new relationship with someone who is not the qualifying child's parent;
- any contact arrangements and whether or not they are being kept to;
- the income or assets of anyone other than the non-resident parent;
- any failure of the non-resident parent to pay child support or maintenance under a court order or written agreement;
- the fact that a non-resident parent pays school fees (because the child support legislation leaves the courts to make orders on tuition fees);[102]
- representations from individuals other than the person with care, non-resident parent or a qualifying child applicant in Scotland.

The CMS must reach a positive conclusion that it is just and equitable to agree to a variation, and not simply that there is no reason not to do so.[103] All factors should be considered, but the CMS (or the First-tier Tribunal on a referral – see p110) decides what weight to give to them.[104] This may mean taking into account circumstances for which either party could have sought a variation, even if s/he did not. For example, since contact costs affect the financial circumstances of a non-resident parent, it may be just and equitable to take these into account when deciding on the variation, even if the application was about something else (and may have been made at the request of the person with care).[105] It may also be just and equitable to take into account voluntary payments by the non-resident parent for expenses that could not have been grounds for a variation.[106] If such wider financial circumstances are taken into account, it must be made clear to all parties on what basis the variation has been decided.

The just and equitable rule can never be used to increase the amount of a variation above the amount justified by the relevant ground.[107] However, the amount may be reduced.[108]

# The effect of the variation

The effect of the variation should not reduce the total amount of child support paid to less than £7, and should not change the fact that the maximum amount of gross income that can be taken into account is the capped amount of £3,000.[109] The following sections examine the effect of a variation on different grounds, including where there is more than one ground. The CMS calls these 'concurrent variations'.

## Special expenses

All special expenses amounts are aggregated (taking account of the threshold rules). This total amount of the non-resident parent's relevant expenses is converted into a weekly amount and deducted from her/his gross weekly income. The calculation is then carried out as normal, using this amount.[110]

If the effect of the variation would be to reduce the child support liability to below the flat rate of £7, the non-resident parent is liable to pay £7.[111]

If the gross weekly income is the capped amount, the effect of the variation is worked out by subtracting the special expenses from the actual gross weekly income. If this results in a figure still above the capped amount of £3,000, the special expenses variation is refused.[112]

---

*Example 5.5*

The situation is as in Examples 5.1 and 5.2. Bronwen has gross weekly income of £628 and pays basic rate child support of £100.48 to Ivan for Ursula and Gretchen. She claims special expenses for the cost of contact with her children, amounting to £2,100 over a six-month period, and for the contribution to the maintenance element of their boarding school fees of £1,500 a term.

Her weekly special expenses are worked out as £80.77 for contact and £28.77 for boarding school costs, totalling £109.54. Both types of special expenses are over the £10 threshold, and so the total amount of £109.54 a week is allowed.

This is deducted from her gross weekly income: £628 − £109.54 = £518.46

Her child support is now worked out in the usual way: 16% x £518.46 = £82.95

Her variation for special expenses has reduced her child support liability from £100.48 a week to £82.95.

---

## Additional income

The amount of any additional income is converted to a weekly amount and added to the non-resident parent's gross weekly income. If this would result in a gross income figure above the capped amount, the gross income to be taken into account is restricted to the capped amount of £3,000.[113]

If a variation on additional income grounds is agreed and the child support without the variation would be the flat rate or £7, the amount of child support is £7 plus the amount calculated on the additional income.[114]

*Example 5.6*

The case in Example 5.3 is referred to the First-tier Tribunal. The tribunal determines that there should be a variation for additional income on the grounds that Marcus has diverted income, with a weekly value of £360. This amount is added to Marcus's gross weekly income of £400 used in the child support calculation. His gross weekly income is now £760. The amount he is now due to pay Helene is £121.60 a week (£760 x 16%).

If Marcus had been paying the flat rate of child support and the variation for additional income of £360 was agreed, the child support due would now be:

Child support at the basic rate for two qualifying children: 16% x £360 = £57.60

The amount of child support payable: £57.60 + £7 = £64.60

## If there is more than one variation

If there is more than one variation element (ie, on both special expenses and additional income grounds, known as a 'concurrent variation'), the results of each variation are added together.[115]

- This aggregate figure is then added to the actual gross weekly income, capping the income at £3,000.
- If the total amount of child support is £7 or less, £7 is payable and is apportioned between the people with care, if appropriate.[116]

*Example 5.7*

Marcus has gross income of £400 a week and pays his ex-wife Helene basic rate child support of £64 a week for their two children. The CMS decides that there should be a variation for additional income on the grounds that he has diverted income, with a weekly value of £360. The CMS also decides that there should be a variation on special expenses grounds as Marcus has contact costs of £32 a week for visiting his children and pays £24 a week for debts of the relationship.

The special expenses Marcus pays are deducted from his additional income: £360 – (£32 + £24) = £304

This amount is added to the gross weekly income: £304 + £400 = £704

Child support at the basic rate for two qualifying children: 16% x £704 = £112.64

The combined effect of the variations is that Marcus now pays Helene an additional £48.64 child support a week.

## When a variation takes effect

If the ground for the variation existed at the initial effective date (see p127) of the child support calculation (ie, when the non-resident parent was notified of the application), the variation takes effect on that date if either:
- the application is made before the calculation is made;[117] *or*
- the application is made within 30 days of the date the calculation decision was notified, or within a longer period if the CMS allows a late application for a revision (see p192).[118]

The exception to this is if the non-resident parent applied for a variation on the grounds of previous debts or payments in respect of certain mortgages, loans or insurance policies before the child support calculation was made, and payments towards these are treated as voluntary payments in the initial payment period (see p147). In this case, the variation takes effect from the date on which the non-resident parent was notified of the amount of her/his child support liability.[119]

If the ground did not apply at the initial effective date of the child support calculation, the variation takes effect from:
- the date the ground arose, if this is after the initial effective date but before the calculation is made;[120] *or*
- the date of the variation application;[121] *or*
- the date on which the ground is expected to arise, if the application for variation is made in advance.[122]

If an application for a variation is made before the child support calculation is made and the ground has ceased to exist by the date the calculation is made, the variation is applied for the period the ground existed.[123]

There may be a number of different grounds, agreed over time, and each may have a different date from when it takes effect.

*Example 5.8*

Tara claims child support. The effective date is 27 August 2018. She is notified of her calculation on 19 September 2018. She takes advice and applies for a variation on the basis that an additional income ground applied on 27 August 2018. She makes this application on 8 October 2018 – ie, within 30 days of her notification of the decision. The variation is agreed and the calculation is revised on 15 November 2018, with effect from 27 August 2018.

Juan, her ex-partner, takes advice and on 3 December 2018 applies for a variation on the grounds that he has been paying off a loan for a car which they bought before splitting up and which Tara needs, as she lives in a secluded cottage. He is also just about to start paying boarding school fees for their eldest child in late December. The variation is agreed and a revision is made on 3 January 2019 in which the element for previous debts takes effect from 3 December and the boarding school fees take effect from 16 December 2018.

Even though the variation for previous debts only applies from December, Juan could ask that the amounts he paid towards the car before the calculation was made be considered as voluntary payments to offset initial arrears. Had Juan taken advice at the same time as Tara and applied for a variation at the same time as she did, on the grounds of previous debts and that his repayments on the car loan were voluntary payments, there could have been a further variation to the calculation, with the decision taking effect from 27 August 2018.

## When a variation is not applied

A variation is not applied for any period when:[124]
- the non-resident parent is liable for the flat or nil rate of child support because s/he or her/his partner receives one of the qualifying benefits (see p60); *or*
- a variation was sought on additional income grounds but the non-resident parent's gross weekly income was already the capped amount of £3,000; *or*
- the non-resident parent applied for the variation on special expenses grounds and:
  - the amount of the expenses is below the threshold (see p93); *or*
  - the non-resident parent is already paying £7 or less child support; *or*
  - after deducting special expenses, the gross weekly income is still above the capped amount of £3,000; *or*
  - the gross weekly income has been estimated because insufficient information was available.

When a variation ceases to have effect because of a change of circumstances, a supersession is carried out. This takes effect from the day on which the change occurred. If there is a further later change that means that a variation might apply again, a further application for a variation must be made (unless the CMS has discretion to reinstate the variation – see below).

## Reinstating a variation

The CMS has the discretion to revise or supersede a child support calculation in order to reinstate a variation that has previously been agreed, without the need for a new application. This is most likely to apply to variations on special expenses grounds, as this discretion can be applied if:[125]
- a variation ceases to have effect, because a change of circumstances means that:
  - the non-resident parent's liability is reduced to the nil rate or another rate that means that the variation cannot be taken into account; *or*

– the child support calculation has been replaced with a default maintenance decision;

*and then:*
- a subsequent change of circumstances means the calculation has been revised or superseded so that the non-resident parent is now liable for a rate which can be adjusted to take the variation into account.

Examples of situations where this could apply include if:
- the non-resident parent is sentenced to a prison term and so becomes liable for the nil rate, but subsequently returns to a basic or reduced rate;
- a variation is agreed and on a subsequent application for a revision or supersession the non-resident parent fails to provide information. Therefore, the child support calculation is replaced by a default decision. Later, the information required is provided and this default maintenance decision is replaced with a calculation. The variation may then be reapplied without a fresh application.

The CMS can reinstate a variation straight away without checking whether the circumstances relating to it have changed. If any party is aware of such changes of circumstances, s/he could apply for a revision or supersession. There is no obligation to investigate, so decisions are made based on the information available to the CMS. There is no time limit on the period between the variation ceasing to apply and being reinstated, provided the circumstances that gave rise to the variation remain unchanged.

*Example 5.9*
Joe obtains a variation from his basic rate child support on the grounds of his contact costs with his children. He is later convicted of a criminal offence and sentenced to six months in prison. He becomes liable to pay the nil rate. On his release, he becomes liable at the reduced rate. The CMS is not satisfied that the circumstances relating to his eligibility are still the same and so does not reinstate the variation. Joe must make a new application for a variation on the grounds of contact costs.

Had a variation been granted on the grounds of previous debts of the relationship, the CMS may have reinstated the variation without Joe having to make a further application, as there is no reason why this ground and its effect should be changed by his imprisonment.

If the calculation ceases, this discretion does not apply. For example, if the parent moves abroad and the CMS ceases to have jurisdiction, but then s/he returns to the UK, a subsequent application must be made for a child support calculation, including an application for a variation. However, in some circumstances, the CMS may be able to reinstate the variation without its being contested (see p107).

## Challenging a decision

A variation is not a separate decision to be challenged; it is applied by a decision revising or superseding the child support calculation decision. Once a variation is applied to the calculation, this decision may then be challenged by applying for a revision within 30 days (and appealing if necessary). The variation is taken into account in the revision/appeal. Any change of circumstances, whether in relation to the variation or other factors, can result in a revision or supersession of the calculation under the normal rules, depending on the circumstances (see Chapter 9). This also applies to decisions referred by the CMS to the First-tier Tribunal for a decision – eg, contentious cases.[126]

If an application is made for a revision or a supersession of a decision that includes a variation:[127]

- there is no preliminary consideration;
- the usual rules on seeking further information and allowing the application to be contested apply; *and*
- the same factors must not be taken into account when considering whether it would be just and equitable to agree to a variation (see p111).

However, the CMS does not have to notify the other parties and invite representations if:[128]

- the revised or superseded decision would not be advantageous to the applicant; *or*
- it considers that representations from the other parties would not be relevant .

The CMS may decide to revise or supersede, or not to revise or supersede, the decision and notifies the applicant and any relevant parties, as appropriate.

# Notes

**1. What is a variation**
1 ss28A(1) and (3) and 28G(1) and (2)
CSA 1991; ss28A-28F and Schs 4A and
4B CSA 1991, as modified by
CS(V)(MSP) Regs

**2. Grounds for a variation**
2 Sch 4B CSA 1991; regs 63-67 CSMC
Regs
3 Reg 68 CSMC Regs
4 Reg 68(3) and (4) CSMC Regs

5 Reg 72(1) CSMC Regs
6 Reg 63 CSMC Regs
7 *CMEC v NC (CSM)* [2009] UKUT 106
(AAC), reported as [2010] AACR 1
8 Reg 63(1) CSMC Regs
9 R(CS) 5/08; *SM v SSWP and FS (CSM)*
[2013] UKUT 445 (AAC)
10 Reg 63(3)(a) CSMC Regs
11 Reg 63(3)(b) CSMC Regs
12 Reg 63(3)(b)(ii) CSMC Regs
13 Reg 64 CSMC Regs

14  Reg 64(2)(d) CSMC Regs
15  Reg 64(2)(a), (b), (f), (g) and (h) CSMC Regs
16  Reg 64(1) CSMC Regs
17  Reg 64(3) CSMC Regs
18  Reg 65(1) CSMC Regs; R(CS) 3/03
19  Reg 65(2) CSMC Regs
20  Reg 65(3)(k) CSMC Regs
21  Reg 2, definition of 'qualifying lender', CSMC Regs; see also CCS/3674/2007, para 23; s376(4) ICTA 1988
22  Reg 65(3) and (4) CSMC Regs
23  CCS/3674/2007, para 19
24  Reg 65(5) CSMC Regs; R(CS) 3/03; R(CS) 5/03; *T v SSWP and A (CSM)* [2017] UKUT 492 (AAC)
25  R(CS) 3/03
26  Reg 66 CSMC Regs
27  Reg 66(6) CSMC Regs
28  Reg 66(2) CSMC Regs
29  Reg 66(3) and (4) CSMC Regs
30  Reg 66(5) CSMC Regs
31  Reg 67(2)(a) CSMC Regs
32  Reg 67(2)(b) CSMC Regs
33  Sch 4B para 4(1) CSA 1991; reg 69(1) CSMC Regs
34  Reg 69(2) CSMC Regs; Parts 3-5 IT(TOI)A 2005
35  DWP, *Child Maintenance: a new compliance and arrears strategy – public consultation,* December 2017
36  Reg 69(5) CSMC Regs
37  DWP, *Child Maintenance: a new compliance and arrears strategy – public consultation,* December 2017
38  Reg 69(7) CSMC Regs
39  Reg 69(8) and (9) CSMC Regs
40  Part 3 IT(TOI)A 2005; HMRC, *Property Income Manual*
41  ss33 and 272 and IT(TOI)A 2005
42  Part 3 IT(TOI)A 2005; HMRC, *Property Income Manual*
43  Reg 69(4) CSMC Regs; s118 ITA 2007
44  ss309, 784, 786, 788(2) and 789(4) IT(TOI)A 2005; Income Tax (Limit for Rent-a-Room Relief) Order 2015, No.1539
45  ss9, 19, 20, 267 and 273 IT(TOI)A 2005
46  Part 4 IT(TOI)A 2005; HMRC, *Savings and Investment Manual*
47  Part 6 IT(TOI)A 2005; HMRC, *Savings and Investment Manual*
48  ss579, 587, 683 and 687 Part 5 IT(TOI)A 2005
49  Part 6 IT(TOI)A 2005
50  Reg 70 CSMC Regs
51  Reg 70(2) CSMC Regs
52  Reg 71(1) CSMC Regs

53  *G'OB v CMEC (CSM)* [2010] UKUT 6 (AAC)
54  *TB v SSWP and SB (CSM)* [2014] UKUT 301 (AAC); *EH v SSWP (CSM)* [2015] UKUT 621 (AAC)
55  R(CS) 6/05; CCS/1769/2007
56  See, for example, *RC v CMEC and WC* [2009] UKUT 62 (AAC), reported as [2011] AACR 38; CCS/1320/2005; CCS/409/2005
57  *PS v SSWP and KH (CSM)* [2015] UKUT 183 (AAC)
58  Reg 71(2) CSMC Regs
59  Reg 21 CSMC Regs
60  Reg 69(6) CSMC Regs

### 3. Applying for a variation
61  s28A(1) CSA 1991
62  s28A(4)(a) CSA 1991
63  s28A(4)(b) CSA 1991
64  s28A(3) CSA 1991
65  *DB v CMEC (CSM)* [2010] UKUT 356 (AAC)
66  *DB v CMEC (CSM)* [2010] UKUT 356 (AAC)
67  R(CS) 2/06
68  Reg 58(1) and (2) CSMC Regs
69  Reg 58(3) CSMC Regs
70  Reg 56(3) and (4) CSMC Regs

### 4. What happens after an application is made
71  s28D(2) CSA 1991
72  s28B CSA 1991
73  s28B CSA 1991; reg 57(1) CSMC Regs
74  Reg 59(1)(a) and (5) CSMC Regs
75  Reg 59(1)(b) CSMC Regs
76  Reg 59(2) CSMC Regs
77  Reg 59(4) CSMC Regs
78  Reg 59(3) CSMC Regs
79  Reg 59(5) CSMC Regs
80  ss12 and 28F(5) CSA 1991
81  s28F(5) CSA 1991
82  s28C CSA 1991; reg 62 CSMC Regs
83  s28C(2) CSA 1991; reg 62(1) CSMC Regs
84  s28C(4) CSA 1991
85  s28C(3) CSA 1991
86  s28C(5) CSA 1991
87  s28C(7) CSA 1991
88  Reg 31(2) and (3) CS(V) Regs
89  s28D(1)(b) CSA 1991
90  *Milton v SSWP* [2006] EWCA Civ 1258
91  R(CS) 3/01
92  s28D(3) CSA 1991
93  R(CS) 5/06

## 5. Decisions

# Chapter 6

## Decisions

This chapter covers:
1. Making decisions about child support (below)
2. The initial child support decision (p122)
3. Default maintenance decisions (p125)
4. Notification of decisions (p126)
5. When liability for child support starts (the 'effective date') (p127)
6. When a calculation ends (p127)

---

## 1. Making decisions about child support

Child Maintenance Service (CMS) officials are responsible for making decisions about child support. In doing so, they must apply the law to the facts of each case. They have no discretion about how some decisions are made – eg, about the amount of child support due or choosing between alternatives, such as whether a person is habitually resident or not.

Some child support decisions, however, are discretionary decisions. The CMS has discretion only if, after deciding on the facts of a case and what the law requires, it still has a choice about what decision to make. There are a limited number of situations where the CMS has discretion – eg, whether a variation would be 'just and equitable' (see p111), or how to collect or enforce payments, including whether to make a deduction from earnings order.

Whenever the CMS makes a discretionary decision, it must take into account the welfare of any child likely to be affected by the decision.[1] Only the welfare of a child must be taken into account (see p8 for who counts as a child), not that of any adults involved. However, it is not just qualifying children or those named in the application who must be considered. The situation of *any* child likely to be affected by the decision must be looked at – eg, a child of the non-resident parent's new family, or another child of the non-resident parent who does not live with her/him.[2]

This duty to consider the welfare of a child also applies to discretionary decisions made by the First-tier Tribunal and Upper Tribunal.

## The welfare of a child

The duty to consider the welfare of children is a general principle in child support law.[3] The legislation does not make it the paramount consideration, or impose a duty on the CMS or First-tier Tribunal/Upper Tribunal to promote the welfare of any children,[4] but considerable weight should be given to this principle.[5] In general, it should be considered along with the other principles of child support – eg, that each parent of a qualifying child has a duty to maintain her/him.[6]

'Welfare' includes the child's physical, mental and social welfare. For example, if imposing a deduction from earnings order (see p158) would prevent a non-resident parent from visiting a child, that child's emotional welfare may be affected. However, an order may mean the parent with care has more money coming in, which may improve the child's physical and social welfare.

Generally, the welfare of a child must be balanced with the benefits of child support being paid for that child or other children. It is likely to be rare that the welfare of a child will justify a decision or action that is contrary to the principle that parents should support their children. However, if the non-resident parent has a child in her/his household who would be adversely affected by the implications of enforcement action, this might mean that certain enforcement action should not be taken. When deciding on enforcement action, the CMS must not use the welfare of the child principle to avoid the full use of its powers, unless it is genuinely appropriate.[7]

The CMS must record its reasons for any decisions it makes on the welfare of all children who could be affected, and it may be useful to ask to see these records. Give the CMS full details as soon as you can about the effect a discretionary decision may have on a child's welfare. If a decision has been made in ignorance of its effect on a child, supply the information and ask the CMS to reconsider. Some decisions that should involve the welfare of the child principle can be challenged (see Chapters 9 and 10). If the decision cannot be appealed (eg, if it is about enforcement), you could consider making a complaint (see Chapter 11) or applying for a judicial review (see p190).

In addition to the general principle of the welfare of children in child support law, the UK must also comply with international obligations, including a commitment to the welfare of children under the United Nations Convention on the Rights of the Child. This means that in instances where more than one interpretation of the law is possible, the one chosen should be that which more closely complies with protecting the welfare of children.[8]

## 2. The initial child support decision

Once an effective application has been made (see p26) and the Child Maintenance Service (CMS) has obtained, or tried to obtain, the necessary information, it can:[9]

- make a calculation;
- make a default maintenance decision (see p125); *or*
- refuse to make a calculation (p124).

Details of the case are entered on the CMS computer system and child support is calculated automatically.

## Waiting for the calculation decision

If the person with care can provide contact details, the CMS aims to start gathering information from the non-resident parent as soon as possible. It aims to make an accurate decision within a month of an application, but some cases may take up to 26 weeks.[10] If the CMS has to trace the non-resident parent, it is likely to take longer before it can make a decision.

### Delays in dealing with applications

Much of the contact with parents to collect and check information needed to make a calculation and collect payments is done by telephone.

The CMS aims to keep people informed about the progress on their case, and contacts applicants at certain stages – eg, to let them know about negotiations with the non-resident parent about collection or if s/he has made a complaint. However, you can contact the CMS on a regular basis for an update on your application.

A delay after the non-resident parent is contacted about the application does not normally delay the starting date of any calculation (see p127), but the date of the decision may be delayed. If the non-resident parent has liability to pay child maintenance under a court order or an agreement, this continues and remains enforceable. Other non-resident parents should consider putting money aside or making voluntary payments (see p147). Parents who are already contributing voluntarily should check whether these payments might be used to offset initial arrears (see p139).

If the non-resident parent is not co-operating, the CMS may make a default maintenance decision (see p125) and may take legal action against her/him (see p38). If you have applied for child support and the CMS does not make a default maintenance decision, request that one be made. If this does not happen, consider making a complaint (see p233). In certain circumstances, the CMS has the option of making a calculation based on an estimate of the non-resident parent's income (see p72).

### Withdrawing the application

If an application is withdrawn or treated as withdrawn (see p27), the CMS cannot make a calculation. If a calculation is made after the application is withdrawn, it can be challenged (see Chapters 9 and 10).

The application cannot be withdrawn after a decision has been made, but the applicant can ask the CMS to cease acting, in which case the calculation is cancelled (see p128).

## Change of circumstances

There is no general requirement to notify the CMS of changes in circumstances. However, both the person with care and the non-resident parent are required to notify the CMS of some changes (see p51). It is an offence for a non-resident parent not to notify the CMS of a change of address.[11]

In practice, any party to a child support calculation (ie, person with care, non-resident person or child applicant in Scotland) may want to tell the CMS of changes or new information that might affect the calculation.

There are also specific rules for when changes of income must be disclosed and which changes result in a calculation being altered (see p77).

If the CMS is told about a change or given new information that relates to before the effective date (see p127), it has discretion on whether to take this information into account. This can be done in the initial calculation, or by making two or more calculations for the different periods.[12]

When making a decision, the CMS takes into account the information that applied at the date the decision would have effect.[13] Any information about a change after the effective date but before the calculation is made can lead to a series of calculations in respect of different periods. The effective date of each calculation is normally the date the change occurred or is expected to occur.[14]

Changes that occur after a calculation is made may result in a revision or supersession, depending on when the change is notified and its significance (see Chapter 9). Changes resulting in a revision or supersession generally take effect from the day on which an event happens or on which a decision is made.

## Refusal to make a calculation

The CMS *must* refuse to make a calculation if:
- the application was made by a person who is not a non-resident parent or a person with care (or, in Scotland, a qualifying child aged 12 or over) (see p7);
- there is a pre-3 March 2003 court order (registered agreement in Scotland) or written agreement (see p18) in force;
- there is a post-3 March 2003 court order (registered agreement in Scotland) that has been in force for less than one year (see p19);
- not all the parties are habitually resident in the UK (see p15);
- there is no non-resident parent, either because both parents live in the same household as the child (see p12) or because the CMS does not accept that the person named is a parent of the child (see p9); *or*
- there is no qualifying child (see p8).

The CMS can also delay making a calculation pending the outcome of a 'test' case (see p227). Otherwise, the CMS must make a calculation.[15]

If there is a change of circumstances so that one of these situations applies for a period beginning after the effective date, the CMS makes a calculation that ends on the date of the change.

If a qualifying child dies before the calculation is made, a decision is still made for the period from the effective date to the date of death (see p27).

The CMS cannot refuse to make a calculation just because it has insufficient information or because it may affect the welfare of a child.[16] The CMS may make a default maintenance decision (see below). If the CMS refuses to make a calculation, the applicant (and, if the applicant is a child in Scotland, any person with care or non-resident parent who had been notified of the application) must be notified in writing of the decision, how to apply for a revision or supersession (see Chapter 9) and the right of appeal (see Chapter 10).[17]

A fresh application may be made after the refusal – eg, if there is a change of circumstances, such as the non-resident parent returning to live in the UK.

# 3. **Default maintenance decisions**

If the Child Maintenance Service (CMS) does not have enough information to make a calculation, or to revise or supersede a decision, it may make a default maintenance decision.[18]

The amount of the default maintenance decision depends on the number of qualifying children applied for:[19]

- £39 per week if there is one qualifying child;
- £51 per week if there are two qualifying children; *or*
- £64 per week if there are three or more qualifying children.

These amounts may be apportioned (see p58) if there is more than one person with care. Any relevant non-resident children (see p65) are ignored.

The 'effective date' of a default maintenance decision is the same as it would have been for a child support calculation decision (see p127).

## When a default maintenance decision ends

A default maintenance decision may be revised at any time – eg, when it is replaced by a calculation.[20] In practice, this only happens when the CMS has sufficient information to determine the case properly (ie, to make a calculation) from the effective date.

# 4. **Notification of decisions**

The Child Maintenance Service (CMS) must notify the person with care and non-resident parent (and child applicant in Scotland) once a child support calculation or interim maintenance decision has been made.[21] This also includes default maintenance decisions (but see below). There are similar rules on notifying revision and supersession decisions (see Chapter 9) and decisions to cancel calculations (see p129). A decision does not have full legal effect until the relevant people are notified of it.[22]

If the CMS corrects an accidental error in a decision or in the record of a decision (see p188), it must also notify the person with care and non-resident parent (and child applicant in Scotland) in writing as soon as practicable.[23]

There is no requirement for decisions to be notified in writing, although in practice most notifications are. The notification of the calculation or interim maintenance decision must include information on:[24]

- the effective date;
- where relevant, the gross weekly income of the non-resident parent, including:
  - whether it is based on historic or current income; *and*
  - if it is based on current income, whether this has been estimated (see p72);
- the number of qualifying children (see p8);
- the number of relevant other children (see p64);
- the weekly rate of child support and any collection fees;
- any variations;
- any adjustments for apportionment (see p58), shared care by the non-resident parent or part-time local authority care (see p79), or maintenance to another relevant non-resident child (see p65); *and*
- the rules for requesting a revision, supersession and appeal.[25]

Notification of a default maintenance decision must state the effective date, the default rate, the number of qualifying children, details of any apportionment and the information needed to make a child support calculation.[26] It should also include details of the right to request a revision, supersession or an appeal.[27]

Unless the people concerned have given written permission, a notification should *not* contain:[28]

- the address of anyone else other than the recipient or information that could lead to her/his being located; *or*
- information on anyone other than people with care, non-resident parents or qualifying children.

If there are errors or someone disagrees with the decision, s/he may challenge it (see Chapter 9). The CMS can also correct an accidental error in a decision or in the record of a decision at any time (see p188).

If there is a court order for maintenance, the court is notified of the calculation.

# 5. When liability for child support starts (the 'effective date')

The date a child support calculation first comes into force and liability begins is called the **'effective date'** or 'initial effective date'.[29] The 'initial effective date' is specified in the notice issued to the non-resident parent informing her/him that an effective application for child support has been made (see p26). The Child Maintenance Service (CMS) may telephone the non-resident parent on or before the initial effective date and then confirm this in writing to the parent's last known address. If the CMS does not telephone the parent, it must send written notice to the parent's last known address at least two days before the initial effective date.[30] The initial effective date is normally expected to be two days after the written notice is issued.[31]

An alleged non-resident parent cannot delay the effective date of a calculation by disputing parentage. The CMS does not make a calculation until the issue of parentage is resolved (see p41) but, if it later decides that the person is the non-resident parent, the calculation is backdated to the initial effective date.

When making a decision, the CMS takes into account the information that applied at the date the decision would have effect.[32]

There are different rules for effective dates after a supersession or revision (see Chapter 9) and for calculations replacing default maintenance decisions (see p125).

# 6. When a calculation ends

A calculation continues until the Child Maintenance Service (CMS):
- cancels it at the request of the person who applied for child support (see p128);
- supersedes it after a change of circumstances means it has ceased to have effect (see p128);
- revises it (see p191); *or*
- supersedes it (see p196).

In some circumstances, this means that the calculation is replaced by another; in others, no further calculation is made. When the cancellation takes effect depends on the grounds on which the supersession or revision was made, or the nature of the request (see p129). Any arrears remaining after a calculation ends may still be collected (see Chapter 8). If an application is made for a child of the non-resident parent who is not named in the existing calculation, a new calculation replaces the old one.

## Requesting a cancellation

A calculation must be cancelled when the applicant requests that the CMS cease acting.[33]

The request may be made verbally or in writing. The CMS must then stop all action, including collecting and enforcing arrears, although the person may specifically ask for action on arrears to continue.

### If the parents are living together

When the request to cancel a calculation is made, reasons need not be given. However, if the reason is that the parent with care and non-resident parent are living together, the CMS should be told. This is because, once all the parties share a household, the non-resident parent is no longer non-resident (see p12), so the child is no longer a qualifying child and the calculation ceases to have effect (see below).

## The calculation ceases to have effect

Some changes of circumstances mean that the calculation is automatically terminated. The CMS must cancel a calculation (including a default decision) if the calculation ceases to have effect because:[34]

- the non-resident parent or person with care dies;
- the only, or all, qualifying child(ren) is (are) no longer a qualifying child(ren); *or*
- the non-resident parent ceases to be a parent of the only, or all, qualifying child(ren).

This means that the calculation is cancelled, for example, when:

- a child aged 16 or over leaves non-advanced education or becomes too old to count as a child (see p8);
- the qualifying child, non-resident parent and parent with care start living together (see p12);
- the qualifying child goes to live with someone else and, as a result, the person with care no longer counts as a person with care;
- the qualifying child is adopted, in which case the non-resident parent is no longer a parent; *or*
- the non-resident parent is no longer considered a parent because of the results of a DNA test or a declaration/declarator of parentage.

## Other cancellations

If the event leading to a possible cancellation requires investigation, cancellation of a calculation requires a formal decision by the CMS, either at its own initiative or following a request or application (see p127). The calculation remains in force until cancelled by a CMS decision (or until it ceases for some other reason).[35]

The CMS must cancel the calculation if the person with care, non-resident parent or qualifying child is no longer habitually resident in the UK (see p15).[36]

If a non-resident parent has successfully contested parentage, the calculation is cancelled and s/he may obtain a refund of any child support paid (see p41).

If an applicant fails to provide the CMS with enough information to make a revision or supersession decision, the CMS *may* cancel the calculation.

## When the cancellation takes effect

If a calculation is cancelled because it ceases to have effect or because of another relevant change (including the circumstances above), the cancellation takes effect from the date the change occurred.[37]

If the cancellation is because the non-resident parent is not considered to be the parent because of a DNA test or declaration/declarator of parentage, the cancellation takes effect from the effective date of the original calculation (see p127).[38]

If a person with care requests that a calculation be cancelled, the cancellation takes effect from the date the request to cancel it was received. A different date may apply, depending on the reason for the cancellation.[39] It may be appropriate to end the calculation on a later date if an applicant has asked for this.

## Notification of the cancellation decision

When the CMS cancels a calculation or refuses to cancel one, it must notify the non-resident parent, person with care and child applicant in Scotland, and must also provide information on revisions and supersessions and on the right of appeal.[40]

If the calculation was made following an application from a child in Scotland and that child is no longer a qualifying child, the CMS must notify the person with care, non-resident parent and any other children aged 12 or over who are potential child applicants that the calculation has been cancelled.[41]

# Notes

1. **Making decisions about child support**
   1 s2 CSA 1991
   2 CCS/1037/1995
   3 s2 CSA 1991
   4 *Brookes v SSWP* [2010] EWCA Civ 420

5 *R v Secretary of State for Social Security ex parte Biggin* [1995] 2 FCR 595, [1995] 1 FLR 851
6 s1(1) CSA 1991; *Brookes v SSWP* [2010] EWCA Civ 420

7 *Brookes v SSWP* [2010] EWCA Civ 420
8 *Smith v SSWP* [2006] UKHL 35

## 2. The initial child support decision

9 s11 CSA 1991
10 www.gov.uk/child-maintenance/how-
   to-apply
11 s14A(3A) CSA 1991
12 Sch 1 para 15 CSA 1991
13 Reg 5 CSMC Regs
14 Sch 1 para 15 CSA 1991; regs 13 and
   18(2)-(4) CSMC Regs
15 s11(2) CSA 1991
16 R(CS) 2/98
17 Reg 24 CSMC Regs

## 3. Default maintenance decisions

18 s12(1) CSA 1991
19 Reg 49 CSMC Regs
20 s16(1B) CSA 1991; reg 14(3) CSMC
   Regs

## 4. Notification of decisions

21 Regs 24 and 25 CSMC Regs
22 *R (Anufrijeva) v SSHD* [2004] 1 AC 604;
   *SSWP v AM (IS)* [2010] UKUT 428 (AAC)
23 Reg 27A(3) CSMC Regs
24 Regs 24(1) and 25(1) CSMC Regs
25 Reg 24(2) CSMC Regs
26 Reg 25(2) CSMC Regs
27 Reg 24(2) CSMC Regs
28 Reg 25(3) CSMC Regs

## 5. When liability for child support starts (the 'effective date')

29 Reg 12 CSMC Regs
30 Regs 7, 11 and 12 CSMC Regs
31 Reg 12 CSMC Regs
32 Reg 5 CSMC Regs

## 6. When a calculation ends

33 ss4(5) and (6) and 7(6) and (7) CSA
   1991
34 Sch 1 para 16 CSA 1991
35 *SM v CMEC* [2010] UKUT 435 (AAC); *GR
   v CMEC* [2011] UKUT 101 (AAC); *TB v
   SSWP and RB (CSM)* [2017] UKUT 218
   (AAC)
36 s44(1) CSA 1991
37 Reg 18(3) CSMC Regs
38 s16(3) CSA 1991
39 s17(4) CSA 1991
40 Regs 24 and 27 CSMC Regs
41 Reg 27(2) CSMC Regs

# Chapter 7

# Collecting and paying child support

**This chapter covers:**
1. Introduction (below)
2. Payment of child support (p132)
3. Collection of other payments (p142)

This chapter explains how child support is collected and paid. Chapter 8 explains what happens if a non-resident parent (the 'paying parent') has arrears, and the enforcement action that can be taken to ensure these are paid.

**Note:** some information about payment of child support in '1993 rules' and '2003 rules' cases that are being closed is relevant to payment arrangements for new '2012 rules' cases. It may also be relevant to enforcement action still being taken against non-resident parents in '1993 rules' and '2003 rules' cases by the Child Support Agency. This chapter therefore includes a number of references to '1993 rules' and '2003 rules' cases. However, for simplicity, it refers only to the Child Maintenance Service. For full details of the process of closing '1993 rules' and '2003 rules' cases, see Chapter 5 of the 2017/18 edition of this *Handbook*.

## 1. Introduction

Once a decision on liability for, and the amount of, child support have been made, payment can be made in different ways. The non-resident parent can pay directly to the person with care without the payment going through the Child Maintenance Service (CMS). Alternatively, the CMS can collect and enforce child support,[1] and certain other maintenance payments (see p142).[2] **Note:** the CMS usually refers to the non-resident parent as the 'paying parent' and the person with care as the 'receiving parent'.

Fees are charged for using the CMS's collection service (see p135) and for some types of enforcement action (see p180).[3] **Note:** the collection service is free for those with remaining cases under the '2003 rules' and '1993 rules' until these are closed (see p2).[4]

If the collection service is being used, a payment schedule is set up. If this breaks down and arrears accrue, debt management procedures may be put in place or the CMS may decide to take enforcement action. If child support is being paid directly and payments are missed, the person with care can inform the CMS, and debt management and enforcement action can also be taken.

The CMS does not have discretion in decisions about liability for child support and the amount due.[5] The amount of child support cannot be altered, except by a revision, supersession, appeal or variation. The CMS does not suspend the current collection just because the non-resident parent states that s/he cannot afford to pay. However, it may agree to lower payments if a decision on a revision, supersession, appeal or variation is pending (see p151).

Decisions on how payment is enforced *are* discretionary and should take into account all the circumstances of the individual case and the welfare of any child likely to be affected (see p122). This should allow scope for negotiation between the CMS and the individuals involved. The CMS should be asked to investigate the circumstances fully in order to allow it to use its discretion appropriately.

## 2. Payment of child support

The Child Maintenance Service (CMS) can require the non-resident parent to pay child support:[6]

- directly to the person with care;
- directly to a child applicant in Scotland;
- to, or via, the CMS, provided the person with care, non-resident parent or child applicant in Scotland has requested this (see below); *or*
- to, or via, another person.

The CMS has broad discretion to decide how payment is to be arranged. This includes the payment of any collection or enforcement fees.[7] Before making these decisions, the CMS must, as far as possible, give the non-resident parent and the person with care an opportunity to make representations and must take these into account.[8]

The CMS prefers the parties to agree that child support should be paid by the non-resident parent directly to the person with care. If direct payments are agreed, once the CMS has calculated the amount owed, the parties make their own arrangement about when and how payments will be made. This is known as 'direct pay'.

If direct payment is agreed, the CMS informs each parent about the amount of any initial arrears and the date regular payments should start. The CMS recommends payment by standing order or a money transfer service (such as PayPal or MoneyGram) if the person with care does not want to disclose financial details to the non-resident parent. The CMS can also advise the person with care about setting up a 'non-geographic' bank account (an account with a central or national sort code rather than one linked to a local branch) and can then pass the account details securely to the non-resident parent. This type of sort code does not give any information about the area in which the person with care lives.[9]

Direct payments are not monitored by the CMS. Both parties should therefore keep careful records of the payments made. If the payment arrangement breaks down, the person with care can ask to use the collection service (see below).

Using the collection service means that the non-resident parent pays child support to the CMS, which then passes it on to the person with care. The collection service is known as **'collect and pay'**. The CMS can only provide the collection service at the request of one of the parties to the calculation.[10] It can only do so if the non-resident parent agrees, or if the CMS thinks that s/he is unlikely to pay otherwise. The CMS can allow the non-resident parent to apply to switch to 'direct pay' without the agreement of the person with care.[11]

**Note:** if the non-resident parent in an existing case that is due to close or transfer to the '2012 rules' (see p2) is subject to enforced methods of payment (such as a deduction from earnings order), the CMS offers her/him a 'compliance opportunity' – ie, an opportunity to comply voluntarily (eg, by paying by direct debit or one of the other voluntary methods of payment – see p137) over the first six months of the '2012 rules' case. During this period, in most cases, half of the child support due is paid by voluntary methods, and half by a deduction from earnings order (see p158) or by deduction from a bank account (see p167) in order to safeguard some payment. The non-resident parent is only then offered the option of 'direct pay' under the '2012 rules' if s/he pays on time and in full throughout the six-month period. If s/he refuses or fails to comply, enforced methods of payment continue.[12]

If the non-resident parent is on benefit at the start of this compliance opportunity, or moves onto benefit during the period, the above does not apply. The case is administered by the CMS's collection service and child support payments are made by deductions from benefit in the usual way (see p137). A decision on whether the non-resident parent is likely to pay, and should be allowed to make direct payments, is made on the information already available. If s/he is considered likely to pay, the case is administered under 'direct pay'. If not, it continues under the collection service, with the collection fees due (see p135).[13]

## The collection service

The person with care, non-resident parent or child applicant in Scotland can request that payment of child support be made via the CMS.[14] The CMS calls this collection service 'collect and pay'. The CMS can only provide the collection service at the request of one of the parties to the calculation.[15] It can only do so if the non-resident parent agrees, or if the CMS thinks that s/he is unlikely to pay otherwise.[16] The non-resident parent can apply to switch to 'direct pay' without the agreement of the person with care at any time.[17]

If the non-resident parent is on benefit, the person with care may want to use the collection service to obtain direct deductions from the benefit. This is particularly useful if a voluntary arrangement cannot be reached. However, there is a collection fee for direct deductions from benefit through the collection service (see p137).

The collection service can be requested at a later date – eg, if payments become irregular. The request can be made verbally or in writing.

If the collection service is being used, the CMS has discretion to decide:

- the method by which the non-resident parent pays;[18]
- the person to whom child support is paid;[19]
- if payments are made through the CMS or someone else, the method by which payment is made to the person with care;[20]
- the timing of payments;[21] *and*
- the amount of payments towards any arrears.[22]

The CMS must notify the non-resident parent in writing of the amounts and timing of payments due, to whom and how s/he must make payment and details of any amount that is overdue and remains outstanding. If an existing '1993 rules' or '2003 rules' case has been closed and outstanding arrears were transferred to the new computer system when the parties applied under the '2012 rules', this notice must also include those outstanding arrears.[23] The notice is sent as soon as possible after the child support calculation is made and again after any change in the details in the notice.[24] A copy is sent to the person with care.

If payments are made to the CMS, only those actually received by it can be passed on. The CMS aims to make the first payment to the person with care within six weeks of making the initial payment arrangements with the non-resident parent. It also aims to transfer payments as soon as it receives them and within one week of receiving them from the non-resident parent.[25]

Using the collection service removes the need for direct contact between the non-resident parent and person with care (although using a non-geographic bank account and having the CMS pass the details to the non-resident parent can also remove the need for direct contact – see p132). It is also supposed to ensure regular payments by starting enforcement action (see p157) as soon as payments are missed, although this does not always happen.

Even if the collection service is used, you should always keep your own records and evidence of payments in case you need to query the accuracy of arrears or the standard of service in handling payments. A payment statement is only issued periodically or on request (see p139).

## Fees

Both the non-resident parent and the person with care must pay regular fees if the 'collect and pay' service is used.[26] These are intended to encourage people to make direct payments instead.[27]

The following fees apply.[28]

- The non-resident parent must pay an additional fee of 20 per cent of her/his child support liability.
- Four per cent of the amount of child support due is deducted before paying the person with care.

The fee charged to the non-resident parent is 20 per cent of the child support liability for each day for which 'collect and pay' arrangements are in place. If s/he is paying child support to more than one person with care and not all are paid by 'collect and pay', the fee is only charged on those payments for which 'collect and pay' has been arranged.[29]

The fee charged to the person with care is deducted by the CMS before it pays the child support to her/him.[30] If the amount actually paid by the non-resident parent is lower than the amount due, the CMS still deducts a fee of 4 per cent of the amount paid before making the payment of child support to the person with care.[31]

### Example

Joe is the non-resident parent of four children who live with his former partner, Susan. Joe has been assessed as liable to pay £35 a week in child support to Susan. If the collection service is used, Joe must, in fact, pay £42 a week (£35 + (20% x £35)) to the CMS.

The CMS also deducts £1.40 (4% x £35) from the child support due to Susan, so she receives £33.60 a week. The balance of £8.40 a week is retained by the CMS.

If the calculation of fees results in a fraction of a penny, this is disregarded if it is less than a half. If a half or over, it is rounded up to the next penny.[32]

In certain circumstances, the CMS can waive the fees for cases which are related to previous '2003 rules' or '1993 rules' cases that were subject to enforced methods of payment (such as a deduction from earnings order) and have been closed as part of the case closure process (see p2). The CMS intends to waive the fees for a limited period to allow the non-resident parent a 'compliance opportunity' (see p133) to determine whether it is appropriate to allow her/him to pay directly. In order to manage the 'compliance opportunity', payments must be administered by 'collect and pay'. Fees can be waived if:[33]

- the person with care, non-resident parent and qualifying child in a '2012 rules' application are the same as in an existing '2003 rules' or '1993 rules' case; and
- a notice of liability ending has been issued on or after 23 May 2016 in relation to the existing case; and

- the existing case was one in which payment was being enforced on the date the notice of liability ending was issued; *and*
- the new application under the '2012 rules' was made before liability in the existing case ended; *and*
- the CMS has specified that child support due under the new '2012 rules' calculation is to be paid by certain methods (eg, standing order, direct debit, automated credit transfer, credit card, debit card, cheque, postal order, banker's draft or cash), or by a combination of one of those methods and a deduction from earnings order (see p158), in order to allow the non-resident parent to demonstrate that s/he is still likely to pay without an enforced method of payment; *and*
- the first payment made in accordance with these payment arrangements is the first payment of child support due under the '2012 rules' calculation.

In such cases, collection fees can only be waived from the effective date of the '2012 rules' calculation to the date the CMS decides that the payment arrangements are to end – ie, the end of the 'compliance opportunity', usually expected to be the first six months of the '2012 rules' calculation. The power for the CMS to waive fees in these cases will end on 22 May 2021.[34]

## If someone is both a person with care and a non-resident parent

In some child support calculations, someone might be both a person with care and a non-resident parent at the same time. This may arise if the qualifying children from a relationship live with different parents after the relationship has ended. In this situation, both parents may be liable to pay child support to each other and a separate calculation is made for each. The CMS can offset their liabilities, but only if the collection service is being used.[35]

*Example*

Ali and Nazia have two children, Mohammed and Faisal. When they separate, Mohammed lives with Ali and Faisal lives with Nazia. Both parents apply to use the collection service. Ali works full time and is liable to pay child support of £60 a week. Nazia works part time and is liable to pay child support of £20 a week.

Instead of the CMS collecting and distributing two sets of payments, it deducts Nazia's liability from Ali's:

£60 – £20 = £40

Ali pays Nazia £40 per week. Nazia does not pay anything.

If someone's liability is offset in this way, collection fees are only calculated on the net amount paid, rather than on the actual liabilities – ie, in the above example, Ali pays £48 a week (£40 plus 20 per cent) and Nazia receives £38.40 a week (£40 minus 4 per cent).

If both parties to a child support calculation are non-resident parents and persons with care and both fall into arrears, these can also be offset so that the CMS only has to pursue the party with the largest debt (see p152).[36]

## Method of payment

The CMS can specify that the non-resident parent make payments by whichever of the following methods it considers appropriate:[37]
- standing order;
- direct debit;
- automated credit transfer;
- credit card;
- debit card;
- cheque;
- postal order;
- banker's draft;
- voluntary deductions from earnings (a deductions from earnings order can also be used as a method of enforcing payment if the non-resident parent has arrears or fails to agree a payment method – see p158); *or*
- cash.

If the collection service is being used, the CMS asks for payment to be made by direct debit or by deductions from earnings.[38] The CMS can direct a non-resident parent to take all reasonable steps to open a bank or building society account for the purposes of paying child support and any collection fees.[39] However, there is no penalty for failing to do so.

When deciding the method of payment, the CMS should give the parties the opportunity to make representations and must take these into account.[40]

If the non-resident parent is receiving certain benefits, the CMS normally deducts the amount for child support directly from the benefit before s/he receives it (see below).[41]

If payment is made via the CMS, the person with care is usually paid by automated credit transfer, unless the CMS considers that it is necessary in the circumstances of the case to use another method.[42] The person with care is asked to provide details of a bank, building society or post office account. If s/he does not have an account, or experiences difficulty opening one, s/he should contact the CMS.

## Deductions from benefit

If a non-resident parent on benefit is required to pay child support at the flat rate (see p60), s/he may pay this directly to the person with care. If the collection service is being used, the CMS will request Jobcentre Plus to make a deduction from her/his benefit for child support.[43] Although child support is calculated weekly, the frequency of the deductions aligns with the frequency of her/his benefit payments.

Deductions can be made from the benefits that qualify a non-resident parent for the flat rate (see p60).[44] **Note:** the government has announced plans to extend this so that deductions can also be made from universal credit (UC) where the non-resident parent has earned income.[45] No date has yet been set for this to be introduced.

If someone should pay at the flat rate but a variation has been made which results in the reduced or basic rate being payable instead, deductions can be made towards the new amount of child support calculated.

If a non-resident parent and her/his partner are on income support (IS), income-based jobseeker's allowance (JSA), income-related employment and support allowance (ESA), UC calculated on the basis that s/he has no earned income, or pension credit (PC) and each is a non-resident parent, the flat-rate deduction of £7 is split between them so that each contributes half the amount to their respective persons with care.[46]

The CMS requests the deduction and Jobcentre Plus must make it in full wherever possible. The parent must be left with at least 10 pence a week (one penny for UC).[47] Partial deductions are not made. The deduction for child support is always made, whatever other deductions are due.

**Note:** deductions from benefit also cover any fee due. If a non-resident parent on benefit is using the 'collect and pay' service (see p133), collection fees are added, making the total deduction £8.40 a week. If the non-resident parent has been offered a 'compliance opportunity' at the start of the '2012 rules' case (see p133) and has been accepted as likely to pay voluntarily, deductions from benefit do not include an element for collection fees.[48] Any amount of the deduction that is for fees is retained by the CMS.[49]

Both the person with care and the non-resident parent are notified that deductions are to be made.

If there are arrears of child support, see p151.

## Timing of payments

The CMS calculates the total amount of child support and any collection fees due to be paid over a 'reference period' of 52 weeks, beginning on the initial effective date (see p127) or on the annual review date (see p74).[50] This total amount due is based on the assumption that the amount of child support will remain unchanged for the 52-week period. The non-resident parent is then required to pay child support in equal instalments. The frequency of payments (usually weekly or monthly) is agreed with the non-resident parent, and is usually at the same frequency as her/his wages are paid if s/he is employed. The non-resident parent is sent a 'payment plan', showing how much is due to be paid, the start and end dates of the reference period and the frequency of payments.[51] The person with care is sent an 'expected payment plan' showing the same information.[52] If payments are to be made by deductions from the non-resident parent's benefits, payments are usually at the same frequency as the benefits are paid. New payment plans are issued if the amount due changes.

Unless undue hardship would be caused to any of the parties, the frequency of payments to the person with care is the same as the frequency set for the non-resident parent's payments (but see p162 for deduction from earnings orders).[53]

Unless payments are to be by direct debit or standing order, the non-resident parent is advised to make each payment three to four days before the due date in order to ensure that payments are received on time and to avoid arrears. Clearance times are allowed for each method of payment, but the CMS aims to make payments to the person with care within a week of receiving them from the non-resident parent.[54] If a delay in payments is caused by maladministration on the part of the CMS, the person with care may be entitled to compensation. S/he must make a complaint first (see Chapter 11).

## Records and evidence of payments

It is important to keep records of both the payments made and received, in case mistakes are made. Records can be in the form of bank statements or receipts if payments are made in cash. If either party disputes the amount that the CMS says is owed, the CMS can be asked to provide a statement of transactions and a breakdown of its calculations.

## Overpayments

An overpayment can arise because:
- a calculation has been changed and the amount of child support due for a past period has been reduced;
- the non-resident parent has paid more than the regular payment due for some other reason (including making voluntary payments in the initial payment period); *or*
- there has been a CMS error.

If the CMS receives an unexpected payment from the non-resident parent, it should check to determine the reason for this – eg, it could be for an overdue collection to offset arrears or an amount towards a future collection.

If there is an overpayment, the CMS has discretion about how it deals with it.[55] The amount may be allocated to reduce arrears due under a previous calculation or, if there are no arrears, it can be used to reduce the amount payable under the current calculation.[56] Adjustments may also be made if there are overpayments of voluntary payments in the initial payment period (see p147).[57] If this is the case, the CMS first makes adjustments to balance out the overpayment.

An adjustment of the amount due under the current child support calculation may reduce the amount to nil.[58] If it does, the parent with care will not receive any more child support until the overpayment has been recovered.

If all, or some, of an overpayment made by the non-resident parent remains after offsetting it against regular child support, arrears and other liability, the CMS can make a refund to the non-resident parent.[59] Refunds are only usually made if there are no overdue collections or arrears on the case. The CMS should refund overpayments made because of CMS error – eg, if a person was told to pay more than the calculation required. In such cases, the non-resident parent may also wish to complain and request compensation (see Chapter 11).

## Recovery of overpayments from the person with care

Allocating overpayments against arrears or regular child support payments is a discretionary decision, and so the person with care may wish to negotiate with the CMS about the rate at which the amount is to be recovered, or for repayment to be made in a different way.

If it is not possible to reduce previous arrears or regular child support payments (perhaps because there is no current calculation and no arrears owed), or if the CMS decides that recovering arrears in this way is not appropriate, it can decide to reimburse all or part of an overpayment directly to a non-resident parent.[60] If the CMS reimburses the non-resident parent, it can recover all, or part, of it from the person with care if s/he has benefited from being overpaid.[61] This also applies to reimbursing overpayments caused by the non-resident parent making voluntary payments.[62]

The CMS aims to recover all overpayments, and contacts the person with care to ask for repayment and to discuss options for how repayment will be made. However, CMS guidance states that recovery of an overpayment from the person with care is not enforceable if there is no current child support calculation in force.[63] If the person with care does not agree to make the repayment, recovery is suspended. An overpayment cannot be recovered from the person with care if s/he was on IS, income-based JSA, income-related ESA or PC at any time during the period in which the overpayment occurred or on the date the non-resident parent was reimbursed.[64] CMS guidance also states that recovery of an overpayment becomes temporarily unenforceable when a person with care starts to receive benefits such as IS or income-based JSA, and it should be suspended. It may be reconsidered for recovery at a future date. In addition, the guidance states that the CMS cannot enforce the recovery of overpayments caused by its own administrative error, but the person with care will be asked whether s/he is prepared to repay them.

All decisions relating to recovery of overpayments are discretionary. When making them, the CMS must consider the welfare of any children likely to be affected by the decision (see p122). Before allocating overpayments against arrears or regular child support payments, the CMS must also consider, in particular:[65]

- the circumstances of the non-resident parent and person with care; *and*
- the amount of the overpayment and the period over which it would be reasonable to adjust the child support payable in order to rectify the overpayment.

If you dispute whether an overpayment should be recovered from you, or if it appears to have been caused by an administrative error by the CMS, you should obtain advice. You may wish to complain (see Chapter 11) about any maladministration, taking into account all the loss and inconvenience caused. You should argue that a past overpayment caused by an error by the CMS should not have an impact on you and your children now.

## Payments made to a third party

The CMS can treat certain payments made to a third party (eg, a mortgage lender) as payments of child support. This can include voluntary payments made between the effective date and the date of the calculation (used to offset any initial arrears – see p146) and payments made after the effective date.[66]

If the person with care agrees to receive payments from the non-resident parent outside the usual child support collection service (eg, if a non-resident parent agrees to pay an urgent utility bill on behalf of the person with care), these may be offset against the amount of child support owed by the non-resident parent.[67] The amount can be offset against any arrears owed, or from her/his ongoing liability if there are no arrears.

For a payment to be offset, it must have been agreed by the person with care and must be for one of the following, in relation to the home in which the qualifying child lives:[68]

- a mortgage or loan either to purchase the property or to pay for essential repairs to it;
- rent on the property;
- mains-supplied gas, water or electricity charges;
- council tax payable by the person with care;
- essential repairs to the heating system; *or*
- essential repairs to 'maintain the fabric' of the home.

Payments can only be offset if child support is collected by the CMS's collection service.[69] Non-resident parents who pay child support directly can reach their own offsetting agreement, but the CMS does not monitor it.[70]

If the CMS intends to reduce ongoing payments of child support to the person with care, it should take the circumstances of both parties and the period over which it would be reasonable to adjust the payments into account.[71] If the current calculation is adjusted, the amount payable may be reduced to nil.[72]

The decision to offset payments made to third parties is discretionary and there is no right of appeal against it. Problems may therefore occur if the person with care denies having agreed to their being made. The CMS's intention is to keep decisions that are not concerned with the actual child support calculation or the underlying liability to pay child support out of the appeals system.[73] However, if you are unhappy, you could complain about how the CMS has used its discretion.

# 3. Collection of other payments

The Child Maintenance Service (CMS) can collect and enforce other forms of maintenance if child support is being collected.[74] Some parents may have, for example, 'top up' maintenance under a court order in addition to child support (see p20).

The CMS's power to collect other maintenance is discretionary. The CMS can only collect other maintenance that falls due after it gives the non-resident parent written notice that it will do so.[75]

The following payments under a court order can be collected by the CMS:[76]
- additional child maintenance in excess of the CMS maximum;
- maintenance for a child's education or training;
- maintenance paid to meet the expenses of a child with a disability;
- maintenance paid for a stepchild – ie, a child living with the person with care who is not a qualifying child, but who was accepted by the non-resident parent as a member of her/his family when the child used to live with her/him;
- spousal or civil partner maintenance for a person with care of a child for whom child support is being collected.

The methods used by the CMS for collecting and enforcing other types of maintenance are the same as for child support.[77] If a non-resident parent is paying more than one type of maintenance and pays less than the total amount required, s/he should stipulate how the amounts are to be allocated. The CMS allocates as requested, except that if arrears of child support are specified, current child support is paid before arrears. If the non-resident parent does not stipulate, the CMS makes the payment of child support a priority.[78]

## Collection of court costs

If the CMS applies to a court to decide whether a person is a parent, the court can order her/him to pay the CMS's costs in bringing the case, including the cost of any DNA tests (see p46). (Also, a non-resident parent may have agreed to pay the DNA test fees to the CMS without a court order.)

The CMS negotiates with the liable person about how these costs should be paid. It initially requests the full amount due, but payment by instalments may be agreed.

Payment of fees and costs can only be enforced through further court action – the rules for enforcement of child support (see p157) do not apply. The relevant court is the county court in England and Wales or the sheriff court in Scotland. If the case is contested, a hearing is arranged in the court with jurisdiction for the area in which the parent lives. A money judgment can be enforced by the usual debt enforcement procedures.

## Notes

### 1. Introduction
1 s29(1) CSA 1991
2 s30(1) CSA 1991
3 DWP, *Supporting Separated Families: securing children's futures*, Cm 8399, July 2012; CSF Regs
4 Reg 4 CS(CEMA) Regs
5 R(CS) 9/98

### 2. Payment of child support
6 s29 CSA 1991; reg 2 CS(C&E) Regs
7 Reg 1(2A) CS(C&E) Regs
8 Reg 6 CS(C&E) Regs
9 CMS factsheet, *Managing Your Payments With Direct Pay*, October 2013, available at www.gov.uk
10 s29(1)(b) CSA 1991
11 ss4(2) and (2A) and 7(3) and (3A) CSA 1991; DWP, *Supporting Separated Families: securing children's futures*, Cm 8399, July 2012
12 Written ministerial statement by the Minister for State, DWP, House of Commons, *Hansard*, 20 May 2013, col 58WS; CS(DOF) Regs, Explanatory Memorandum
13 CS(DOF) Regs, Explanatory Memorandum
14 s29(1)(b) CSA 1991
15 s29(1)(b) CSA 1991
16 ss4(2) and (2A) and 7(3) and (3A) CSA 1991
17 ss4(2) and (2A) and 7(3) and (3A) CSA 1991; DWP, *Supporting Separated Families: securing children's futures*, Cm 8399, July 2012
18 Reg 3 CS(C&E) Regs
19 Reg 2 CS(C&E) Regs
20 Reg 5 CS(C&E) Regs
21 Reg 4 CS(C&E) Regs
22 Reg 4 CS(MPA) Regs
23 Reg 7(1) CS(C&E) Regs
24 Reg 7(2) CS(C&E) Regs
25 CMS leaflet CMSB013GB, *Receiving Child Maintenance*, October 2013
26 s6 CMOPA 2008; CSF Regs 2014
27 DWP, *Supporting Separated Families: securing children's futures*, Cm 8399, July 2012
28 DWP, *Supporting Separated Families: securing children's futures*, Cm 8399, July 2012
29 Reg 7(2) CSF Regs 2014
30 Reg 7(3) CSF Regs 2014
31 DWP, *Government Response to the Consultation Supporting Separated Families: securing children's futures*, Cm 8742, November 2013; reg 7(3) CSF Regs 2014
32 Reg 7(5) CSF Regs 2014
33 Reg 12A CSF Regs 2014; CS(DOF) Regs, Explanatory Memorandum
34 Reg 1(2) CS(DOF) Regs
35 s41C(3) CSA 1991; reg 5 CS(MPA) Regs
36 Reg 7 CS(MPA) Regs
37 Reg 3(1) CS(C&E) Regs
38 CMS leaflet CMSB009GB, *Paying Child Maintenance*, October 2013
39 Reg 3(2) CS(C&E) Regs
40 Reg 6 CS(C&E) Regs
41 CMS leaflet CMSB009GB, *Paying Child Maintenance*, October 2013
42 Reg 5(1) CS(C&E) Regs
43 s43 CSA 1991
44 s43 CSA 1991; Sch 9B SS(C&P) Regs

45  DWP, *Child Maintenance: a new
compliance and arrears strategy – public
consultation,* December 2017
46  Sch 1 para 4(2) CSA 1991; reg 44(2) and
(3) CSMC Regs
47  Reg 35(l) SS(C&P) Regs; Sch 9B
SS(C&P) Regs; Sch 7 para 2(4)
UC,PIP,JSA&ESA(C&P) Regs
48  CS(DOF) Regs, Explanatory
Memorandum
49  Regs 14 and 15 CSF Regs 2014
50  s29(3)(ca) and (3A) CSA 1991; reg 4
CS(C&E) Regs, as substituted by reg
4(1) CS(MOC&NCR)Regs
51  CMS leaflet CMSB009GB, *Paying Child
Maintenance,* October 2013
52  CMS leaflet CMSB013GB, *Receiving
Child Maintenance,* October 2013
53  Reg 5(3) CS(C&E) Regs
54  CMS leaflet CMSB009GB, *Paying Child
Maintenance,* October 2013
55  Regs 8 and 9 CS(MPA) Regs
56  Reg 8 CS(MPA) Regs
57  Reg 9 CS(MPA) Regs
58  Regs 8(3) and 9(3) CS(MPA) Regs
59  s41B(2) CSA 1991
60  s41B(2) CSA 1991
61  s41B(3) and (4) CSA 1991
62  s41B(7) CSA 1991
63  CSA online procedures, release No.153,
December 2012
64  Regs 10A and 10B CS(AIAMA) Regs
65  Regs 8(2) and 9(2) CS(MPA) Regs
66  Regs 6 and 7 CS(MPA) Regs
67  Reg 6 (1) CS(MPA) Regs
68  Reg 6(3)(a)-(f) CS(MPA) Regs
69  s41C(3) CSA 1991
70  CS(MPA) Regs, Explanatory
Memorandum
71  Reg 7(2) CS(MPA) Regs
72  Reg 7(3) CS(MPA) Regs
73  CS(MPA) Regs, Explanatory
Memorandum, para 7.11

**3. Collection of other payments**
74  s30 CSA 1991; CS(CEOFM) Regs
75  Reg 5 CS(CEOFM) Regs
76  Reg 2 CS(CEOFM) Regs
77  Regs 3 and 4 CS(CEOFM) Regs
78  s30(3) CSA 1991

# Chapter 8

. . . . . . . . . . . . . . . . . . . . . . . . . . . . . . . . . . . . . . . . . . . . . . . . . . . . . . . . . .

# Arrears

This chapter covers:
1. Arrears (below)
2. Enforcement action (p157)
3. Fees for enforcement action (p180)
4. Delays in collection and enforcement (p182)

**Note:** some enforcement action against non-resident parents in '1993 rules' and '2003 rules' cases is still being pursued by the Child Support Agency. This chapter therefore includes a number of references to how enforcement action on such cases differs from action on '2012 rules' cases. However, for simplicity, it refers only to the Child Maintenance Service.

For full details of the process of closing '1993 rules' and '2003 rules' cases, see Chapter 5 of the 2017/18 edition of this *Handbook*.

## 1. Arrears

The Child Maintenance Service (CMS) can only act on arrears if child support is being collected and paid through its collection service (see p133).[1] If the collection service is being used, the CMS can take enforcement action as soon as payments are missed. If a non-resident parent pays child support directly to the person with care ('direct pay'), the person with care must notify the CMS that payments have stopped. The CMS is otherwise not aware of this. The CMS may then decide to take enforcement action. If it does, it also starts managing ongoing future payments through the collection service.

If direct payment arrangements break down, the case may be moved onto the collection service (see p133). The CMS will ask for payment records for the time direct payment was in place, it will pursue arrears due for this time and it charges fees (see p135) on these arrears.

If direct payment is being used, the CMS does not continue to pursue action on arrears, even if those arrears arose from a past period when the collection service was being used. However, it can add the arrears to the payment schedule. If the person with care wants the CMS to pursue the arrears, the case must remain

. . . .

managed on the collection service. Alternatively, if a private family-based arrangement for child maintenance is made instead, the CMS closes the case, then treats it as an 'arrears-only' case and pursues the arrears.

The CMS cannot take enforcement action on non-payment of maintenance in a private agreement. If a private agreement breaks down, the person with care can apply to the CMS for child support instead. The CMS can pursue all arrears of child support from the date the child support calculation is requested, but not any missed payments under the private agreement before that date.[2]

The CMS's priority is to collect arrears in cases where child support is still in payment, so that children for whom child support is being paid can benefit from the arrears recovered. Historic arrears in cases where child support is no longer being paid are a lower priority, although the CMS still aims to collect them.[3]

If the non-resident parent now resides in another European Union country, the CMS can enquire about assets and enforce certain arrears that accrued while both parents were resident in the UK (see p16).

If '1993 rules' and '2003 rules' cases close as part of the case closure process (see p2) and a new application for child support is made, any outstanding arrears from the closed cases are verified at that point and further action is considered.[4]

## Initial arrears

As the first child support calculation is usually made after its effective date (see p127), there are almost always initial arrears.

The CMS draws up a 'payment plan', which shows payments for the following 12 months, including initial arrears. The proposed schedule is discussed and agreed with the non-resident parent. Written confirmation of the collection schedule is issued once the non-resident parent has agreed to it.[5]

The written notification states:[6]

- the amount due and to whom it is to be paid;
- how it is to be paid – ie, method, day and interval between payments;
- any amounts that are overdue and outstanding.

The CMS may request payment of the initial arrears as a lump sum. If a non-resident parent cannot pay this all at once, s/he may negotiate an agreement to pay in instalments or a collection schedule to cover both the initial payment and ongoing liability (see p149).

A parent who fails to pay the outstanding arrears within seven days of the written notification of the amount due may face further enforcement action.

If you think the calculation is wrong, you may be able to challenge the decision (see Chapters 9 and 10). If you object to the way the CMS is dealing with collecting the amount you owe, you can make a complaint (see Chapter 11).

**Note:** if a court order made on or after 3 March 2003 has been in force for more than a year and there is an application to the CMS, any payments due under that order which the non-resident parent has made after the effective date are treated as payments of child support.[7] This helps to avoid additional liability for child support accumulating if there is a gap between the effective date (at which point the court order ceases to have effect) and the date the calculation is actually made. If the payments made under the court order are at a higher rate than those due under the calculation, this is treated as an overpayment of child support and the calculation can be adjusted accordingly.

## Voluntary payments made in the initial period

If the non-resident parent makes voluntary payments through the CMS (or, if the CMS agrees, directly to the person with care or a third party) after the effective date, but before the calculation is made and notified, these may be offset against arrears of child support.[8] The CMS may seek the views of the parties when considering whether a payment should be classed as a voluntary payment.[9] By accepting a payment as a voluntary payment, the CMS can be deemed to have agreed to its being made directly to the person with care or a third party.[10] As these are discretionary decisions, the CMS must consider the welfare of any child likely to be affected (see p122). There is no right of appeal against these decisions.

Only the following types of payment can be offset:[11]

- in lieu of child support;
- in respect of a mortgage or loan on the child's home, or for repairs or improvements to the property;
- rent on the child's home;
- mains gas, water or electricity at the child's home;
- council tax payable at the child's home;
- repairs to the heating system at the child's home; *or*
- repairs to the child's home.

Payments can be made by cash, standing order, cheque, postal order, debit card or other method or arrangement from an account of the non-resident parent or on her/his behalf – eg, credit card.[12]

If the payments are made to the CMS, it passes them on to the person with care. Once the CMS has made the calculation, the voluntary payments are offset against the initial arrears.

If the payments are made directly to the person with care or a third party, the CMS checks with the person with care whether payments have been made.[13] This is normally done by phone. If the person with care confirms the payments, this is usually accepted without any further need for proof. If there is a dispute about whether a payment has been made, the CMS asks the non-resident parent to verify the payments by providing bank statements, duplicates of cashed cheques, receipts, paid bills or invoices, or a written or verbal statement from the person with care.[14] It is in the interests of both parties to ensure payments are recorded, and the CMS should explain to the non-resident parent the importance of keeping a record and provide a form on which to do so.

If either party disagrees with a decision about offsetting, s/he can make a complaint (see Chapter 11).

If offsetting means that the non-resident parent has overpaid child support, the calculation may be adjusted to compensate her/him, or a refund may be made.[15]

If the non-resident parent makes payments outside the usual collection service after the calculation is made (eg, if s/he pays an urgent bill on behalf of the parent with care), see p141.

## Arrears notice

The CMS may begin to consider action to recover arrears when:
- a payment from the non-resident parent to the CMS is not received; *or*
- child support is being paid by 'direct pay' or 'maintenance direct' and the person with care notifies the CMS that a payment due has not been received.

The CMS aims to begin action within three days of a payment being missed.[16] The CMS contacts the non-resident parent to discuss the issue, normally by telephone at first and followed up in writing if no response is received. The non-resident parent may request an appointment at a local office to discuss payment face to face with CMS staff.

If the non-resident parent has missed one or more child support payments, the CMS must send her/him an arrears notice stating the amount of all the outstanding arrears owed. The notice also explains the rules about arrears and requests payment of the outstanding amount.[17]

The arrears notice only shows the total amount of outstanding arrears, but the non-resident parent can ask the CMS at any time to provide an itemised list of payments due but not received.[18]

If you have received an arrears notice, you should check that the amount owed is correct and tell the CMS of any mistakes. If you think that the balance is incorrect, ask for a payment statement (see p139) and compare this with your own records. It is important to keep the CMS informed so that it does not start enforcement action in the meantime.

The non-resident parent can contact the CMS to negotiate payment by instalments (see p149). Once an arrears notice has been issued, another does not have to be sent if arrears remain uncleared, unless the non-resident parent has paid all the arranged payments for a 12-week period.[19]

The CMS does not send an arrears notice if direct pay arrangements are in place, or the collection service is being used but no enforcement action is being taken, and the CMS has notified the non-resident parent during the previous 12 months that it will consider taking collection and enforcement action if payments are missed. In this case, the CMS can take enforcement action and start managing ongoing payments if the non-resident parent has missed one or more payments.[20]

## Negotiating repayments

If you have received an arrears notice, you should contact the CMS to negotiate an agreement to pay the arrears.

You can contact the CMS before this point – eg, when you receive the collection schedule or if you have difficulty making ongoing payments. The CMS does not normally agree to defer payment of current liability, although it may do so if a revision, supersession or appeal is pending (see p151).

If you intend to pay the arrears, the CMS may:

- accept a delayed payment, setting a time limit by when payment must be received; *or*
- reschedule the amount to include it within the arrears.

If you indicate that a change of circumstances is causing difficulty in making payments, the CMS may investigate whether there should be a supersession (see p196). In all cases, a parent who wants to co-operate should try to renegotiate an agreement in good time before any anticipated change in circumstances – eg, redundancy. If you have paid regularly and the change would reduce the amount due, the CMS may accept a lower amount. You could also try to negotiate a suspension in payments if personal circumstances make it difficult or insensitive to enforce recovery – eg, if you are unemployed, sick or in prison.

The CMS has the discretion to make an agreement with a non-resident parent about how arrears will be recovered, so to avoid other methods of recovery, you should come to an agreement (see above) as soon as possible and comply with it.

There are no set rules on the level of payments or how quickly the arrears must be cleared. Although CMS staff always begin by requesting full payment of the outstanding arrears, it may be possible to reach an agreement to pay the amount in instalments. The CMS aims to agree repayment plans that are affordable and that will be kept to.

In making these discretionary decisions, the CMS must take into account the welfare of any child likely to be affected (see p122) and should consider:

- the needs of the non-resident parent or any new family;
- any representations from the non-resident parent about hardship;
- the needs of the person with care and the qualifying child.

If you have other financial priorities (eg, fuel) or other large debts, you should get independent money advice: preparing a financial statement and sending it to the CMS may assist in reaching an agreement. However, existing arrangements with other creditors may have to be renegotiated to take into account the child support calculation. As the CMS has several methods of recovery, it is unlikely to agree to a non-resident parent making low payments over a very long period. It is in a non-resident parent's interests to come to an agreement in order to avoid further enforcement action, and to keep the CMS informed so that it does not assume that s/he is refusing to co-operate. For more information on preparing a financial statement and negotiating with creditors, see CPAG's *Debt Advice Handbook*.

The CMS aims to collect arrears within two years, at a rate of up to 40 per cent of a non-resident parent's net income. It can use its discretion and take into account the non-resident parent's particular circumstances, if appropriate to do so.[21]

It may accept a plan to pay arrears by instalments over more than two years, but it is likely to obtain a liability order (see p174) if there will be more than £1,000 outstanding at the end of two years. A liability order gives the CMS the power to use a wide range of methods to enforce payment, should the plan not be completed. The CMS may also consider other methods of recovery.

Repayments spread over several years may help non-resident parents who are in financial hardship, but this means that the person with care will receive payments very late and may want to make representations to the CMS. No interest is paid to the person with care in respect of arrears. If arrears have accrued because of CMS delay or error, the person with care (or a child applicant in Scotland) may, however, wish to make a complaint and request compensation (see Chapter 11).

The person with care and qualifying children are not consulted about the level at which arrears are collected, but are informed when the decision has been made. This practice may be contrary to the European Convention on Human Rights' protection of private property,[22] but there has been no reported caselaw on this point (see also p183 on the fact that a person with care cannot directly enforce the payment of child support).

### If the non-resident parent does not reach an agreement or defaults

The CMS aims to take prompt action on arrears. If a repayment agreement is not reached, legal enforcement should begin. There is no set timescale for how quickly action should begin if no arrangement has been agreed, but it should begin as quickly as possible.[23]

If the non-resident parent fails to reach or keep a repayment agreement:

- a penalty payment may be imposed,[24] although in practice, this power is not currently used; *and*
- a deduction from earnings order or other method of enforcement may be considered (see p157).

The CMS informs her/him of its powers to collect and enforce child support.

From 5 August 2008, interest is no longer added to child support arrears and any outstanding liability for interest has been removed.[25]

## If there is a revision, supersession, variation or appeal pending

The CMS can suspend the collection of arrears if a decision on a revision, supersession, variation or appeal is pending. If the calculation is likely to be reduced, the CMS may agree to suspend collection of some of the ongoing payments. However, this does not happen often; the CMS prefers to speed up considering the case and aims to supersede calculations to reflect changes quickly in order to minimise arrears.[26]

If you are a non-resident parent and have requested a revision, supersession or appeal and you are having problems paying current child support or any arrears, ask the CMS for lower regular payments.

## Payment of arrears

Arrears do not have to be paid by the same method as ongoing child support payments – eg, they could be collected via the CMS, with ongoing payments made directly to the person with care. However, in practice, the CMS prefers to use the same method of payment for both.

Arrears of child support may be retained by the CMS and not passed to the person with care if they are in respect of a period before 12 April 2010 during which time the person with care (or her/his partner) was in receipt of income support (IS), income-based jobseeker's allowance (JSA), income-related employment and support allowance (ESA) or pension credit (PC). (Before this date, child support payments were treated as income for means-tested benefits).

The CMS can keep any arrears payments that would not have been passed to the person with care had the child support been paid when due[27] – ie, the CMS can retain an amount equal to the difference between the amount of benefit that was paid to the person with care and the amount that would have been paid had the non-resident parent not been in arrears.[28] Payments of arrears are allocated between the CMS and the person with care in the same way as overpayments (see p139).

## If the non-resident parent is on benefit

If the non-resident parent is in receipt of one of the benefits (except if s/he, or her/his partner, gets IS, income-based JSA, income-related ESA, universal credit (UC) or PC[29]) that would qualify her/him for the flat rate (see p60), a deduction of £1.20 may be made from the benefit towards any child support arrears. This is, in effect, a £1 payment towards arrears, plus a 20 per cent collection fee. The amount of the deduction that is for fees is retained by the CMS.[30]

Deductions for arrears are separate to other deductions made from benefit and are not affected by the priority rules to decide which deductions should be made first. For more information on the priority rules on deductions from benefit, see CPAG's *Welfare Benefits and Tax Credits Handbook*.

Deductions for arrears are in addition to deductions for flat rate child support. However, no deductions from benefit for arrears are currently made if a non-resident parent has ongoing liability to pay child support. **Note:** the government has announced that it intends to introduce powers to continue deductions from benefit at an amount equivalent to the flat rate (plus collection fees) where ongoing liability ends but there are arrears on a case.[31] At the time of writing, no date had been set for this.

If a non-resident parent (or her/his partner) is on IS, income-based JSA, income-related ESA, UC or PC, arrears action is suspended. If a person with care believes that the arrears should be pursued in some other way, s/he should contact the CMS to explain her/his reasons. If the CMS is unwilling to take action, a complaint may be made (see Chapter 11).

## Offsetting arrears

'Offsetting' is a way of balancing payments or arrears that are owed by a person with care and a non-resident parent to each other, so that the CMS only has to pursue arrears from one of them. Similarly, the amount of child support a non-resident parent is required to pay can be reduced to take account of arrears owed to her/him by the other person for a period when s/he was a person with care. Offsetting therefore reduces any arrears due under any current or previous child support calculation made in respect of the same relevant people – ie, a person with care, non-resident parent and child applicant in Scotland.[32]

Arrears may be offset if:
- a non-resident parent becomes a parent with care (see p153); *or*
- arrears are owed by both parties to a calculation (see p153).

Arrears can only be offset in this way if the collection service is being used. Those with an arrangement to pay child support directly can reach their own offsetting agreements, but the CMS does not monitor them.[33]

Offsetting is a discretionary power. The decision to offset arears does not require the agreement of either parent, but the CMS should notify all relevant parties to the calculation when it is considering offsetting and ask for their views. They are given 14 days in which to respond. The CMS should take into account parents' wishes and should also have regard to the welfare of any child likely to be affected by the decision (see p122).[34]

If there are no arrears of child support due, or an amount remains to be offset after any arrears have been taken into account, the CMS can reduce the amount payable under the current calculation. When reducing ongoing payments to the person with care, the CMS should take into account the circumstances of all the parties and the period over which it would be reasonable to adjust payments. Payments can be reduced to nil.[35]

If the current child support calculation is reduced, either the person with care or the non-resident parent can contact the CMS at any time to ask that it be reviewed. The CMS should then discuss with both parties alternative ways of collecting any outstanding arrears.[36]

### A non-resident parent becomes a parent with care

When a qualifying child for whom child support is payable moves households, so that the non-resident parent becomes the parent with care and vice versa, the CMS can offset the new non-resident parent's liability to pay child support against any arrears owed to her/him by the other parent.[37] The amount payable by the new non-resident parent can be reduced to nil.[38]

*Example*
Stephen and Zoe divorced five years ago. They have one child, Luke, who has lived with Zoe since the divorce. Zoe applied for child support and used the collection service. However, Stephen has not paid child support regularly for the past few years. Luke decides that he wants to live with Stephen, who becomes the parent with care. Zoe is now the non-resident parent. If Stephen applies for child support, the amount that Zoe must pay to Stephen each week can be reduced as a way of recovering the arrears still owed to her.

### Arrears are owed by both parents

Offsetting can also be used if both parents in a calculation owe each other arrears.[39]

*Example*
Luke has lived with his father, Stephen, for two years. His mother, Zoe, made regular child support payments for the first year, but when Stephen moves in with his new partner, she starts to miss payments. Luke then returns to live with Zoe, who becomes the parent with care again. At this time, Zoe owes Stephen £1,000 in arrears. However, there are still £500 arrears that are yet to be recovered from when Stephen was the non-resident parent and did not make regular payments. Rather than both sets of arrears being pursued, Stephen's arrears are deducted from Zoe's.
Zoe has to pay Stephen £500 in arrears. Only Zoe is pursued for arrears. Stephen's liability under the current calculation could be reduced to recover these.

Offsetting of arrears may also apply if the qualifying children from a relationship live with different parents. In this situation, both are parents with care and non-resident parents in relation to different children.

If both are liable to pay child support, but one falls into arrears, the ongoing payments of the other parent can be reduced.[40]

### Accepting part payment in full and final settlement

In certain circumstances, the CMS can treat a part payment of arrears of child support owed by a non-resident parent as 'full and final settlement' of all the arrears owed.[41] This flexibility is intended to act as an incentive for the non-resident parent to pay at least something, where s/he may not otherwise have done so.

Before accepting a part-payment offer from the non-resident parent, the CMS must obtain the written consent of the person with care (or child applicant in Scotland, and person with care of that child).[42]

The decision to accept an offer of part payment is discretionary. The CMS only uses this power if an offer is made by the non-resident parent or suggested by the person with care. It then investigates the circumstances of the non-resident parent, and also considers the likely success of continued enforcement action in recovering the full arrears.[43] (The CMS has conducted a trial of using the power more actively to contact parents to try to reach agreements between them on making or accepting part payments of outstanding arrears. However, the CMS does not intend to continue this approach.[44]) The CMS must also consider the welfare of any child likely to be affected (see p122).

If the CMS intends to accept the offer, it prepares a written agreement setting out:[45]

- the name of the non-resident parent;
- the name of the person with care (or child applicant in Scotland) if her/his consent is required (see below);
- the amount of arrears and the period to which they relate;
- the amount that the CMS proposes to accept as settlement of those arrears;
- who the amount will be paid to and by what method; *and*
- the date by which the payment must be made.

A copy is sent to the non-resident parent and to each person with care (or child applicant in Scotland) affected for their agreement.[46]

If the CMS considers the offer to be unreasonable, it may decide not to contact the person with care. In some circumstances, it may insist on the full amount of the arrears being paid – eg, if it thinks that the non-resident parent has the ability to pay and there is a reasonable prospect of recovering the arrears.[47]

If there are arrears due both to a person with care and to the Department for Work and Pensions (DWP) (ie, because, for a period prior to 12 April 2010, the person with care would have received less benefit if the child support due had been paid), any part payment agreed is allocated to pay the person with care first. **Note:** if it is only the DWP that will not be paid in full if the offer is accepted, the CMS does not need the consent of the person with care (or child applicant in Scotland) before accepting the offer.[48] In such a case, the CMS has discretion to decide whether the amount offered is reasonable in the non-resident parent's current financial circumstances.

If the non-resident parent has arrears that are due to more than one person with care, these are treated as separate amounts.[49] The CMS does not ask the non-resident parent to identify which person with care should receive receive the part payment.[50] If the non-resident parent does not state a preference, the CMS apportions the payment between them. Each person with care is notified of how much of the part payment s/he will receive if s/he agrees to accept this as a full and final payment. If one or more person with care rejects the offer, the CMS may apportion the amount between those who have accepted it. Arrears due to those who have rejected the offer remain outstanding and are pursued by the CMS.

If the offer is accepted and the agreed payment made, the person with care cannot change her/his mind and ask the CMS to reinstate and pursue the arrears. So a person with care may wish to accept an offer where, for example, s/he would rather receive some arrears than wait for the enforcement process to run its course. If the non-resident parent pays all the agreed amount, her/his liability on any outstanding arrears ends and the CMS cannot take further action on them.[51] If the non-resident parent fails to make all of the agreed part payment, s/he remains liable for the full amount of the outstanding arrears and the CMS pursues recovery.[52] The CMS can make a further proposed agreement for part payment in the future, even if the non-resident parent has failed to keep to the terms of a previous agreement. The new agreement replaces any previous one.[53]

The part payment offered must be paid in one lump sum. (At some point in the future, part payments may be able to be made by instalments.[54] However, there are no plans to introduce this at present.)

## Writing off arrears

The CMS has the power to write off certain arrears if it considers that it would be unfair or inappropriate for it to enforce the liability.[55] The power to write off arrears is limited, and the CMS does not intend to undertake a large-scale write-off of arrears. Before 10 December 2012, a decision not to pursue recovery resulted in the arrears being suspended, but the liability still remained. Suspended arrears can be revived by the CMS in certain circumstances, but many arrears have remained on record, even though there is no prospect of their ever being collected. The CMS also has various initiatives to pursue arrears in historic cases where a child support liability is no longer in force, although this action is a lower priority.[56] A person with care may be asked if s/he wishes arrears to be written off as part of the process of closing a '2003 rules' or '1993 rules' case (see p2).

The CMS can only write off arrears if it considers that it would be unfair or inappropriate for it to enforce the liability and:[57]

- the person with care (or child applicant in Scotland) has requested that the CMS stop taking action on the arrears; *or*
- the person with care (or child applicant in Scotland) has died; *or*
- the non-resident parent died before 25 January 2010 and it is not possible to recover the arrears from her/his estate; *or*
- the arrears have accrued from an interim maintenance assessment (see previous editions of this *Handbook* for details of these) in force between 5 April 1993 and 18 April 1995. These arrears are not legally recoverable;[58] *or*

- the CMS has advised the non-resident parent that the arrears have been permanently suspended and that no further action will ever be taken to recover them. This may happen if, for example, the arrears resulted from a delay (which was not the non-resident parent's fault) in establishing child support liability.

The CMS has discretion whether to use this power to write off arrears. Before doing so, it must consider all the circumstances of an individual case, the principles of child support law and the welfare of any child affected by the decision.

If the non-resident parent has arrears that are due to more than one person with care, these are treated as separate amounts and separate decisions are made.[59]

If it is considering writing off arrears, the CMS must give written notice to the person with care and non-resident parent (and a child applicant in Scotland).[60] The notice must set out:[61]

- the person with care (or child applicant in Scotland) who is owed the arrears;
- the amount of arrears and the period to which they relate;
- the reasons why the CMS believes that it would be unfair or inappropriate to enforce the arrears;
- the effect of writing off the arrears; *and*
- an explanation of the right to make representations to the CMS about the proposal to write off the arrears within 30 days of receiving the notice.

The notice is treated as being received two days after it was sent by the CMS to the person's last known or notified address.[62]

When making its decision, the CMS must consider any representations made by any relevant party.[63] If no representations are made within 30 days, the CMS can decide to write off the arrears.[64] It must give written notice of its decision to the person with care and non-resident parent (and a child applicant in Scotland). If the CMS does not write off the arrears, it may continue to pursue recovery. There is no right of appeal against its decision.

## Arrears in closed cases

The DWP has said that it will use the closure of existing '1993 rules' and '2003 rules' cases (see p2) to validate arrears and prioritise recovery action.[65]

If a case has been closed and there are arrears, but no ongoing liability for child support in a new '2012 rules' case, action to recover the outstanding arrears is expected to be treated as a low priority. **Note:** the government has consulted on plans to collect or write off outstanding arrears arising from '1993 rules' and '2003 rules' cases,[66] but no date has yet been set for any new action to come into effect.

Arrears that arise from '1993 rules' or '2003 rules' cases remain outstanding unless the person with care states that s/he does not want them to be collected. As part of the transition process, the person with care is asked whether s/he wants the arrears written off (see p155).

Arrears are only transferred if there is an ongoing liability for child support under a '2012 rules' application. Before being transferred, the arrears are checked for accuracy. Only arrears that have been validated in this way are transferred. This process could take up to six months. Existing enforcement action is expected to continue while this is going on. The parties are informed of any balance of arrears that is transferred to the new case.

Once arrears have been validated and transferred, no new enforcement action is started by the CMS unless the non-resident parent has failed to pay her/his ongoing liability. This means that, once enforcement action in the existing case has ended, no further enforcement action will be started until the CMS accepts that a direct payment arrangement is not suitable in the case.[67]

## 2. Enforcement action

The Child Maintenance Service (CMS) should usually consider enforcement action as soon as it is clear that the non-resident parent has failed to keep to the agreed payment arrangements for child support and any fees due and has not responded to warnings.[68]

In many cases, in order to enforce payment, the CMS must first obtain a **liability order** from the county court or, in Scotland, sheriff court (see p174). However, for an increasing number of enforcement options, the CMS does not need a liability order and no court action is required.

A liability order is *not* required for:
- a deduction from earnings order. This is usually appropriate when the non-resident parent is employed (see p158);
- making deductions from bank or building society accounts. This is likely to be used if the non-resident parent is not an employee (see p167);
- collecting arrears from a deceased person's estate (see p172).

However, the CMS must first obtain a liability order (see p174) if it wants to:
- take control of and sell goods (see p175);
- disqualify the non-resident parent from driving (see p178);
- imprison the non-resident parent (see p178).

**Note:** the rules on collecting and enforcing payments of child support also apply to payment of any fees for enforcement action due, except that the CMS cannot seek to disqualify the non-resident parent from driving or to imprison her/him when enforcement action is being taken solely to recover fees.[69]

A decision concerning collection and enforcement cannot be challenged by seeking a revision and then an appeal to the First-tier Tribunal.[70] However, in limited circumstances, a deduction from earnings order (see below) can be appealed to a magistrates' court (England or Wales) or the sheriff court (Scotland). Orders to deduct amounts from bank accounts (see p167) can be appealed in the family court (England and Wales) or the sheriff court (Scotland). It may be possible to challenge other decisions by judicial review (see p190). A complaint can also be made about the way the CMS has used its discretion (see Chapter 11).

The government has indicated that, since 18 June 2011, the CMS can enforce certain arrears that accrued while both parents were resident in the UK if the non-resident parent now resides in another European Union (EU) country. The CMS may also make enquiries about assets a non-resident parent may own in another EU state.[71]

The CMS can also assist parents with care to obtain a court order for ongoing maintenance, which can then be enforced by applying (in England and Wales) to the Reciprocal Enforcement of Maintenance Orders (REMO) Unit at the office of the Official Solicitor and Public Trustee or HM Courts and Tribunals Service Maintenance Enforcement Business Centres, or (in Scotland) the Scottish government's Central Authority and International Law Team.[72]

# Deduction from earnings orders

## When a deduction from earnings order is made

The CMS may make a deduction from earnings order to the non-resident parent's employer, instructing it to make deductions from her/his wages or salary and pay them to the CMS.[73] The CMS does not need a court order to do this and it is the first enforcement option that is likely to be used against an employed non-resident parent who cannot provide a good reason for the arrears, or who has failed to agree a method of payment with the CMS.[74]

A non-resident parent can also choose a voluntary deduction from earnings order as the method for making regular child support payments, even if s/he is not in arrears (see p137).

*Earnings*

'**Earnings**' include wages, salary, fees, bonuses, commission, overtime pay, occupational pension or statutory sick pay, any other payment made under an employment contract and a regular payment made to compensate for loss of wages.[75] Earnings do not include a payment by a foreign government or the government of Northern Ireland,[76] or a payment to a special member of a British reserved armed force.[77] 'Net earnings' is the amount remaining after income tax, national insurance (NI) and contributions towards a pension scheme have been deducted.[78]

A deduction from earnings order may not be made if there is good reason not to use one.[79] For what is considered 'good reason', see p165.

The best way for a non-resident parent to avoid a deduction from earnings order being imposed is to negotiate an arrears agreement (see p149) and keep to it wherever possible. However, making ongoing payments in full may be enough to prevent an order from being made. Any objection by a non-resident parent to an order is likely to be rejected if it is unlikely that regular payments would be made using a different method.

The decision to make a deduction from earnings order is discretionary and the welfare of any children must be considered (see p122).[80] If warned of an order, the non-resident parent should tell the CMS, preferably in writing, how any children would be affected.

A deduction from earnings order can be made while the non-resident parent is waiting for a decision on a revision, supersession or appeal. The CMS should consider the grounds of the revision, supersession or appeal before making one. A non-resident parent can also make representations about the amount and method of payments (see p137 and p145). The CMS may accept lower payments, but may still impose an order.

A deduction from earnings order cannot be made if the employer is based outside the UK and has no place of business in the UK, but can be made in Great Britain against an employer in Northern Ireland and vice versa.[81]

A deduction from earnings order cannot be made if the non-resident parent is in the armed forces. Instead, the CMS can request the armed forces to make deductions for child support under armed forces law, known as a deduction from earnings request, which sets limits on the amounts that can be deducted.[82]

If the full amount requested by the CMS cannot be deducted from earnings, the CMS uses other methods to collect and enforce the remainder.

**Note:** a deduction from earnings order may also be made as part of the 'compliance opportunity' arrangements (see p133) that may be offered to a non-resident parent in an existing '2003 rules' or '1993 rules' case. If an application is made under the '2012 rules' before the date the existing case closes, the CMS may allow the non-resident parent to pay a portion of the '2012 rules' child support liability by a voluntary method of payment for a period of time and make a deduction from earnings order for the remainder. In this situation, the CMS does not have to consider whether there is good reason not to make an order, and there is therefore no right of appeal on this ground against the order being made.[83]

If a deduction from earnings order is made, the non-resident parent can appeal against it to the magistrates' court in England and Wales, or sheriff court in Scotland (see p165).

## Information the non-resident parent must provide

The non-resident parent must provide the name and address of her/his employer, the amount of her/his earnings and anticipated earnings, place of work and the nature of her/his work within seven days of being asked to do so in writing by the CMS.[84] Once a deduction from earnings order is in force, s/he must inform the CMS within seven days of leaving employment or becoming employed or re-employed.[85] Failure to take all reasonable steps to comply with any of these requirements is an offence, punishable by a fine of up to £500.[86]

For these purposes, information sent to the CMS is treated as having been given or sent on the day that it is received.[87] Any notice sent from the CMS is treated as though it was given or sent on the day that it was posted.[88]

## What the employer must do

A copy of the deduction from earnings order must be served on the employer and the non-resident parent.[89] The employer must comply with it within seven days of receiving it,[90] and can be fined up to £1,000 for providing false or misleading information, or deliberately withholding information from the CMS.[91]

The order must state:[92]

- the name and address of the non-resident parent;
- the name of the employer;
- the non-resident parent's place of work, employee number and NI number (if known by the CMS), and the nature of her/his work;
- the normal deduction rate(s) (see p161) and the date on which each takes effect;
- the protected earnings proportion (see p161);
- the address to which the deductions must be sent.

An employer must inform the CMS in writing within 10 days of being served with an order if it does not, in fact, employ the non-resident parent.[93]

If a parent who is subject to a deduction from earnings order leaves her/his job, the employer must notify the CMS within 10 days.[94] If an employer finds out that an order is in force against an employee (eg, on becoming her/his employer), it must notify the CMS within seven days of becoming aware of this information.[95] Failure to take all reasonable steps to comply with any of these requirements is an offence, punishable by a fine of up to £500.[96]

The employer must inform the non-resident parent in writing of the amount of each deduction no later than the date of the deduction or, if not practicable, by the following payday.[97] If the deduction will always be the same amount, this can be done by a standing statement given at least annually.[98] If the employer does not give notice of the deduction, the non-resident parent can complain to an employment tribunal, which can order the employer to pay the non-resident parent a fine up to the total amount of the unnotified deductions, even if paid to the CMS.[99] This fine does not affect deductions already paid to the CMS.

For other duties about providing information, see p35. The CMS and the child maintenance section of the gov.uk website provide further information for employers.

Employers can manage deduction from earnings orders through a self-service website.[100]

If an employer implements a deduction from earnings order incorrectly and you dispute this, you should ask the CMS to intervene.

For these purposes, information sent to the CMS is treated as having been given or sent on the day that it is received.[101] Any notice sent from the CMS is treated as though it was given or sent on the day that it was posted.[102]

## How much is deducted

The deduction from earnings order states a 'normal deduction rate' and a 'protected earnings proportion'.[103]

The **'normal deduction rate'** is the amount that will be deducted each payday, provided it does not bring the parent's net earnings below a certain amount (the protected earnings proportion). The normal deduction rate can include the current child support liability and an amount for any arrears, penalty payments (see p150) and any fees due. There are no special rules on how quickly the CMS should aim to clear the liability, although often the maximum deduction rate of 40 per cent of net income is applied (see p149). You may wish to discuss with the CMS how it has chosen to apply its discretion.

**Note:** more than one normal deduction rate can be set, each applying to a different period.[104]

The **'protected earnings proportion'** is 60 per cent of net earnings.[105] Deductions must not reduce earnings below this level.

The CMS does not know the non-resident parent's net income or pay frequency, as it receives only gross income information from HM Revenue and Customs. The employer is therefore responsible for calculating the protected earnings proportion. The CMS provides employers with pay frequency options for weekly, fortnightly, four-weekly and monthly pay, from which the employer selects the normal deduction rate corresponding to the parent's pay frequency.[106] If the parent is paid at a different frequency, the CMS must cancel the order (see p164).[107]

These amounts also apply to deduction from earnings orders made after 10 December 2012 in 'arrears only' cases under the '1993 rules' and '2003 rules' (ie, cases where there are arrears outstanding but no regular ongoing child support liability), provided the CMS gives written notice to the non-resident parent. Any deduction from earnings order made before this date continues under the previous rules until it is cancelled or lapses.[108]

**Note:** if an order is made as part of a 'compliance opportunity' (see p159), payments under the order do not need to be made in equal instalments.

## Payment

The employer must pay the CMS monthly by the 19th of the month following the month in which the deduction is made.[109] This means that there is always a delay before the person with care receives the first payment from the CMS. The person with care receives monthly payments, even if the non-resident parent is having weekly deductions made. These monthly payments may not always be for the same amount (see p163).

The payment by the employer may be made by credit transfer, cheque or any other method to which the CMS agrees.[110] The deduction from earnings order reference number must be given so that the CMS can identify the person with care.

It is an offence, punishable by a fine of up to £500, for an employer to fail to take all reasonable steps to pay the CMS on time.[111]

### Administration of the deductions

An employer can deduct a charge for administrative costs each time a deduction is made under a deduction from earnings order.[112] This means that employees paid weekly can be charged more for administrative costs. The charge must not exceed £1 per deduction and can be made even if this would bring someone's earnings below the protected earnings proportion.

Each payday, the employer should make a deduction from net earnings at the normal deduction rate plus any administration charge. If deducting the normal deduction rate would reduce net earnings below the protected earnings proportion, the amount of the deduction is the excess of net earnings over the protected earnings proportion.[113]

If the employer fails to make a deduction, or it is less than the normal deduction rate, arrears build up and are deducted at the next payday in addition to the normal deduction, applying the same rules for protected earnings.[114]

If, on a payday, the non-resident parent is paid for a longer period than that for which the normal deduction rate is set, the deduction is increased in proportion to the length of the pay period.[115]

Such fluctuations in deductions may mean that the person with care receives irregular payments.

### Example

Ed is due to pay child support of £48 a week and has net earnings of £240 a week. When a deduction from earnings order is considered, there are arrears of £432. The order shows a normal deduction rate of £60 (child support due plus £12 towards arrears) and a protected earnings proportion of £144. The employer can deduct £1 administrative costs for weeks in which a deduction is made.

| Payday | Net pay £ | Child support due £ | Deduction £ | Pay £ | Unpaid £ |
|--------|-----------|---------------------|-------------|-------|----------|
| 5/7    | 240       | 60                  | 61          | 179   |          |
| 12/7   | 250       | 60                  | 61          | 189   |          |
| 19/7   | 160       | 60                  | 17          | 143   | 44       |
| 26/7   | 160       | 104                 | 17          | 143   | 88       |
| 2/8    | 240       | 148                 | 97          | 143   | 52       |
| 9/8    | 250       | 112                 | 107         | 143   | 6        |
| 16/8   | 250       | 66                  | 67          | 183   |          |
| 23/8   | 240       | 60                  | 61          | 179   |          |
| 30/8   | 120       | 60                  | Nil         | 120   | 60       |
| 6/9    | 240       | 120                 | 97          | 143   | 24       |
| 13/9   | 240       | 84                  | 85          | 155   |          |
| 20/9   | 250       | 60                  | 61          | 189   |          |
| 27/9   | 240       | 60                  | 61          | 179   |          |

In the week of 19/7, the full deduction cannot be made, as this would take income below the protected earnings proportion. A deduction is made of £16 plus a £1 administration fee. The amount of the deduction from earnings order outstanding is added to the next amount due on 26/7. As earnings are again low, the full deduction cannot be taken and is carried forward.

In the week of 30/8, earnings are too low for a deduction to be made and, therefore, there is no deduction and no administrative charge.

## Payment to the person with care

When payments under the order have reached the CMS, they should be passed on to the person with care within approximately 10 days. If s/he was on income support, income-based jobseeker's allowance, income-related employment and support allowance or pension credit in the period to which the arrears relate, some of the payments may be retained in lieu of benefit paid.[116] This only applies to arrears of child support payments that were due to be made before 12 April 2010 (when child support was taken into account as income for means-tested benefits).

*Example*

Following on from the previous example, Ed's ex-wife Claire will receive the following payments.

| Month | Payment by the 19th of the month £ | Current liability paid (£48 a week due) £ | Arrears paid (assigned to oldest debt) £ |
|---|---|---|---|
| July | | Nil | Nil |
| August | 156 | 156 | Nil |
| September | 328 | 192 | 136 |
| October | 300 | 192 | 108 |

By the time Claire gets the first payment from the deduction from earnings order in August, s/he is owed £624 (£432 + £192 (July)), but because of Ed's fluctuating earnings, s/he receives less than the amount due. It is only in September that s/he begins to obtain arrears of child support, even though the order was put in place in July.

## Priority of orders

A deduction from earnings order takes priority over an attachment of earnings order made by a county court and any arrestment of earnings under Scottish law.[117] In England and Wales, if a deduction from earnings order is served on an employee who is already subject to an attachment of earnings order made by a magistrates' court to recover a fine, council tax or maintenance, the earliest order has priority.[118]

Any deductions under a lower priority order are taken from the net earnings left after deductions under the first order have been made.

## Reviews, cancellations and lapsed orders

The CMS must review a deduction from earnings order if there is a change in the amount of the calculation, or if any arrears, penalty payments and any collection or enforcement fees included have been paid off.[119] This does not apply if a normal deduction rate that takes into account the change has already been specified (see p161). An order can be changed on this review.[120] An employer must comply with the change within seven days of the new order being served on it.[121] The usual penalties for failing to comply apply.

If the non-resident parent is paid at a frequency other than weekly, fortnightly, four-weekly or monthly, the CMS *must* cancel the order.[122] In existing '1993 rules' and '2003 rules' cases, this only applies if there are only arrears and no ongoing liability and the non-resident parent has been notified in writing.

The CMS *can* cancel the order if:[123]

- no further payments are due under it;
- liability in an existing case has ended under the case closure process (see p2);

- it was made as part of a 'compliance opportunity' (see p159) and the non-resident parent receives any benefit that means that the flat rate applies (see p60);
- it is ineffective or there appears to be a more effective way of collecting the payments;
- it is defective (see p166) or does not comply with a procedural requirement;
- the CMS did not have, or has ceased to have, jurisdiction to make it; *or*
- using it to enforce a default maintenance decision or interim maintenance decision is no longer appropriate, given the compliance or attempted compliance of the non-resident parent.

The CMS can also cancel the order if:[124]
- it has agreed with the non-resident parent an alternative method for payment of the child support and any fees due; *and*
- it considers it is reasonable to cancel the order.

If the order was made as part of a 'compliance opportunity' (see p159), the CMS can also cancel it if:[125]
- the non-resident parent receives any benefit that means that the flat rate applies (see p60); *or*
- the non-resident parent has made payments by the agreed voluntary method for the agreed period and the CMS considers that it is reasonable in the circumstances to cancel the order.

If an order is in force for a '1993 rules' or '2003 rules' case and there are outstanding arrears when that case closes and an application is made under the '2012 rules', the order is treated as cancelled when the arrears are transferred to the '2012 rules' computer system. The order therefore continues until the arrears are validated. If there are no outstanding arrears, the order is treated as cancelled on the date the first deduction is made under an order under the '2012 rules'.[126]

The CMS must send written notice of cancellation to the non-resident parent and employer.[127]

A deduction from earnings order lapses when a non-resident parent leaves the employment.[128] The CMS can revive it if s/he finds a new job with the same or a different employer.[129] If it is revived, copies of the notice must be served on the parent and new employer.[130] Any shortfall under the order before the revival cannot be carried over to the revived order.[131]

## Appeals

A non-resident parent can appeal against a deduction from earnings order to the magistrates' court in England and Wales or sheriff court in Scotland.[132] The appeal must be made within 28 days of the order being made (56 days if the parent is not resident in the UK).[133] An appeal can only be made on the grounds that:

- the order is 'defective' (see below);
- the payments made to the parent are not earnings (see p158);[134] *or*
- unless the order is made as part of a 'compliance opportunity' (see p159), there is 'good reason' not to use an order (see below).[135]

A deduction from earnings order is **defective** if it is impracticable for an employer to comply with it because it does not include the correct information required.[136] Many orders may include incorrect information (such as errors in names, addresses and dates), but an appeal will not succeed on this basis if the employer can still comply with it. Although some early appeals were upheld because the order was unsigned, a signature is not legally required.

When determining whether there is a **good reason** not to use an order, the CMS must consider whether making the order is likely to result in the disclosure of the parentage of a child and the likely impact of this on the non-resident parent's employment or on any relationship between the non-resident parent and a third party.[137] The impact of a third party becoming aware of the non-resident parent's deduction from earnings order is not considered to be a good reason in any other circumstances.[138]

A good reason for not imposing an order may also exist if a relative of the non-resident parent or parent with care is employed by the same employer as the non-resident parent and s/he is likely to find out about the order. If her/his employment or family relationships may be adversely affected as a result, this should be a good reason not to impose an order.[139]

The fact that a non-resident parent may prefer a different method of payment or would prefer the employer not to be informed about her/his child support liability are not considered good reasons to refrain from using a deduction from earnings order.[140]

In England and Wales, there is no specific application form for the appeal. In Scotland, the form of the application for an appeal is laid out in the sheriff court child support rules.[141]

Once the application is made, the court notifies the CMS. The CMS checks the deduction from earnings order and contacts the employer to check the earnings. If the order is based on incorrect amounts, the CMS varies and reissues it. If the case gets as far as a court hearing, the magistrates/sheriff may quash the order or specify which payments, if any, constitute earnings.[142] The court cannot question the child support calculation itself.[143]

Even if the court quashes the order, it cannot order the CMS to repay deductions to the non-resident parent.[144] For this reason, if deductions are being made from payments that are not earnings, or on the basis of an incorrect normal deduction rate or protected earnings proportion, it may be better to challenge the order by judicial review.

Either party can be represented by a lawyer. The CMS appoints its own staff to conduct deduction from earnings order appeals and appear at related court hearings.[145] The non-resident parent can also be represented by a lay person, if the magistrate or sheriff accepts that s/he is suitable. An authorised lay representative does not have the full rights of a legal representative, but may be entitled to expenses.

**Note:** if the CMS has not properly exercised its discretion in making a deduction from earnings order, a complaint can be made (see Chapter 11) and/or judicial review can be sought (see p190).

## Deductions from bank accounts

If a non-resident parent has failed to pay child support, the CMS can make an order requiring a bank or building society to make deductions from her/his current or savings account and pay the CMS. The CMS can make an order without the non-resident parent's consent, and without applying to court or obtaining a liability order.[146] The deductions can be either regular (see p168) or made as a lump-sum payment (see p169).[147] As soon as a non-resident parent is in arrears, a deduction order becomes possible as a method of enforcement.

Deduction orders are intended to be an option for all appropriate cases where there are arrears.[148] An order may be made if a non-resident parent is self-employed and a deduction from earnings order is not possible.

The CMS has discretion to choose the most suitable account from which to make deductions. Generally, regular deduction orders are directed at current accounts and lump-sum deduction orders at savings accounts. The use of deduction orders on more complex accounts, such as notice accounts or stocks and shares accounts, may also be considered.[149]

A lump-sum or regular deduction order cannot be made in respect of an account which is used wholly or partly for business purposes. This does not apply if a regular deduction order is made in respect of an account belonging to a non-resident parent who is a sole trader.[150] **Note:** the government has announced that it intends to introduce powers to make deduction orders against business accounts.[151] It is expected that this would only be done after deductions have been sought from other accounts. No date for this power to be introduced has yet been set.

The CMS cannot currently make a deduction order in respect of a joint account,[152] but the government intends that this will be possible in the future.[153] At the time of writing, no date for this has yet been set. However, the government has indicated that:

- before making deductions from a joint account, the CMS will investigate ownership of the funds;
- account holders will be given time (14 days for proposed regular deduction orders and 28 days for lump- sum deduction orders) to make representations to the CMS;
- joint account holders will have enhanced review and appeal rights.

The bank or building society can take an amount from the non-resident parent's account to cover the administrative costs of setting up and paying a deduction order. The maximum amounts that can be charged are:[154]

- £10 for each deduction made under a regular deduction order;
- £55 for each deduction made under a lump-sum deduction order.

## Regular deduction orders

A regular deduction order can be used to collect both arrears and ongoing child support payments that will become due under the calculation that is in place.[155]

When a regular deduction order is made, a copy is served on both the bank or building society and the non-resident parent. The order must specify the amount of the regular deduction and the dates on which deductions are due to be made.[156]

If there is a current child support calculation, or arrears are being collected for an arrangement which is no longer in force, the maximum that can be deducted is 40 per cent of the non-resident parent's gross weekly income (net weekly income in '1993 rules' and '2003 rules' cases). If a default maintenance decision has been made, the maximum that can be deducted is £80 a week.[157]

When the power to make deductions from a joint account has been brought fully into force (see p167), before a regular deduction will be able to be made from a joint account, each account holder should be given an opportunity to make representations on the making of the order and the amounts to be deducted.[158]

It is an offence, punishable by a fine of up to £500, for a person not to comply with the requirements of a regular deduction order, unless s/he can show that all reasonable steps were taken to comply.[159]

### Priority of payments

If the non-resident parent's account is subject to other deduction orders, such as a third-party debt order, these are generally paid first before a regular deduction order is dealt with. The exception to this is if a third-party debt order is served on the bank or building society after the regular deduction order, but on or before the date a payment is due to be made under the deduction order. In this case, the deduction order is paid first on that occasion, unless the bank or building society has already taken steps to process the other orders. For future payments, it is assumed that the other orders take priority.[160]

### Minimum amounts

A deduction cannot be made if the amount of credit in the relevant account is below a certain level on the date a deduction is due to be made. The minimum amounts are:

- £40, if deductions are made monthly;
- £10, if deductions are made weekly;

- if deductions are made for any other period, £10 for each whole week in that period, plus £1 for each additional day in that period.

In addition to these amounts, there must be sufficient funds in the account to pay the administrative costs.[161]

### Reviews and variations

A non-resident parent or a bank or building society can apply to the CMS for a review of a regular deduction order if:[162]
- the parent does not have a beneficial interest in some or all of the money in the account; *or*
- there has been a change in the amount of the child support calculation; *or*
- any amounts payable under the order have been paid; *or*
- there has been a change in the non-resident parent's current income (net weekly income in '1993 rules' and '2003 rules' cases);[163] *or*
- because of an official error, an incorrect amount has been specified in the order.

A regular deduction order can be varied to change the amount that is deducted if:[164]
- the CMS accepts that the non-resident parent has made a payment of child support arrears, or a payment towards an enforcement fee, and no alternative method of payment is in place; *or*
- there has been a successful appeal against a child support calculation; *or*
- the order has been changed following a successful review or appeal to the county court (sheriff court in Scotland) against making the order; *or*
- there are arrears that are not included in the order.

## Lump-sum deduction orders

If it is established that the non-resident parent owes arrears of child support, the CMS considers whether a lump-sum deduction order is the most appropriate method of recovering them.

Once the CMS has decided to make a lump-sum deduction order, it serves an interim order on the non-resident parent's bank or building society, or other third party. This acts as an instruction to secure funds up to the amount of the order in a specified account until further notice. The bank or building society is expected to prevent the funds from being moved or reduced below the amount that is ordered or, if funds are already below this amount, not to allow them to decrease further (unless the CMS permits it to do so – eg, because of hardship).

Once funds have been secured, a copy of the order is served on the non-resident parent. Both the bank or building society and the parent have 14 days from the date the order is served in which to make representations to the CMS.

The order is treated as having been served on the parent at the end of the day on which the copy is posted to her/his last known address.[165]

When issuing the order and instructing the bank or building society to secure funds, the CMS should take into account:[166]

- any hardship that may be caused to the non-resident parent's partner or a relevant child;
- any written, contractual obligations regarding the money that were made before the order was made;
- any other circumstances that the CMS considers appropriate in the particular case.

Once the power to make deductions from a joint account has been brought fully into force (see p167), the CMS should also ensure that the amount deducted from a joint account does not exceed an amount that is fair, given all the circumstances, especially the amounts contributed to the account by each of the account holders.[167]

### Priority of payments

In **England and Wales**, if there is a final lump-sum deduction order and another interim third-party debt order, a bank or building society must comply with them in the order in which they were served on it. If an interim lump-sum deduction order is served after an interim third-party debt order, the final versions of these other orders take priority.[168]

In **Scotland**, a bank or building society must give priority to the lump-sum deduction order and any other orders, according to the order in which they were served on it.[169]

### Minimum amounts

A deduction should not be made if the amount of credit in the relevant bank account is below a minimum level. The current minimum level is £55 plus the amount of administrative costs charged by the bank or building society.[170] The administrative costs must not be more than £55.[171]

### Variations

A non-resident parent or her/his bank or building society can ask the CMS to use its discretion to vary the order in certain circumstances. These include if:[172]

- the CMS accepts the parent's agreement to make a payment;
- there has been a revision or supersession of, or a successful appeal against, the child support calculation;
- there has been an appeal to the county court (sheriff court in Scotland) against making an order, or against a refusal by the CMS to consent to funds being moved or reduced;

- the CMS agrees that hardship may be caused to the parent's partner or to a relevant child;
- the parent is under a written contractual obligation, made before the lump-sum deduction order was made.

## Lapsed and discharged orders

A **regular deduction order lapses** (but is treated as remaining in force for certain purposes) if the CMS considers it reasonable in all the circumstances and:[173]
- an alternative method of payment of the child support due, including any fees, has been agreed between the CMS and the non-resident parent; *or*
- on two consecutive deduction dates (or more if the CMS decides this is appropriate), there have been insufficient funds in the account to make the deduction.

A **regular deduction order may be discharged** by the CMS if it considers it appropriate in all the circumstances, and *must* be discharged if:[174]
- the account specified in the order has been closed;
- the child support calculation is no longer in force and the amount due, including any fees, has been paid in full;
- the non-resident parent has complied with any alternative methods of payment agreed with the CMS for a period it considers appropriate;
- the CMS has reviewed the order and the amount to be deducted has been reduced to nil or a court has set aside the order on appeal;
- six months have passed since the order lapsed, unless an appeal has been made (see the bullet point below);
- an appeal has been made against a lapsed order and one month has passed since the appeal was concluded *or* the time limit for a further appeal expired, whichever is the later; *or*
- the non-resident parent has died.

The order is discharged immediately after the payment of the last deduction prior to discharge.

A **lump-sum deduction order lapses** (but is treated as remaining in force for certain purposes) if the CMS considers it reasonable in all the circumstances and:[175]
- there is no money in the account (including if the amount has reduced to nil because the CMS has given permission for money to be used, for instance, in cases of hardship – see p170); *or*
- an alternative method of payment of the child support due, including any fees, has been agreed between the CMS and the non-resident parent.

A **lump-sum deduction order may be discharged** by the CMS if it considers it appropriate in all the circumstances, and *must* be discharged if:[176]

- the account specified in the order has been closed;
- the amount of arrears specified in the order, including any fees, has been paid in full;
- the non-resident parent has paid the total amount of arrears due, including any fees, by an alternative method of payment agreed with the CMS;
- after considering representations about making an interim order, the CMS has decided not to make a final order;
- six months have passed since the order lapsed, or since a deduction was made if the amount of the deduction was for all the funds in the account but less than the amount due under the order (unless an appeal has been made – see the bullet point below);
- an appeal has been made against a lapsed order and one month has passed since the appeal was concluded *or* the time limit for a further appeal expired, whichever is the later; *or*
- the non-resident parent has died.

### Appeals

A non-resident parent has the right to appeal against a regular deduction order or a lum-sum deduction order and related decisions made by the CMS. The appeal is made to the family court in England and Wales or the sheriff court in Scotland.

You can appeal against:[177]

- the making of a regular deduction order;
- any decision by the CMS on a request to review a regular deduction order;
- a refusal to waive the requirement to freeze or protect funds which are the subject of an interim lump-sum deduction order;
- the making of a final lump-sum deduction order.

There is a time limit of 21 days from the date the final lump-sum deduction order is received in which to appeal against its being made. This time limit cannot be extended by the court.[178] A non-resident parent is considered to have received the final lump-sum deduction order two days after it was posted.

### Recovery of arrears from an estate

The CMS can request the payment of arrears of child support (and any collection fees) from a deceased person's estate without having to apply to court or obtain a liability order. The decision to recover arrears is a discretionary one. The person must have died on or after 25 January 2010. Any arrears for which s/he was liable immediately before death become a debt payable to the CMS from her/his estate.[179] The CMS can contact the administrator or executor of the estate to request payment.

The CMS aims to avoid legal action where possible when using this power and to avoid delaying or obstructing the administration of an estate.[180]

It is understood that the CMS is notified electronically when other government departments are informed of the death of a non-resident parent. However, the person with care may also wish to inform the CMS of the death of a non-resident parent who owes arrears of child support.

The administrator or executor has the same rights of appeal, following the same procedures and time limits, as the non-resident parent had before s/he died.[181]

The CMS must disclose relevant information to enable the administrator or executor to make a decision about whether to pay or appeal the arrears. The CMS has discretion to decide whether the information requested is essential and, therefore, whether it should be disclosed.[182] Any application for information should be in writing and give reasons. The CMS should not disclose the address of any person involved in the case unless s/he has given written consent, and should also prevent the disclosure of any information that could lead to the person with care, or any other relevant person, being located.[183]

It is intended that child support arrears will be treated in the same way as other debts – eg, unpaid utility or council tax bills. It does not appear that they take priority over other payments.

Before making a claim on an estate, the CMS should thoroughly check the amount of outstanding debt, including completing any outstanding reassessments relating to periods before the death.[184] Administrators of the estate should check that the CMS has carried out this process and that the amount of debt to be recovered is accurate.

## When arrears should not be recovered

The CMS should not pursue arrears from an estate without the consent of the person with care. If s/he does not wish to pursue the arrears, the CMS should not take any further action.[185] For further details on when arrears may be written off, see p155. The CMS also has a duty to take into account the welfare of any child likely to be affected (see p122). This includes children of the non-resident parent who may not have been the subject of the child support calculation, or other dependent children who would otherwise benefit from the estate. When the CMS registers its claim against the estate, it may not be aware of other children or the potential implications for them. If the CMS later becomes aware of any potentially adverse impact on other children, it should reconsider whether to pursue the arrears.[186] The CMS also takes into account the administrative cost of recovering arrears in this way.[187]

If the arrears recovered from an estate would be retained by the CMS in lieu of any benefit paid, they should not be pursued if this would have a detrimental effect on a person with care or a qualifying child. This only applies to arrears relating to a period before 12 April 2010, when child support was counted as income for means-tested benefits. The CMS should contact the person with care to establish what impact the recovery would have before approaching the administrators of the estate.[188]

## Obtaining a liability order

If a deduction from earnings order is inappropriate (eg, because the non-resident parent is not employed) or one has been made but proved ineffective, the CMS may apply to the magistrates' court in England and Wales, or sheriff court in Scotland, for a liability order.[189] Either party can be represented in the court proceedings by a lawyer or by another person.

A liability order provides legal recognition of the debt, and allows the CMS to take further enforcement measures. A liability order is required before the CMS can take action to:

- take control of and sell goods (see p175);
- disqualify the non-resident parent from driving (see p178);
- imprison the non-resident parent (see p178).

The CMS must give the non-resident parent seven days' notice of its intention to seek a liability order (28 days if s/he is not resident in the UK).[190] The notice must state the amount of child support outstanding, including any collection or enforcement fees.

If the court decides that the payments are due but have not been made, it must make the order.[191] The court cannot question the child support calculation itself.[192] When making a liability order, the court can take into account payments made by the non-resident person by a method other than that specified by the CMS.[193]

An order (including one made in Northern Ireland) can be enforced anywhere in the UK.[194]

If the court makes the liability order, it usually orders the non-resident parent to pay the CMS's legal expenses.

### Time limits

Since 12 July 2006, there has been no time limit for applying for a liability order. Debts that were older than six years on 12 July 2006 (ie, that became due on or before 12 July 2000) and were not subject to a liability order cannot be enforced through a liability order and will be recovered by other methods.[195] The six years do not begin to run until the non-resident parent is notified of the calculation. Although a calculation can be backdated, liability does not exist until it is made.[196]

The CMS does not need to act on a liability order immediately after it is granted. If an order is made, there may be a long delay before the CMS takes any further action. Action that directly aims to recover money (eg, taking control of goods) must be taken within six years from the date of the order.[197] The six-year time limit does not apply to action that does not, in itself, recover money, such as imprisonment or disqualification from driving.[198]

### England and Wales

The non-resident parent is sent a summons giving 14 days' notice of the hearing. The magistrates decide whether or not to issue the liability order, but cannot consider whether the parent is liable or the calculation has been properly made.[199] If an appeal against a decision of the CMS on those issues is pending, however, the court may decide to adjourn.

The court may decide not to issue an order if the non-resident parent appears to be co-operating. However, the CMS may still ask for the order to be granted on the understanding that it will not be enforced if the parent continues to co-operate. If the parent does not attend the court, the CMS may still obtain the order, unless the application has not been properly made. It is unusual for a non-resident parent to attend a liability order hearing. If s/he does attend, the court may adjourn and arrange another hearing to ensure that there is sufficient time for her/him to speak.

There is a set form for the court order. It must specify the outstanding amounts of child support, fees and other forms of maintenance.[200]

### Scotland

A CMS litigation officer can sign the liability order application instead of a solicitor.[201] Court officials serve notice of the application on the non-resident parent.[202] The parent has 21 days to object to the liability order being made. This should be done in writing by returning the notice stating the grounds of the objection and enclosing evidence. If objections are received, a hearing is held. Even if the parent does not attend, the sheriff must still consider her/his objections.[203] The court cannot question the non-resident parent's liability for child support, or the calculation itself. An extract of the liability order may be issued 14 days after the order is actually made. All the forms used in this procedure are included in the sheriff court child support rules.[204]

## Taking control of goods and other enforcement action

If a liability order has been made, in **England and Wales**, the CMS can decide to instruct enforcement agents to take control of the non-resident parent's goods or take court action (see below). In **Scotland**, a liability order can be enforced by 'diligence' (the term for various processes of debt enforcement in Scottish law – see p176).[205]

The CMS aims to use the full range of sanctions available, including removing a driving licence, imprisonment and taking control of goods, where appropriate.[206]

### England and Wales

If a liability order has been made, the amount on the order can be enforced in England and Wales by **taking control of and selling the non-resident parent's goods**.[207] The enforcement agent (a private bailiff) carrying this out must give the person written notice at least seven clear days before taking action. The notice must include details of the liability order and the debt.[208] It must also explain how payment of the debt in full can be made to avoid the taking and subsequent sale of goods.[209]

Certain items cannot be taken. These include:[210]

- tools, books, vehicles and other items necessary for work, up to a total value of £1,350; *and*
- clothing, bedding, furniture, household equipment and provisions reasonably required to meet the basic domestic needs of the non-resident parent and every member of her/his household.

Fees can be charged at each of the stages involved in the process.[211]

For more information about bailiffs, including how to complain about them, see CPAG's *Debt Advice Handbook*.

Once a liability order has been made, the CMS can **register the order as if it were a judgment debt**.[212] This record is publicly available and damages the non-resident parent's credit rating (see also p54 for when the CMS can disclose information directly to credit reference agencies). The CMS can also use the county court to recover any amount that remains unpaid.[213]

A **charging order** allows a debt to be registered against the non-resident parent's property (and certain other assets, such as land, stocks, shares and any interest s/he may have in a trust). When the property is sold, the debt due under the liability order can be recovered from the proceeds of the sale. In some cases, it may not be possible to register a charge, in which case a caution against dealings may be obtained to prevent the property from being sold without the CMS's knowledge. Once a charge or caution has been registered, the CMS can consider applying to the court for an order of sale, forcing the non-resident parent to sell the property and pay the debt.

A **third-party debt order** can be obtained by the CMS if it is aware that the non-resident parent has a bank account or is owed money by a third party. The order freezes funds in the account and requires that person to release funds to the CMS up to the amount of the liability order.

## Scotland

In Scotland, the CMS can ask sheriff officers to issue a 'charge for payment', a formal request in writing demanding that the non-resident parent pay the debt within a specific period, usually 14 days. If s/he does not, various enforcement processes (known as 'diligence') can be used. The law of diligence can be complex. The following is not a full statement of the law, but a summary of the processes that can be used by the CMS.[214] If you are subject to diligence action by the CMS, get help from a money adviser.

The CMS can ask the sheriff court to freeze money or goods through an **arrestment**. This prevents money in an account being used, and prevents any money owed to the non-resident parent being paid into the account. A company holding any goods owed to the parent can be required to cancel the transaction and transfer the money used to pay for the goods to the CMS instead.

The sheriff court can also make an **attachment order**, preventing the non-resident parent from selling or transferring belongings. If the parent still does not pay the arrears, the goods can be seized and sold at public auction and the proceeds paid to the CMS.

The CMS can instruct sheriff officers to register the debt against any heritable property (eg, a house, garage, land or business premises). This is known as **inhibition**, and prevents the non-resident parent selling or transferring the property until s/he has paid the debt.

## Orders preventing the disposal of assets

In England, Wales and Scotland, the CMS can take action to prevent a non-resident parent disposing of assets or transferring them out of the UK in order to avoid paying child support arrears.[215] The CMS may apply to the High Court or family court (England and Wales) or the Court of Session or sheriff court (Scotland) if a non-resident parent:

* has arrears of child support; *and*
* on or after 6 April 2010, has disposed of, or is about to dispose of, assets with the intention of avoiding paying child support.

Disposing of assets includes any conveyance, assurance or gift of property of any description. It does not include assets transferred under a will or codicil.[216]

If the asset has already been disposed of, the court can make an order to 'set the transaction aside' or, in Scotland, to 'reduce the disposition' – ie, to reverse the disposal.[217] If the parent is about to dispose of an asset, the court can make a restraining order (England and Wales) or an interdicting order (Scotland) to prevent this.[218]

The court can review any disposal of assets by the non-resident parent, except if the asset was given as part of a contract with an innocent party who acted in good faith.[219] For example, if the parent disposes of a sum of money to purchase goods from an individual who had no knowledge of her/his intention to avoid paying child support, the transaction cannot be reversed. An asset transferred to another as part of a marriage agreement can, however, be reviewed by the court.[220]

If the court is satisfied that the CMS would be able to take action to recover arrears from the asset in question, the burden of proof is on the non-resident parent to show that s/he did not dispose of, or was not about to dispose of, the asset with the intention of avoiding paying child support.[221] If an order is made in Scotland, the parent can apply to the court to have it reviewed, varied or recalled at any time.[222]

## Disqualification from driving or imprisonment

If all the methods of recovery have failed, the CMS may take action to disqualify the non-resident parent from driving or to imprison her/him (but not both).[223]

Before taking action, every attempt must be made to contact the parent. If no phone contact has been successful during the enforcement action, a face-to-face visit may be appropriate. These powers are only used as a last resort.[224] Suspended prison sentences and suspended disqualifications from driving are significantly more common than actual committals and disqualifications.[225]

The power is discretionary and when deciding whether to take this action, the CMS must consider the welfare of any child likely to be affected (see p122).

**Note:** the government plans to introduce a power for the CMS to take action to disqualify the non-resident parent from holding or obtaining a passport or other UK travel authorisation for up to two years.[226] This is intended to be used where all methods of recovery have failed and arrears of at least £1,000 remain outstanding. The process would be similar to that for taking action for imprisonment or disqualification from driving. No date has yet been set for this coming into force.

## Action for disqualification from driving or imprisonment

In England and Wales, if taking control of goods and/or other enforcement action has been tried, but an amount is still due under the liability order, the CMS can apply to the magistrates' court (or sheriff court) to issue either an order disqualifying her/him from driving or a warrant committing the non-resident parent to prison.[227] The CMS can only do this if the other proceedings have been tried unsuccessfully. It is not enough that they have been considered, but not pursued.[228]

The hearing must take place in the presence of the parent.[229] The court can summon her/him to appear in court and produce her/his driving licence.[230] If s/he does not appear, the court may issue a warrant (citation in Scotland) for her/his arrest.[231] The CMS should explain why it considers disqualification or imprisonment appropriate in the circumstances.

The court must enquire into the parent's means, whether s/he needs a driving licence to make a living and whether there has been 'wilful refusal or culpable neglect' on her/his part.[232] It can only disqualify her/him from driving or commit her/him to prison if there has been 'wilful refusal or culpable neglect'[233] and the decision whether to do so is at the court's discretion. The CMS must prove beyond reasonable doubt that the non-resident parent has the ability to pay and has wilfully refused.[234]

A written statement from an employer is accepted as proof of earnings.[235]

### Disqualification from driving

If the court decides that there has been wilful refusal or culpable neglect and disqualification from driving is appropriate, an order is issued.[236] The order may be issued, but its implementation suspended on conditions – eg, regular payments. The order states the amount outstanding, including child support, court costs and any other charges.[237] If the amount is paid in full, the order is revoked.

The maximum period of disqualification is two years.[238] If, after the order has been issued, part payment is made, the period of disqualification may be reduced.[239] If the amount is paid in full, the order must be revoked. If the arrears have not been paid in full at the end of the period of disqualification, the CMS may apply again for disqualification or imprisonment.[240]

### Imprisonment

If the court decides that there has been 'wilful refusal or culpable neglect' and it is appropriate, a warrant for imprisonment is issued.[241] If the court decides on committal rather than disqualification from driving, it should explain the reasons why this is preferred.

A warrant cannot be issued against a non-resident parent who is under 18.[242]

Instead of immediate committal to prison, the court usually fixes a term of imprisonment and postpones it on conditions, usually of regular payments.[243] A warrant of commitment is issued, stating the total amount outstanding, including child support, fees, court costs and any other charges.[244] If the amount is paid in full, the non-resident parent will not be imprisoned.

The maximum period of imprisonment is six weeks.[245] If, after the warrant has been issued, part payment is made, the period of imprisonment is reduced by the same proportion as that by which the debt has been reduced.[246]

If the parent is imprisoned, s/he can be released immediately if the liability order debt is paid in full. If part of the debt is paid, the prison sentence can be reduced.[247] Advisers should check whether the payment needs to be made to the prison or to the CMS.

The court cannot write off the arrears, so if full payment is not made, arrears still exist following the period of imprisonment. If a warrant is not issued or the court does not fix a term of imprisonment, the CMS can renew the application at a later date on the grounds that the non-resident parent's circumstances have changed.

The ability to apply to court for a warrant for imprisonment is not a one-off power. If the non-resident parent builds up a new debt (eg, by not keeping up with current child support payments), the CMS can go back to court to request a warrant in respect of each new debt.[248]

## Bankruptcy

A non-resident parent may have child support arrears when s/he is made bankrupt. The CMS is not a creditor that can be bound by an individual voluntary arrangement (in England and Wales, this is a binding compromise agreement with creditors to avoid the consequences of bankruptcy) made by a non-resident parent who has failed to pay child support. Any liability for arrears of child support cannot, therefore, be reduced by means of an individual voluntary arrangement.[249]

The CMS cannot take enforcement action while a non-resident parent is being made bankrupt. Therefore, if the CMS is notified of bankruptcy, any ongoing enforcement action must cease until the bankruptcy order has been made.

In this case, the CMS may decide not to enforce the order because it may not be practical – eg, a charging order/inhibition of sale may not be effective, as any property may already have been sold to pay creditors. The CMS may obtain a liability order to remind the non-resident parent that responsibility for child support cannot be avoided.

As part of bankruptcy proceedings, the non-resident parent can inform the court of her/his child support liabilities. The administrator of the bankruptcy should take this liability into account when deciding how much money the parent needs to meet her/his basic living expenses. This decision is made before any available funds are distributed among creditors.

Bankruptcy in England and Wales may not prevent the CMS considering further enforcement measures, such as disqualification from driving or imprisonment – eg, further action may be pursued if the non-resident parent has a steady income. In these circumstances, the parent must show that s/he cannot afford to meet her/his child support liability. This may be more difficult if the administrator of the bankruptcy has already made provision for the current child support payments when deciding how much money the parent needs to meet basic living expenses. However, in the vast majority of cases, the CMS still pursues child support.[250]

If a non-resident parent is sequestrated in Scotland, any child support debt is wiped out and is no longer recoverable.[251]

# 3. **Fees for enforcement action**

If the Child Maintenance Service (CMS) takes certain enforcement action, fees are imposed on the non-resident parent as follows:[252]
- £50 for making a deduction from earnings order (see p158);
- £50 for making a regular deduction order (see p168);
- £200 for making a lump-sum deduction order (see p169);
- £300 for applying for a liability order (see p174).

Enforcement fees may be waived by the CMS if:[253]
- an additional fee would otherwise be due because:
  - more than one deduction from earnings order is sought by the CMS because the non-resident parent has more than one employer or has recently changed jobs;

- more than one regular deduction order or lump-sum order is sought because the non-resident parent has more than one bank or building society account, or has recently changed accounts;
- the amount being collected under a deduction from earnings order or regular deduction order has changed;
- the CMS has sought a liability order, but it was not granted;
- the CMS's action to impose a deduction from earnings order, regular deduction order or lump-sum deduction order has been successfully challenged by the non-resident parent by appeal or judicial review;
- due to error or maladministration by the CMS, the deduction from earnings order, regular deduction order or lump-sum deduction order has lapsed or been discharged;
- a deduction from earnings order is made because the non-resident parent has chosen to use this as the method of paying her/his child support liability;
- a deduction from earnings request (see p159) is made for a non-resident parent in the armed forces when that parent is deployed on operational duty.

**Note:** there are no fees for enforcement action on remaining cases under the '2003 rules' and '1993 rules' until these are closed (see p2).

From 23 May 2016, enforcement fees can also be waived in certain circumstances (see p135) while the non-resident parent is being offered a 'compliance opportunity' (see p133) to prove that s/he will pay voluntarily in order to be allowed to use 'direct pay' in a '2012 rules' case. In such cases, if a deduction from earnings order is imposed during the compliance period to cover a portion of the payments due, the fee for the order can be waived.[254] At the end of the compliance opportunity, if the order is varied (ie, because the non-resident parent has not complied and it has to be varied to cover the full amount of child support due), an enforcement fee of £50 is due. This fee is only due the first time the deduction from earnings order is varied, and can be waived by the CMS for one of the usual reasons listed above.[255] The power to impose and waive these fees in these circumstances ends on 22 May 2021.[256]

An enforcement fee is payable to the CMS, not the person with care. It is recovered by the CMS from any arrears owed by the non-resident parent before the balance is paid to the person with care.[257] If an enforcement fee is charged, the CMS must send the non-resident parent a notice as soon as possible stating the amount of the fee and the enforcement action in respect of which it has been imposed.[258]

**Note:** the rules on collecting and enforcing payments of child support also apply to payment of fees, except that the CMS cannot seek to disqualify a non-resident parent from driving or imprison her/him where enforcement action is being taken against her/him solely to recover fees.[259]

# 4. **Delays in collection and enforcement**

Many cases may accumulate arrears. In recent years, the Child Maintenance Service (CMS) has said that it has been pursuing a more vigorous and effective approach to enforcement and taking enforcement action more quickly in response to a non-resident parent's failure to pay.

If you are a person with care and concerned about the speed of pursuit, contact the CMS and explain the effects of this on the welfare of the child(ren). In particular, you may want to request that a deduction from earnings order be issued. If a deduction from earnings order or another form of enforcement is refused, the reasons for this should be explained.

**Note:** enforcing the obligation to pay child support is at the discretion of the CMS.[260] This means that a person with care cannot decide which method of enforcement is used. If you believe that there has been undue delay by the CMS, or that it has not used its discretion reasonably or rationally, you can make a complaint (see Chapter 11). Judicial review (see p190) could also be considered. Get specialist advice before considering an application for judicial review.

If arrears of over £100 have built up because of CMS maladministration, the person with care may be eligible for an advance payment (see below). This may be in addition to any payment of compensation (see p234).

## Advance payments

An advance payment of child support is not compensation. The payment is to ensure that a person with care is not worse off as a result of maladministration by the CMS. Essentially, it is advance payment of arrears that the CMS is collecting from the non-resident parent. The decision on whether or not to make an advance payment is discretionary and there are no guidelines in the legislation. Some details of when the CMS considers making an advance payment are available on the child maintenance section of the gov.uk website.

For an advance payment to be considered, there must be clear evidence of maladministration by the CMS. 'Maladministration' may include:[261]

- rudeness;
- delay;
- refusing to answer reasonable questions;
- knowingly giving advice which is misleading or inadequate;
- incompetence;
- bias – eg, because of gender or ethnicity; *or*
- disregarding guidance that should be followed.

A request for an advance payment could also be considered even if the CMS is not able to recover arrears from the non-resident parent. This could apply if arrears of child support have become unenforceable – eg, because enforcement action was not taken within the time limits, or the non-resident parent has subsequently moved abroad and is outside the CMS's jurisdiction. If the arrears could have been collected had the CMS taken timely action, a request for an advance payment can be made. Although the power is discretionary, the Independent Case Examiner (ICE – see p238) has recommended payment in such cases.[262]

The CMS may consider an advance payment on its own initiative or at the request of the person with care. If an advance payment is to be made, the amount is the arrears that would have been due but for the maladministration. Allowances are made for normal processing time, so only delay over and above this is considered.

If a decision is made not to make a payment, there is no right of appeal. You can provide further information to support the case, complain (see Chapter 11), contact your MP or possibly seek a judicial review (see p190). If a complaint is made, the CMS may still refuse to make an advance payment. However, ICE and the Ombudsman have the power to recommend advance payments, so it may be worthwhile moving to the next stage of the complaints procedure if you have reasonable grounds.

Where maladministration has occurred, there is also provision for the CMS to pay compensation or a consolatory special payment (see p234).

## Enforcement by the person with care

Although there is no provision in child support legislation for the person with care to bring her/his own court action against the non-resident parent for the child support due, it may be possible to do so. In practice, however, such action may be difficult. The European Court of Human Rights has confirmed that only the CMS has the legal standing to enforce child support, and that a lack of direct access to the courts by a person with care to enforce child support payments from a non-resident parent does not breach the right to a fair hearing under the European Convention on Human Rights.[263]

If you have lost out because of CMS delay or maladministration, it may be possible to sue the CMS for negligence. If you are considering doing either of the above, get legal advice. Using the complaints procedure is more likely to be an effective means of obtaining redress within a reasonable timescale (see Chapter 11).

# Notes

## 1. Arrears

1  ss4(2)(b) and 7(3)(b) CSA 1991
2  CMS leaflet CMSB006GB, *What Happens if a Paying Parent Doesn't Pay Child Maintenance?* November 2013
3  DWP, *Preparing for the Future, Tackling the Past: child maintenance – arrears and compliance strategy 2012–2017*, January 2013
4  DWP, *Supporting Separated Families: securing children's futures*, Cm 8399, July 2012; DWP, *Preparing for the Future, Tackling the Past: child maintenance – arrears and compliance strategy 2012-2017*, January 2013
5  CMS leaflet CMSB009GB, *Paying Child Maintenance*, October 2013
6  Reg 7 CS(C&E) Regs
7  Reg 8A CS(MAJ) Regs
8  s28J CSA 1991
9  Reg 2(2) CS(VP) Regs
10  *DP v CMEC (CSM)* [2012] UKUT 63 (AAC)
11  Reg 3(b) CS(VP) Regs
12  Reg 3(a) CS(VP) Regs
13  Regs 2(2) and 4(b) CS(VP) Regs
14  Reg 4(a) CS(VP) Regs
15  s41B(1A) and (2) CSA 1991; reg 9 CS(MPA) Regs
16  DWP, *Preparing for the Future, Tackling the Past: child maintenance – arrears and compliance strategy 2012–2017*, January 2013
17  Reg 3(3) CS(MPA) Regs
18  Reg 3(3)(a) CS(MPA) Regs; DWP, *Child Support (Miscellaneous Amendments) Regulations 2012: government response to consultation*, March 2012
19  Reg 3(4) CS(MPA) Regs
20  Reg 3A CS(MPA) Regs
21  DWP, *Child Maintenance Frequently Asked Questions*, August 2012
22  First Protocol, Art 1 European Convention on Human Rights
23  DWP, *Preparing for the Future, Tackling the Past: child maintenance – arrears and compliance strategy 2012-2017*, January 2013
24  s41A CSA 1991 and reg 7A CS(C&E) Regs; Sch 7, para 3(1) UC,PIP,JSA&ESA(C&P) Regs
25  s43 CMOPA 2008

26  DWP, *Preparing for the Future, Tackling the Past: child maintenance – arrears and compliance strategy 2012–2017*, January 2013
27  s41(2) and (2A) CSA 1991; reg 8 CS(AIAMA) Regs
28  Reg 8 CS(AIAMA) Regs
29  s43 CSA 1991; Sch 9B SS(C&P) Regs
30  Sch 9B para 3(1) SS(C&P) Regs
31  DWP, *Child Maintenance: a new compliance and arrears strategy – public consultation*, December 2017
32  Reg 7(1) CS(MPA) Regs
33  Child Maintenance and Enforcement Commission, *Child Maintenance and Other Payments Act Summary of Responses to the Consultation on Draft Regulations*, November 2009, para 3
34  Child Maintenance and Enforcement Commission, *Child Maintenance and Other Payments Act Summary of Responses to the Consultation on Draft Regulations*, November 2009, para 3
35  Reg 7(3) CS(MPA) Regs
36  Child Maintenance and Enforcement Commission, *Child Maintenance and Other Payments Act Summary of Responses to the Consultation on Draft Regulations*, November 2009, para 3.5
37  Reg 5 CS(MPA) Regs
38  Reg 7(3) CS(MPA) Regs
39  Reg 5(2) CS(MPA) Regs
40  Reg 5(2) CS(MPA) Regs
41  s41D CSA 1991
42  s41D(3) and (5)-(7) CSA 1991
43  DWP, *The Draft Child Support Management of Payments and Arrears (Amendment) Regulations 2012: government response to consultation on draft regulations*, October 2012
44  DWP, *Child Maintenance: a new compliance and arrears strategy – public consultation*, December 2017
45  Reg 13D(1) and (2) CS(MPA) Regs
46  Reg 13D(3) CS(MPA) Regs
47  DWP, *The Draft Child Support Management of Payments and Arrears (Amendment) Regulations 2012: government response to consultation on draft regulations*, October 2012
48  Reg 13C(1) CS(MPA) Regs
49  Reg 13B CS(MPA) Regs

50 DWP, *The Draft Child Support Management of Payments and Arrears (Amendment) Regulations 2012: government response to consultation on draft regulations*, October 2012
51 Reg 13E(1) and (2) CS(MPA) Regs
52 Reg 13E(3) CS(MPA) Regs
53 Reg 13E(4) and (5) CS(MPA) Regs
54 DWP, *The Draft Child Support Management of Payments and Arrears (Amendment) Regulations 2012: government response to consultation on draft regulations*, October 2012
55 s41E CSA 1991
56 DWP, *Preparing for the Future, Tackling the Past: child maintenance – arrears and compliance strategy 2012–2017*, January 2013
57 s41E(1) CSA 1991 and reg 13G CS(MPA) Regs
58 DWP, *Preparing for the Future, Tackling the Past: child maintenance – arrears and compliance strategy 2012–2017*, January 2013
59 Reg 13F CS(MPA) Regs
60 The duties on the CMS to give written notice do not apply to someone who cannot be traced or who has died: regs 13(2) and 13H(2) CS(MPA) Regs
61 Reg 13H CS(MPA) Regs
62 Reg 13H(5) CS(MPA) Regs
63 Reg 13I CS(MPA) Regs
64 Reg 13H(4) CS(MPA) Regs
65 DWP, *Supporting Separated Families: securing children's futures*, Cm 8399, July 2012; DWP, *Preparing for the Future, Tackling the Past: child maintenance – arrears and compliance strategy 2012–2017*, January 2013
66 DWP, *Child Maintenance: a new compliance and arrears strategy – public consultation*, December 2017
67 DWP, *Supporting Separated Families: securing children's futures*, Cm 8399, July 2012

## 2. Enforcement action
68 CMS leaflet CMSB006GB, *What Happens if a Paying Parent Doesn't Pay Child Maintenance?*, November 2013
69 Reg 13 CSF Regs
70 *KA v CMEC* [2009] UKUT 99 (AAC)
71 House of Commons, *Hansard*, Written Answers, 20 July 2011, col 1063W
72 *Child maintenance: cases where someone lives overseas (England and Wales)*, House of Commons Library, January 2018
73 s31 CSA 1991
74 CMS leaflet CMSB006GB, *What Happens if a Paying Parent Doesn't Pay Child Maintenance?*, November 2013

75 Reg 8(3) and (4) CS(C&E) Regs
76 Reg 8(4)(a) CS(C&E) Regs
77 Reg 8(4)(b) CS(C&E) Regs
78 Reg 8(5) CS(C&E) Regs
79 s29(4)(a) CSA 1991
80 *R v Secretary of State for Social Security ex parte Biggin* [1995] 2 FCR 595, [1995] 1 FLR 851
81 Sch 1 para 10 CS(NIRA) Regs
82 CSA(CA)O; Army Act 1955; Air Force Act 1955; Naval Forces (Enforcement of Maintenance Liabilities) Act 1947; Merchant Shipping Act 1970
83 Regs 3(3) and 6 CS(DEOAMMA) Regs
84 Reg 15 CS(C&E) Regs
85 Reg 15(1) CS(C&E) Regs
86 s32(8) and (11) CSA 1991; reg 25(ab) and (b) CS(C&E) Regs
87 Reg 1(3)(a) CS(C&E) Regs
88 Reg 1(3)(b) CS(C&E) Regs
89 s31(6) CSA 1991
90 s31(7) CSA 1991
91 s14A CSA 1991; reg 4(2)(b) CSI Regs; CMS online guide, *Make Child Maintenance Deductions From an Employee's Pay*
92 Reg 9 CS(C&E) Regs
93 Reg 16(1) CS(C&E) Regs
94 Reg 16(2) CS(C&E) Regs
95 Reg 16(3) CS(C&E) Regs
96 s32(8) and (11) CSA 1991; reg 25(aa), (b) and (c) CS(C&E) Regs
97 Reg 13 CS(C&E) Regs; s8(2)(b) ERA 1996
98 s9 ERA 1996
99 s12(3)-(5) ERA 1996
100 https:// childmaintenanceservice.direct.gov.uk
101 Reg 1(3)(a) CS(C&E) Regs
102 Reg 1(3)(b) CS(C&E) Regs
103 Reg 9 CS(C&E) Regs
104 Reg 9(d) CS(C&E) Regs
105 Reg 11(2) CS(C&E) Regs
106 Regs 10(1) and (2) and 11 CS(C&E) Regs, as substituted for '2012 rules' cases and other 'arrears only' cases by reg 4(4) CS(MOC&NCR) Regs
107 Reg 10(3) CS(C&E) Regs, as substituted for '2012 rules' cases by reg 4(4) CS(MOC&NCR) Regs
108 Regs 1(4), 11 and 12 CS(MOC&NCR) Regs
109 Reg 14(1) CS(C&E) Regs
110 Reg 14(2) CS(C&E) Regs
111 s32(8) and (11) CSA 1991; reg 25(aa) CS(C&E) Regs
112 Reg 12(6) CS(C&E) Regs
113 Reg 12(2) CS(C&E) Regs
114 Reg 12(4) CS(C&E) Regs
115 Reg 12(3A) CS(C&E) Regs
116 Reg 8 CS(AIAMA) Regs

117  Reg 24(2)(a) and (4) CS(C&E) Regs
118  Reg 24(2)(b) CS(C&E) Regs
119  Reg 17 CS(C&E) Regs
120  Reg 18 CS(C&E) Regs
121  Reg 19 CS(C&E) Regs
122  Regs 10(3) and 20(1)(g) CS(C&E) Regs, as substituted for '2012 rules' cases and other 'arrears only' cases by regs 4(4) and (6) and 11 CS(MOC&NCR) Regs
123  Reg 20(1) CS(C&E) Regs
124  Reg 20(1A) CS(C&E) Regs
125  Reg 36 CS(C&E) Regs, as inserted by reg 3(3) CS(DEOAMMA) Regs, modifying reg 20 by inserting paras (1)(i) and (1B) until 21 May 2021
126  Reg 4 CS(DEOAMMA) Regs, amending reg 12 CS(MOC&NCR) Regs until 21 May 2021
127  Reg 20(2) CS(C&E) Regs
128  Reg 21(1) CS(C&E) Regs
129  Reg 21(4) CS(C&E) Regs
130  Reg 21(5) CS(C&E) Regs
131  Reg 21(6) CS(C&E) Regs
132  Reg 22(1) CS(C&E) Regs
133  Reg 22(2) CS(C&E) Regs
134  Reg 22(3) CS(C&E) Regs
135  Reg 22(3A) CS(C&E) Regs
136  Reg 8(1) CS(C&E) Regs
137  Reg 3(4) CS(C&E) Regs
138  Reg 3(6)(c) CS(C&E) Regs
139  Reg 3(5) CS(C&E) Regs
140  Reg 3(6) CS(C&E) Regs
141  r5 and Form 6 AS(CSR)
142  Reg 22(4) CS(C&E) Regs
143  s32(6) CSA 1991
144  *Secretary of State for Social Security v Shotton* [1996] 2 FLR 241
145  ss48 and 49 CSA 1991; r6 AS(CSR)
146  ss32A and 32F CSA 1991
147  Reg 25A CS(C&E) Regs
148  Child Maintenance and Enforcement Commission, *Deduction Order Review, Research Report No.2*, March 2011, pp2 and 4
149  Child Maintenance and Enforcement Commission, *Deduction Order Review, Research Report No.2*, March 2011, p16
150  Reg 25X CS(C&E) Regs
151  DWP, *Child Maintenance: a new compliance and arrears strategy – public consultation*, December 2017
152  Child Maintenance and Enforcement Commission, *Deduction Order Review, Research Report No.2*, March 2011, p15
153  DWP, *Child maintenance: deduction orders against joint accounts – government response to public consultation*, October 2017
154  Reg 25Z CS(C&E) Regs
155  s32A CSA 1991
156  Reg 25B(1) CS(C&E) Regs

157  Reg 25C CS(C&E) Regs, as amended by reg 4(7) CS(MOC&NCR) Regs for '2012 rules' cases
158  s32B CSA 1991
159  s32D CSA 1991
160  Reg 25H CS(C&E) Regs
161  Reg 25D CS(C&E) Regs
162  Reg 25G CS(C&E) Regs, as amended by reg 4(7) CS(MOC&NCR) Regs for '2012 rules' cases
163  Reg 25G(2)(d) CS(C&E) Regs, as amended by reg 4(5) CS(MA) Regs for '2012 rules' cases
164  Reg 25I CS(C&E) Regs
165  Reg 25A(3)(b) CS(C&E) Regs
166  Reg 25N(1) CS(C&E) Regs
167  s32F(3)(b) and (4) CSA 1991
168  Reg 25P(1) and (2) CS(C&E) Regs
169  Reg 25P(6) CS(C&E) Regs
170  Reg 25Q CS(C&E) Regs
171  Reg 25Z(b) CS(C&E) Regs
172  Regs 25R and 25N CS(C&E) Regs
175  Reg 25S CS(C&E) Regs
176  Reg 25U CS(C&E) Regs
177  Reg 25AB CS(C&E) Regs
178  *AH v SSWP (CSA)* [2017] EWFC 9
179  s43A CSA 1991; reg 11 CS(MPA) Regs
180  Child Maintenance and Enforcement Commission, *CMOPA 2008: summary of responses to the consultation on the draft regulations*, November 2009, para 4.9
181  Reg 12 CS(MPA) Regs
182  Reg 13 CS(MPA) Regs
183  Reg 13(3) CS(MPA) Regs
184  Child Maintenance and Enforcement Commission, *CMOPA 2008: summary of responses to the consultation on the draft regulations*, November 2009, para 4.11
185  Child Maintenance and Enforcement Commission, *CMOPA 2008: summary of responses to the consultation on the draft regulations*, November 2009, para 4.6
186  Child Maintenance and Enforcement Commission, *CMOPA 2008: summary of responses to the consultation on the draft regulations*, November 2009, para 4.8
187  DWP, *Preparing for the Future, Tackling the Past: child maintenance – arrears and compliance strategy 2012–2017*, January 2013
188  Child Maintenance and Enforcement Commission, *CMOPA 2008: summary of responses to the consultation on the draft regulations*, November 2009, para 4.7
189  s33 CSA 1991
190  Reg 27 CS(C&E) Regs
191  s33(3) CSA 1991
192  s33(4) CSA 1991
193  *Bird v SSWP* [2008] EWHC 3159 (Admin)
194  Reg 29 CS(C&E) Regs; r3 AS(CSR)

195 Reg 28(2) and (2A) CS(C&E) Regs;
DWP, *Preparing for the Future, Tackling
the Past: child maintenance – arrears and
compliance strategy 2012–2017*, January
2013
196 *R (Sutherland) v SSWP* [2004] EWHC 800
(Admin)
197 s9 Limitation Act 1980
198 *CMEC v Mitchell* [2010] EWCA Civ 333
199 *Farley v CSA and Another* [2006] UKHL 31
200 Reg 29(1) and Sch 1 CS(C&E) Regs
201 *Secretary of State for Social Security v Love*
[1996] SLT 78
202 r2 AS(CSR)
203 *Secretary of State for Social Security v
Nicol* [1996] SLT 34
204 Forms 1-4 AS(CSR)
205 ss35(1) and 38(1) CSA 1991
206 DWP, *Preparing for the Future, Tackling
the Past: child maintenance – arrears and
compliance strategy 2012–2017*, January
2013
207 s35 CSA 1991; Part 3 TCEA 2007
208 Regs 6-8 Taking Control of Goods
Regulations 2013, No.1894
209 Sch 12 para 58 TCEA 2007
210 Reg 4 Taking Control of Goods
Regulations 2013, No.1894
211 Taking Control of Goods (Fees)
Regulations 2014, No.1
212 s33(5) CSA 1991
213 s36 CSA 1991
214 s38 CSA 1991
215 s32L CSA 1991
216 s32L(8) CSA 1991
217 s32L(2) CSA 1991
218 s32L(1) CSA 1991
219 s32L(5) CSA 1991
220 s32L(5) CSA 1991
221 s32L (7) CSA 1991
222 s32L(11)(b) CSA 1991
223 s39A CSA 1991
224 DWP, *Preparing for the Future, Tackling
the Past: child maintenance – arrears and
compliance strategy 2012–2017*, January
2013
225 DWP/National Statistics, *CSA Quarterly
Summary Statistics for Great Britain*,
December 2015
226 s27 CMOPA 2008; Department for
Work and Pensions, *Child Maintenance: a
new compliance and arrears strategy –
public consultation*, December 2017
227 ss39A(2) and 40(1)-(11) CSA 1991
228 s39A(1) CSA 1991; *Karoonian v CMEC
and Gibbons v CMEC* [2012] EWCA Civ
1379
229 s39A(3) CSA 1991
230 Reg 35(1) CS(C&E) Regs
231 s40(11) CSA 1991
232 s39A(3) CSA 1991

233 ss40(3) and 40A(1) CSA 1991
234 *Karoonian v CMEC and Gibbons v CMEC*
[2012] EWCA Civ 1379
235 ss40(11) and 40A(8) CSA 1991; reg
35(2) CS(C&E) Regs
236 s40B CSA 1991
237 Reg 35(4)-(5) and Sch 4 CS(C&E) Regs
238 s40B(1) CSA 1991
239 s40B(5) CSA 1991
240 s40B(7) CSA 1991
241 ss40 and 40B CSA 1991
242 ss40(5) and 40A(3) CSA 1991
243 ss40(3) and 40B(1) CSA 1991
244 Sch 3 CS(C&E) Regs
245 ss40(7) and 40A(5) CSA 1991
246 Reg 34(5) and (6) CS(C&E) Regs
247 CMS leaflet CMB006GB, *What Happens
if a Paying Parent Doesn't Pay Child
Maintenance?*, November 2013
248 CMS leaflet CMB006GB, *What Happens
if a Paying Parent Doesn't Pay Child
Maintenance?*, November 2013
249 *CMEC v Beesley* [2010] EWCA Civ 1344;
s382(5) Insolvency Act 1986, as to be
amended by s142 WRA 2012
250 DWP, *Preparing for the Future, Tackling
the Past: child maintenance – arrears and
compliance strategy 2012–2017*, January
2013
251 Independent Case Examiner, *Annual
Report 1 April 2011 – 31 March 2012*,
July 2012

### 3. Fees for enforcement action
252 Reg 10 CSF Regs 2014
253 Reg 12 CSF Regs 2014
254 Reg 12A CSF Regs 2014; CS(DOF) Regs,
Explanatory Memorandum
255 Regs 10(2) and 12(1A) CSF Regs 2014
256 Reg 1(2) CS(DOF) Regs
257 Reg 11 CSF Regs 2014
258 Reg 7(1B) and (4) CS(C&E) Regs
259 Reg 13 CSF Regs 2014

### 4. Delays in collection and enforcement
260 *Kehoe v UK* [2009] 48 EHRR, [2008] 2
FLR 1014
261 CSA leaflet CSL308, *How Do I Complain
About the Service I Get From the Child
Support Agency?*, October 2013
262 Independent Case Examiner, *Annual
Report 1 April 2008/09*, July 2012
263 *Kehoe v UK* [2009] 48 EHRR, [2008] 2
FLR 1014

# Chapter 9

· · · · · · · · · · · · · · · · · · · · · · · · · · · · · · · · · · · · · · · · · · · · · · · · · · · · · · ·

# Challenging a decision: revisions and supersessions

This chapter covers:

## 1. Changing a decision

Most decisions can be changed or challenged by a revision or supersession. However, there are some decisions that cannot (see p190).

The Child Maintenance Service (CMS) can also correct an accidental error in a decision or in the record of a decision at any time. The correction is then treated as part of the record of the decision.[1]

A supersession or revision is a decision that changes an earlier decision.

- **A revision** means that the decision which is wrong or which has been challenged is itself changed. The revised decision usually takes effect from the date the original decision had effect.
- **A supersession** means that the original decision is replaced by a new decision, which takes effect from a later date.

As with all decisions, revisions and supersessions are made by officials who work for the CMS and who make decisions on behalf of the Secretary of State for Work and Pensions. A revision or supersession usually happens because the CMS is told that something is wrong or has changed since the initial decision was made. The CMS may also initiate a revision or supersession itself.

If a decision is challenged within 30 days of the decision (or of the date an accidental error in the decision was corrected), it may be revised. Outside this time period, a decision can only be revised if the CMS accepts a late application (see p192), or in special circumstances where the original decision was wrong in such a way that it can be revised at any time – eg, if there has been an official error (see p194). If these special circumstances are not met, the decision may be superseded instead. A decision can also be superseded if circumstances have changed since it was made.

The table below shows when decisions are revised and superseded.

If the original decision is not incorrect, but the CMS has not dealt with the case properly in some way, a complaint can be made at any time (see Chapter 11). In some cases where the original decision is wrong (eg, where maladministration has led to an official error), it may be appropriate to make a complaint as well as applying for the decision to be revised.

### Revisions and supersessions

| Why is the decision being challenged? | When? | What can be done? |
|---|---|---|
| The decision is wrong for any reason. | Within 30 days of being told the decision. | The decision can be revised. |
| The CMS made a mistake (an 'official error'), or it was misled or did not know about something that would have affected its decision, or someone is not a parent of a child to whom a calculation relates. | At any time. | The decision can be revised. If the CMS did not know something or was misled, the decision can only be revised in certain circumstances (see p191). If these do not apply, the decision can be superseded. |
| The decision is wrong for any reason (other than one of the above reasons). | More than than 30 days after being told the decision. | The decision may be superseded. A late application for for a revision to be considered can also be made (see p192). |
| Something that affects the decision has changed. | At any time. | The decision can be superseded. |

A variation is an element of the child support calculation. This means that if an application for a variation is made after a calculation is in force and the CMS accepts it, it then revises or supersedes the original calculation to include the variation. See Chapter 5 for details.

For how to change a decision on deductions of child support from benefits, see CPAG's *Welfare Benefits and Tax Credits Handbook*.

Decisions of the First-tier Tribunal and the Upper Tribunal (see Chapter 10) can also be superseded or revised, but only in certain circumstances (see p192 and p196).

If a non-resident parent thinks the revision or supersession may reduce the amount of child support, s/he may try to negotiate lower payments pending the decision, although this is usually difficult (see p151).

## Challenging a decision that cannot be revised or superseded

Decisions that cannot be revised or superseded are mainly about information gathering, collection and enforcement (including decisions about fees), and refusals to make an interim or default maintenance decision.

If you want to challenge a decision that cannot be revised or superseded, provide the CMS with further information and ask it to reconsider. If the decision involved the CMS exercising its discretion, there may be further information that could be put to the CMS about the welfare of any child affected (see p122). If the CMS refuses to change the decision, a complaint can be made. An accidental error in a decision or in the record of a decision can also be corrected at any time.[2]

There may be other occasions that do not involve a decision, but where the behaviour of CMS staff or others is unsatisfactory – eg, if there is intimidating or unnecessarily intrusive questioning, or unwarranted demands for evidence and documentation. In these cases, you could make a complaint (see Chapter 11).

Some decisions on the enforcement of arrears cannot be revised or superseded, but can be appealed to a court (see p158).

### Judicial review

Judicial review is the legal procedure that allows a court to examine the way in which a public body has exercised its decision-making power to ensure that it has done so lawfully.[3] A person affected by a decision or action of a public body or one of its officers can ask the High Court (or Court of Session in Scotland) to carry out a judicial review of the decision or action.

A judicial review looks at the validity of the process by which a decision was made rather than the actual result of the decision.

The court can 'set aside' the decision and can also order the public body which made the decision to consider it again in a lawful way. Judicial review is not usually possible if there is a right to raise the issue in an appeal to the First-tier Tribunal, Upper Tribunal or court. Otherwise, judicial review of a CMS decision (eg, on enforcement) may be sought. Legal advice must be obtained as soon as possible after the decision is made.

In England and Wales, an application must be made to the High Court promptly and, in any event, within three months of the decision being challenged.[4] In Scotland, an application must be made within three months (or a longer time if the Court of Session considers it equitable in the circumstances).[5] The court's permission must be obtained before making an application.[6]

Judicial review of a child support decision may succeed if:[7]
- the CMS makes an error in law (illegality) – eg, does something it has no power to do; *or*

- the CMS fails to take into account a relevant matter or takes an irrelevant matter into account, or where a decision is 'so outrageous in its defiance of logic or of accepted moral standards that no sensible person who had considered the question could have arrived at it' (irrationality); *or*
- there has been procedural unfairness.

## Challenging a decision about benefit entitlement

Some CMS decisions depend on a decision of another part of the Department for Work and Pensions (DWP). For example, a non-resident parent in receipt of income support, income-based jobseeker's allowance, income-related employment and support allowance, universal credit calculated on the basis that s/he has no earned income, or the guarantee credit of pension credit pays the flat rate (see p60) of child support. Provided the DWP pays one of these benefits, even if the non-resident parent has other income, there can be no application for a variation on additional income grounds (see p98). A parent who believes that the other parent is fraudulently claiming a benefit cannot directly challenge a DWP decision to award it, but can raise the issue with the CMS, which contacts the other part of the DWP, which then investigates. The result is reported to the CMS, but not to the person who made the allegation. That person cannot appeal to the First-tier Tribunal against the DWP decision,[8] although a judicial review could be sought.

## 2. Revisions

The Child Maintenance Service (CMS) can revise a decision:[9]
- on its own initiative; *or*
- if requested by a person with care, non-resident parent or child applicant in Scotland; *or*
- if a person applies for a variation.

### Decisions that can be revised

Most child support decisions can be revised, including:[10]
- a decision to make a calculation (including a variation on a calculation), an interim decision or a default maintenance decision;
- a decision not to make a calculation, unless the CMS has made an interim or default maintenance decision instead (in which case, this decision can be revised). A refusal to make an interim or default maintenance decision cannot be revised;
- a decision of the First-tier Tribunal to make, or refuse to agree to, a variation to a calculation following a referral by the CMS;
- any supersession decision made by the CMS (see p196);

- a decision which has previously been revised if any of the circumstances on p191 apply to the revised decision.

A decision cannot be revised because of a change in circumstances after the date the decision was made, or because of an expected change.[11] Instead, the decision may be superseded (see p196) or a new child support application should be made. For revisions of default maintenance decisions, see p125.

**Note:** under the test case rules (see p227), the CMS may refuse to follow the law as decided by the Upper Tribunal or the courts, or may even suspend a decision on revision while an appeal is being brought in another case.

## When a decision can be revised

A decision can be revised on any grounds, provided it is within the time limit (see below), or at any time in certain circumstances (see p193).

### Time limits for a revision on any grounds

The CMS can revise a decision if:

- a person applies within 30 days of the decision (or of the date an accidental error in the decision or in the record of the decision was corrected); *or*
- a person applies for a variation within 30 days, provided the grounds for variation existed from the date of the decision being revised; *or*
- the CMS initiates the revision within 30 days of the original decision.

If someone applies within the 30-day time limit, but the CMS refuses to carry out a revision because there is insufficient information or evidence, it may allow her/him more time to provide this. (The CMS generally allows 14 days to provide information and extends this to 16 days to allow for the time taken to reach the CMS by post.) If the CMS does not allow this extra time to provide information and evidence, it could still revise the decision at a later date if it accepts a late application for a revision (see below).

If the time limit is missed, it may be possible to make a late application (see below).[12] In addition, there are certain situations in which the original decision was wrong in such a way that it can be revised at any time (see p193).

### Late applications

The CMS can extend the 30-day period for applying for a revision if it considers that:[13]

- the application has merit; *and*
- it was not practicable to apply within the time limit because of 'special circumstances' (see p193); *and*
- it is reasonable to allow the application.

'Special circumstances' are not defined. Include as much detail as possible to explain why an application is late. The application for an extension must identify the decision you want revised and explain why an extension should be granted.[14] The longer the delay in applying for a revision, the more compelling the special circumstances must be.[15]

There is no absolute time limit for seeking a revision on any grounds.

When the CMS is considering whether to accept a late application, any days before an accidental error in a decision or in the record of a decision is corrected are not counted towards the time limit.[16]

An application that is refused may not be renewed,[17] although the CMS may have power to reconsider a refusal to extend.[18] If a late application for a revision is refused, the CMS considers whether the decision can be revised on one of the grounds on which a decision can be revised at any time (see below) or whether it can be superseded.[19]

If the CMS refuses to accept a late application for an 'any grounds' revision, this means it has considered whether to revise the original decision and a mandatory reconsideration notice should be issued. There is no right of appeal against the decision not to extend the time limit, but an appeal to the First-tier Tribunal can be made against the original decision.[20]

**Note:** because a supersession (see p196) cannot usually lead to a decision being backdated to the original effective date, if possible you should make a late application for a revision. However, in case this is not accepted, an application for a supersession can be made at the same time, if appropriate. For example, a decision may be based on the wrong information about a child's education. If you have missed the deadline for applying for a revision, you can make a late application (giving special reasons) and also apply for a supersession on the grounds that there has been a mistake about a fact (see p196).

Judicial review of a refusal to extend the time limit for making a revision may also be possible (see p190).

## Revisions at any time

There is no time limit and the CMS can revise a decision at any time if:

- an appeal has been made in time (or within the time allowed for late appeals) and it has not yet been determined.[21] If an appeal is lodged, the CMS checks to see whether the decision should be revised;
- there has been an 'official error' (see p194);[22]
- the decision is wrong because of a misrepresentation or failure to disclose a material fact (see p194) and, because of this, the decision is more advantageous to the person who misrepresented or failed to disclose than it would otherwise have been;[23]
- it is an interim maintenance decision or default maintenance decision;[24]
- the decision is wrong because a child support calculation has been made for someone who was not, at the time it was made, a parent of a qualifying child.[25]

If the CMS makes a decision which is then appealed and, while that appeal is pending, the CMS makes a second decision on the same case, when the First-tier Tribunal decides the appeal on the first decision, the CMS can revise its second decision at any time if it would have been made differently had the CMS known about the tribunal's decision.[26]

The CMS can also revise a decision at any time if the information on historic income (or unearned income for a variation) given to it by HM Revenue and Customs (HMRC) has since been amended.[27]

### Official error

'Official error' is a mistake made by an officer of the CMS, another part of the Department for Work and Pensions or HMRC, which was not caused, or contributed to, by anyone outside these bodies.[28] This includes mistakes of law (see p197), except those only shown to be an error by a decision of the Upper Tribunal or court, as well as mistakes of fact, such as:

- a mistake of arithmetic;
- a wrong assumption about a person's circumstances where there was no evidence for it;
- a mistake made because CMS staff did not pass information or evidence to the officer who made the decision, when they should have done.

**Note:** if the official error appears to be accidental (eg, a mistake of arithmetic), the CMS can be asked to correct this. The CMS can correct an accidental error in a decision, or in the record of a decision, at any time. If the CMS does this, the time limit for requesting a revision of the decision begins from the date of the correction.[29]

### Misrepresentation and failure to disclose

A **'misrepresentation'** is a written or spoken statement of fact which is untrue.[30] This applies to an untrue statement, even if the person making it believes it to be true.[31]

There is only a **'failure to disclose'** a fact if there is a legal duty to report that fact to the CMS.[32] Therefore, a person who is asked to give information, but does not, has failed to disclose that information. However, if a person is not asked for the information, there can be no failure to disclose unless it is one of the facts that a parent with care or non-resident parent must always report. There is no general duty to report all changes of circumstances to the CMS, but there are some changes which must be reported (see p51).

The CMS can only consider a revision if the original decision was more advantageous to the person who misrepresented or failed to disclose.[33]

## How to apply for a revision

The notification of a decision also explains how to ask for a revision of that decision.[34] The request for a revision may be made by telephone. However, unless the issue is straightforward, it is best to follow up any telephone call with a letter to the CMS, confirming the reason for the request.

The CMS is not required to notify the parties that it is considering a revision or to inform one party that the other has applied for a revision. However, if there is an application for a variation that has had a preliminary consideration[35] or a request for a revision of a calculation with a previously agreed variation,[36] the other parties are usually contacted and asked for their representations.

There are rules about what information the CMS should disclose (see p52).

If you request a revision, you must show that there are grounds for the decision to be reviewed,[37] unless you are applying within the time limit or a late application is accepted (see p192) (in which case, it is enough that you simply think that the decision is wrong).

Provide a full explanation of your reasons for seeking the revision, and any supporting information or evidence.

If you do not provide sufficient information or evidence for the CMS to make a decision, the CMS may allow more time in which to do so (see p192).

The CMS may decide to:

- revise the decision; *or*
- make a default maintenance decision (see p125); *or*
- refuse to revise the decision.

If someone has applied for a revision and also lodges an appeal (see Chapter 10), the CMS can still consider whether the decision should be revised. If it is revised and the revised decision is more advantageous for the person appealing, the appeal lapses.[38] S/he can then decide to lodge a fresh appeal against the revised decision within the usual time limits. The CMS should try to inform all the relevant people that the appeal has lapsed.[39] If the revised decision does not benefit the person appealing, the appeal goes ahead against the decision as revised.[40]

## The revised decision

All the parties must be notified of the decision and given the usual details (see p126).[41] If there is more than one person with care in relation to a non-resident parent, this means all of them must be notified. The normal rules on information disclosure apply (see p52).[42]

If the decision is revised, this normally has the same effective date as the decision it replaces.[43] However, if the effective date of that decision was wrong, the revised decision has the effective date that the replaced decision should have had.[44]

If a revision is refused, the notification of the decision must include the reasons for the refusal and details of how to appeal.

The time limit for appealing against a decision that has been revised runs from the date of the notice of the revised decision.[45]

## 3. Supersessions

The Child Maintenance Service (CMS) can supersede a decision at any time, with or without an application, if certain rules are met. Usually a decision is superseded because of a change in circumstances. There is no general duty to tell the CMS of all changes of circumstances. See p51 for the changes that must be notified. A decision can also be superseded if it was wrong in law (see p197).

The main difference between a revision and a supersession is that a superseded decision generally takes effect from the date on which it is made (see p200), whereas a revision generally takes effect from the effective date of the decision being revised. However, there are exceptions to this general rule.

A child support calculation is likely to be subject to regular supersessions. See p74 for the rules about annual reviews and p76 for the rules about periodic current income checks.

### Decisions that can be superseded

Most child support decisions (whether made by the CMS, the First-tier Tribunal or the Upper Tribunal) can be superseded.[46] Decisions that can be superseded include:

- a decision to make a child support calculation (including a variation of a calculation), an interim decision or a default maintenance decision (see p126);
- a decision of a First-tier Tribunal on a CMS referral of a variation application;
- a revised decision (see p191).

It may also be possible to supersede other CMS decisions, depending on how the CMS (or the First-tier Tribunal or Upper Tribunal) interprets the rules. See p191 for which decisions can be revised.

### When a decision can be superseded

The CMS can normally supersede a decision if:[47]

- there has been a relevant change of circumstances since the decision had effect, or it is expected that there will be such a change. In some circumstances, there must be a significant change in the amount of the calculation as a result (see p198);

- it was made in ignorance of, or was based on a mistake about, a material fact; *or*
- there is an application for a variation of the calculation.

A decision made by the CMS can also be superseded if it is wrong in law (see below). If a person thinks that a decision of the First-tier Tribunal or Upper Tribunal is wrong in law, s/he must appeal against it.[48]

If the CMS is notified of a change of circumstances, it does not have to consider anything apart from that change when it is considering whether to supersede the decision. If the CMS is acting on its own initiative to supersede the decision, it does not have to consider anything other than the change that caused it to act).[49] It does not have to investigate whether all the other circumstances are still correct. However, the CMS might decide to incorporate the supersession process into a 'case check', which could result in other changes or errors being identified, and subsequent revisions or supersessions being carried out.

Under the 'test case rules', the CMS may refuse to follow the law as decided by the Upper Tribunal or courts, or even suspend a supersession decision, while an appeal is being brought in another case. See p227 for details.

## Wrong in law

A decision that is wrong in law can constitute an official error and also be grounds for a revision (see p194). A decision is wrong in law if:[50]

- when making it, the CMS misinterpreted or overlooked part or all of an Act of Parliament, a regulation or relevant caselaw;
- there is no evidence to support it;
- the facts are such that no reasonable person applying the law could have come to such a conclusion;
- there is a breach of 'natural justice' – ie, the procedure used has led to unfairness, or the officer who took the decision appeared to be biased;[51]
- the CMS has not given sufficient reasons for the decision;
- when exercising its discretion, the CMS took something irrelevant into account or ignored something relevant – eg, the welfare of the child (see p122).[52]

A decision is also wrong in law if the regulation under which it is made was not made lawfully. Such a regulation is said to be *ultra vires* (outside the powers). The courts and tribunals can decide that a regulation is *ultra vires*,[53] and the First-tier and Upper Tribunals have done so in benefit cases.

A decision is also wrong in law if it is contrary to European law – ie, European Union (EU) law and the European Convention on Human Rights (ECHR). EU law will rarely be relevant to child support issues. Caselaw has established that European law on the equal treatment of men and women in social security matters does not apply to child support.[54]

ECHR law is more likely to be relevant. The CMS, courts and the First-tier and Upper Tribunals are required to interpret Acts of Parliament consistently with the ECHR as far as possible, and must not act in a way which is incompatible with an ECHR right.[55] They cannot use the ECHR to overrule an Act of Parliament, but the courts can issue a 'declaration of incompatability'.[56] Courts and tribunals can override regulations which are incompatible with the provisions of the ECHR. In practice, however, few challenges using these principles have succeeded.

## When a decision cannot be superseded

The CMS cannot supersede a decision:
- which can be revised instead (see p191);[57]
- refusing to make or cancelling a child support calculation.[58] A further application for a calculation should be made instead.

In a case in which gross income is determined on the basis of current income (see p71), a decision cannot be superseded on the basis that there has been, or it is anticipated that there will be, a change in the non-resident parent's current income, unless there is at least 25 per cent difference.[59] This 'tolerance level' does not apply if the superseding decision:[60]
- is made by the CMS as part of an annual review of gross income or a periodic check of current income;
- is made because of an error of law; or
- supersedes a calculation decision that was based on an estimate of current income.

The CMS intends calculations to remain in place for a reasonable period. In many cases, the calculation is likely to remain in place for the year ahead.

## Deciding whether to request a supersession

Before requesting a supersession because of a change of circumstances, you may wish to establish whether a fresh calculation would be to your advantage. Unless it is a change that must be reported to the CMS (see p51), you need only tell the CMS about the changes in your favour. If the change only relates to one party, the CMS may not tell the other person. However, if it does, s/he might tell the CMS about other changes. These may cancel out the effect of the changes which led you to ask for a supersession.

If you believe that the other parent's circumstances have changed (eg, a non-resident parent no longer has children living with her/him), you can ask for a supersession and for the CMS to investigate (see Chapter 3). The CMS does not have to, but any changes it is aware of must be taken into account when it decides whether or not to supersede.

## How to apply for a supersession

A party to the calculation can apply for a supersession at any time. There are no time limits. If an application is made, the CMS must consider it and supersede if the conditions on p196 are met.

The CMS itself can initiate a supersession. It must take into account the welfare of any children affected (see p122) when considering whether or not to do so. The CMS learns of some changes automatically from Jobcentre Plus or may do so from a third party.

If the supersession is in relation to an application for a variation that has had a preliminary consideration (see p106),[61] or a supersession of a previously agreed variation,[62] the other relevant parties are contacted and notified of the grounds of the application and any relevant information or evidence the applicant has given. They are not told details of any long-term illness or disability of a relevant other child (if the application for variation was made on that basis), harmful medical evidence or the address of a relevant person or qualifying child if that would cause a risk of harm or undue distress.[63]

Otherwise, the other party is not notified of the application for a supersession. The normal rules about disclosure apply to the information given in any notification (see p52).[64]

The CMS does not have to check all the facts again. It can just consider the issues raised in the application.[65] You should therefore include all available information and evidence that supports your case for the decision to be changed in the application. Information provided may need to be verified in the normal way (see Chapter 3).

## The superseding decision

The CMS may decide that:
- there are no grounds for a supersession to be made;
- there are grounds for a supersession, but the calculation remains unchanged;
- there are grounds for a supersession and the calculation should be changed; *or*
- the calculation should be cancelled.

If the decision results in a supersession, whether or not a new calculation is made (including an interim maintenance decision – see p109 – or default maintenance decision – see p125), the parties must be notified of the decision and given the usual details (see p126).[66] The notice must also state how to apply for a revision or supersession, and how to appeal.[67]

If a supersession is refused, notification is also given, including the reasons for the refusal and the right to challenge the decision.[68]

A party can ask for a supersession decision to be revised and can then, if the decision is one against which there is a right of appeal, appeal to the First-tier Tribunal (see Chapter 10). **Note:** an appeal against a decision can normally only be made if the CMS has first considered an application for a revision (a 'mandatory reconsideration' – see p204).

If the CMS intends to cancel the case, it must notify each party and, if the reason for cancellation is a child applicant in Scotland's ceasing to be a qualifying child, inform any other potential child applicants in the case.[69]

## Effective date of the superseding decision

The general rule is that a supersession takes effect from the day on which the decision is made or the application for the supersession/variation was made.[70] However, the effective date may be different in certain circumstances (see the table below, but note that this does not cover all the circumstances in which a calculation is cancelled – see p127).

| Circumstances | Effective date |
|---|---|
| Gross income is based on current income and the non-resident parent is required to report a change because her/his current income has changed by at least 25 per cent. | The day on which the change occurred.[71] |
| There is a new qualifying child in relation to the non-resident parent. | The day that would be the initial effective date (ie, two days after the day on which written notification would be sent to the non-resident parent) if a new application were made for that child, if there were no calculation already in force.[72] |
| The application is made by one of the parties. | The day the application is received by the CMS.[73] |
| The CMS has acted on its own initiative. | If the CMS acts on the basis of information provided by a third party, the day that information is provided.[74]<br>In any other case, the day on which the decision is made.[75] |
| There is an anticipated change in circumstances. | The day on which the change is expected to occur.[76] |
| There is an expected change in circumstances which is a ground for a variation. | The day on which the change is expected to occur.[77] |
| A qualifying child dies or ceases to be a qualifying child. | The day on which the change occurred.[78] |

| | |
|---|---|
| A relevant other child (or a child supported under other maintenance arrangements) dies or ceases to be a qualifying child for child support purposes. | The day on which the change occurred.[79] |
| A person with care ceases to be a person with care in relation to a qualifying child. | The day on which the change occurred.[80] |
| A person with care, non-resident parent or a qualifying child ceases to be habitually resident in the UK. | The day on which the change occurred.[81] |
| A non-resident parent (or her/his partner) becomes or stops being entitled to a benefit that qualifies her/him for the flat rate. | The day on which the change occurred.[82] |
| The CMS is superseding a decision given by the First-tier Tribunal or the Upper Tribunal following the CMS's having served notice that a test case which could have affected that decision was pending before the Upper Tribunal or a court. | The day on which the decision of the First-tier Tribunal or Upper Tribunal would have taken effect had it been decided in accordance with the decision in the test case.[83] |
| The CMS is superseding a decision of the First-tier Tribunal or the Upper Tribunal on the ground that it is wrong because of a misrepresentation about, or a failure to disclose, a material fact, and the decision is more advantageous to the person who misrepresented or failed to disclose than it would otherwise have been but for that error. | The date on which the First-tier Tribunal or Upper Tribunal decision took, or was to take, effect.[84] |
| A decision of the CMS is superseded because it is shown to have been wrong by the Upper Tribunal or a court. | The date of the relevant Upper Tribunal or court decision.[85] |

# Notes

## 1. Changing a decision

1 Reg 27A CSMC Regs
2 Reg 27A CSMC Regs
3 *West v Secretary of State for Scotland*, 1992 SC 385, 1992 SLT 636, reported as *West v Scottish Prison Service*, 1992 SCLR 504
4 r54.5 The Civil Procedure Rules 1998
5 s27A Court of Session Act 1988
6 s27B(1) Court of Session Act 1988
7 *Council of Civil Service Unions v Minister for the Civil Service* [1984] 1 WLR 1174, [1984] 3 All ER 935
8 s12(2) SSA 1998; reg 25 SS&CS(DA) Regs

## 2. Revisions

9 ss16 and 28G CSA 1991; reg 14(1)(a) and (d) CSMC Regs
10 s16 CSA 1991
11 Reg 14(2) CSMC Regs
12 Reg 15 CSMC Regs
13 Reg 15(4) CSMC Regs
14 Reg 15(3) CSMC Regs
15 Reg 15(5) CSMC Regs
16 Reg 27A(4) CSMC Regs
17 Reg 15(7) CSMC Regs
18 See CIS/93/1992
19 DWP, *Mandatory Consideration of Revision Before Appeal: government response to public consultation*, September 2012
20 *R(CJ) and SG v SSWP (ESA)* [2017] UKUT 324 (AAC); *AO v SSWP and JA (CSM)* [2017] UKUT 499 (AAC)
21 Reg 14(1)(c) CSMC Regs
22 Reg 14(1)(e) CSMC Regs
23 Reg 14(1)(b) CMSC Regs
24 Reg 14(3) CSMC Regs
25 Reg 14(1)(g) CSMC Regs
26 Reg 14(3A) CSMC Regs
27 Reg 14(1)(f) CSMC Regs
28 Reg 14(4) CSMC Regs
29 Regs 14(1)(a) and 27A CSMC Regs
30 R(SB) 9/85
31 R(SB) 2/92 (*Page and Davis v CAO*)
32 CCS/15846/1996
33 Reg 14(1)(b) CSMC Regs
34 Reg 24(2) CSMC Regs
35 Reg 57 CSMC Regs

36 Reg 61 CSMC Regs
37 R(I) 1/71
38 s16(6) CSA 1991; Sch para 1(1) CSMC Regs
39 Reg 15C(12) SS&CS(DA) Regs
40 Sch para 1(2) CSMC Regs
41 Reg 26(1) CSMC Regs
42 Reg 25(3) CSMC Regs
43 s16(3) CSA 1991
44 Reg 16 CSMC Regs
45 r22(2) TP(FT) Rules

## 3. Supersessions

46 s17(1) CSA 1991
47 Reg 17(1)-(3) CSMC Regs
48 Reg 17(1)(c) CSMC Regs
49 s17(2) CSA 1991; reg 17(6) CSMC Regs
50 R(A) 1/72; R(SB) 11/83
51 *R v Gough* [1993] AC 646, [1993] 2 WLR 883, [1993] 2 All ER 724
52 *Wednesbury Corporation v Ministry of Housing and Local Government (No.2)* [1965] 3 WLR 956, [1965] 3 All ER 571
53 *CAO v Foster* [1993] AC 754, [1993] 2 WLR 292, [1993] 1 All ER 705
54 R(CS) 3/96; R(CS) 2/95; CCS/17/1994. These concerned the application of Art 141 of the EC Treaty (formerly Art 119), and Council Directives 75/117 and 79/7. The Sex Discrimination Act 1975 also has no effect. CCS/6/1995
55 ss3 and 6 HRA 1998
56 s4 HRA 1998
57 Reg 17(4) CSMC Regs
58 Reg 17(5) CSMC Regs
59 Reg 23(1) and (2) CSMC Regs
60 Reg 23(3) CSMC Regs
61 Reg 59 CSMC Regs
62 Reg 61(1) CSMC Regs
63 Reg 59(1)(a) and (5) CSMC Regs
64 Reg 25(3) CSMC Regs
65 s17(2) CSA 1991; reg 17(6) CSMC Regs
66 Reg 26(1) CSMC Regs
67 Reg 24(2) CSMC Regs
68 Regs 24(2) and 26(2) CSMC Regs
69 Reg 27 CSMC Regs
70 s17(4) CSA 1991
71 Reg 18(4) CSMC Regs
72 Reg 18(5) CSMC Regs
73 Reg 18(6)(a) CSMC Regs

74  Reg 18(6)(b) CSMC Regs
75  Reg 18(6)(c) CSMC Regs
76  Reg 18(2) CSMC Regs
77  Reg 18(2) CSMC Regs
78  Reg 18(3)(a) CSMC Regs
79  Reg 18(3)(a) CSMC Regs
80  Reg 18(3)(b) CSMC Regs
81  Reg 18(3)(c) CSMC Regs
82  Reg 18(3)(d) CSMC Regs
83  Reg 30 CSMC Regs
84  Reg 31 CSMC Regs
85  Reg 32 CSMC Regs

# Chapter 10

· · · · · · · · · · · · · · · · · · · · · · · · · · · · · · · · · · · · · · · · · · · · · · · · · · · ·

# Challenging a decision: appeals

This chapter covers:

---

## 1. Considering an appeal

Most decisions made by the Child Maintenance Service (CMS) can be appealed to an independent appeal tribunal: the First-tier Tribunal (Social Entitlement Chamber).

Before you can appeal, you must apply for a revision, asking the CMS to reconsider its decision. This is called a **'mandatory reconsideration'**. In order to be sure of having a right to appeal, you should request a mandatory reconsideration and should do so within the time limit (see p192).

If you appeal without first seeking a mandatory reconsideration, the CMS can treat the appeal as if it were a request for a mandatory reconsideration.[1] If the CMS does not do this, ask for a mandatory reconsideration as soon as possible, explaining why it is late, if necessary.

The CMS issues a letter, outlining its response to your request (a 'mandatory reconsideration notice'). Two copies are sent – you must send one of them to the First-tier Tribunal with the appeal.

**Note:** the CMS can correct an accidental error in a decision or in the record of a decision at any time (see p188).[2] A mandatory reconsideration of the corrected decision must be requested before an appeal to the First-tier Tribunal can be made.

## Who can appeal

Usually, anyone who is a party in a child support calculation (ie, a person with care, a non-resident parent or, in Scotland, a child applicant) has the right to appeal.[3]

Regardless of who appeals, all the parties in a child support calculation are also parties in the appeal and have the same rights, except that only the person making the appeal (the 'appellant') can ask to withdraw the appeal. Because an appeal can be withdrawn without the consent of any other party (see p214), it is best for each person who wishes to challenge a decision to bring her/his own appeal. The appeals can be heard together.

The CMS may also refer an application for a variation to the First-tier Tribunal in certain cases (see p110).

If a person with a right of appeal dies, the executor or administrator of her/his estate can can continue with any appeal that this already underway.[4]

## Decisions that cannot be appealed

Only decisions and, in some cases, refusals to make decisions, can be appealed. It is not possible to appeal if no decision has been made – eg, because of a delay. Instead, a complaint (see Chapter 11) or an application for a judicial review could be considered. Similarly, decisions about fees and some decisions about the method of collection or the enforcement of payment cannot be appealed. If you are uncertain whether you can appeal against a decision, get advice straight away.

## Parentage disputes

If someone denies when s/he appeals, or during the course of the appeal, that s/he is the parent of a child named in the child support application, the appeal is not dealt with by the First-tier Tribunal, but by the family court (in England and Wales) or sheriff court (in Scotland).[5] If there are other grounds for appeal apart from the dispute about parentage, the tribunal deals with those issues and the parentage issue is dealt with by the court. If the appeal is sent to the tribunal and it involves a denial of parentage, the tribunal should transfer that issue to the court.[6] For more information about parentage disputes, see p41.

---

# 2. Appealing to the First-tier Tribunal

When the Child Maintenance Service (CMS) makes a decision, each party (ie, the person with care, non-resident parent and, in Scotland, child applicant) must be sent a notice of that decision and information on the right to challenge it.[7]

If you are unhappy with a decision, you must first ask the CMS to reconsider it (see p204). Once you have received the mandatory reconsideration notice, if you are still unhappy you can appeal by sending a notice of appeal directly to the First-tier Tribunal. Form SSCS2 should be used, if possible, which is available from the gov.uk website.[8] Take care to provide all the required information.

The notice of appeal must include:[9]

- the name and address of the person making the appeal;
- the name and address of any representative (see p214);
- an address to which documents about the appeal may be sent or delivered;
- the name and address of any respondent (ie, the other party), if you know it;
- the grounds of the appeal – ie, the reasons why you disagree with the CMS.

You must also send a copy of:[10]

- the mandatory reconsideration notice;
- any statement of reasons sent by the CMS for the decision; *and*
- any available documents supporting the appeal that have not already been supplied to the CMS or the other party.

The appeal will not be accepted by the First-tier Tribunal unless the mandatory reconsideration notice is included. Documents supporting the appeal are normally accepted by the tribunal after the notice of appeal has been sent, but should be sent as soon as practicable.

If there was a long delay before the CMS sent you the mandatory reconsideration notice and you think you have been placed at a disadvantage (eg, if it is now more difficult to obtain evidence), tell the tribunal.[11]

There are strict time limits for making an appeal, which can be extended in certain circumstances (see below).

There is a CMS leaflet that explains the appeal process.[12]

## Time limits

An appeal must normally be received by the First-tier Tribunal within one month of your being sent the the the mandatory reconsideration notice.[13] The tribunal can extend this time limit, but there is still an absolute time limit within which the appeal must be made (see below).

*Month*

'Month' means a complete calendar month from the day of notification.[14] When calculating time, if something has to be done by a certain day, it must be done by 5pm that day. If a time limit ends on a day other than a working day, it must be done by the next working day to meet the time limit.[15]

If you are appealing against a refusal to revise a decision following a late application for a revision (see p192) where time was not extended, this one-month time limit runs from the date of notification of the original decision, not the date on which the CMS notified you of its refusal to revise. However, if the CMS refused to revise a decision following an application for a revision that was made within the time limit (see p192) or the extended time limit, the one-month time limit runs from the date on which the notice of refusal to revise was issued.

A notice of a decision counts as having been sent on the second day after the day it was posted.[16]

## Late appeals

If an appeal is not made within the one-month time limit, the First-tier Tribunal can extend the time limit, provided neither the CMS nor the other party objects and the tribunal does not direct otherwise.[17] The time limit can only be extended by 12 months – ie, there is an absolute time limit of 13 months from the date of the mandatory reconsideration notice being sent in which to appeal.[18] **Note:** in very exceptional circumstances (eg, if you did not receive notice of the decision), it may be possible to argue that the tribunal has discretion to accept an appeal outside this absolute time limit. You must show that you did everything you could have done to appeal in time.[19]

If you appeal outside the one-month time limit and the CMS or the other party objects, the tribunal decides whether the appeal should be admitted. It should bear in mind the overriding objective that appeals should be dealt with fairly and justly (see p210). It does not have to be satisfied that there are special reasons for why the appeal is late.[20] There is no guarantee that the tribunal will admit the appeal, so make sure you appeal in time wherever possible.

If a notice of appeal is submitted outside the time limit, in addition to the information listed on p206, it must also include the reasons why it is late and a request for it to be accepted.[21] It is best to include as much detail as possible about why there may be special reasons for the appeal being late and why it would be fair for it still to be admitted.

If the First-tier Tribunal decides that an appeal cannot be admitted because it was made outside the time limit, you can appeal to the Upper Tribunal (see p223) against this decision.[22]

## After an appeal is made

When the First-tier Tribunal receives your appeal, the regional office of HM Courts and Tribunals Service (HMCTS) sends you an acknowledgement. This advises you that HMCTS has also sent a copy of the appeal and any accompanying documents to the CMS and the other party(ies).[23] HMCTS checks that the appeal is validly made – ie, that the correct information has been included, the appeal has been made on time and the form has been signed. If the appeal is not validly made, HMCTS returns it to you and you have 14 days to complete it properly or provide the required information. If you do not do so, the appeal may be 'struck out' (see p213).[24]

HMCTS informs you that a hearing can be arranged at the nearest appeals venue. If it is not the most convenient venue for you, request that the venue be changed to a different one. This should be done promptly, as the later the request is left the more likely it is to be refused. In general, a request for a change of venue made in good time is likely to be agreed by HMCTS.

When the CMS receives a copy of the appeal, it may revise the decision. See p195 for further information.

If the CMS does not revise the decision, it should prepare a 'response' to the appeal. This should be sent to the tribunal, and copied to you and the other parties as soon as reasonably practical. Before sending the response, the CMS should check with you and the other party whether you (s/he) want your (her/ his) address, or any information that could lead to it being identified, removed from the papers (see p209).[25]

The CMS must send the response to the tribunal within 42 days of the date on which the CMS received the copy of the notice of appeal.[26] The response should state:[27]

- the name and address of the official who made the decision;
- the name and address of that official's representative (if any) – known as a 'presenting officer';
- an address where documents for the CMS can be sent or delivered;
- the name and address of the other party(ies) and her/his representative (if any).

The response should explain what parts of the grounds put forward for the appeal the CMS disagrees with, and why.[28] The response may also indicate whether the CMS thinks the case requires a hearing or could be decided by just considering the papers.[29]

The response must have the following attached to it:[30]

- a copy of any written record of the decision being appealed, and any statement of reasons for it, if they were not already sent with the appeal;
- copies of all documents relevant to the case that the CMS has.[31]

If any delay in the CMS sending the response to the tribunal is causing hardship, you can apply to the tribunal for a direction instructing the CMS to provide the papers.

Once you and the other party(ies) receive the copy of the response from the CMS, you (s/he) can make a written submission and supply any further documents in reply. This is your opportunity to explain your case in detail, and to provide any documents or other evidence to back it up. Your written submission should be sent to the tribunal within one month of receiving the CMS's response. The tribunal sends a copy of any written submission to the CMS and other parties.[32]

Although this one-month time limit is in the rules, it is unlikely that the tribunal will refuse to accept further evidence and submissions after this has passed, especially if there is to be an oral hearing (see p217) at which submissions and further evidence may be expected to be presented. It is more helpful to the tribunal to send evidence ahead of the hearing, even if this is late, than to present it on the day of the hearing, especially if there is a large quantity of evidence (which is likely to lead to an adjournment of the hearing and further delay).

### Confidentiality

If either the person with care or non-resident parent wants her/his address, or the address of the child, to be kept confidential, s/he should inform the CMS or tribunal on the notice of appeal, or within 14 days of receiving an appeal enquiry form.[33] The CMS and tribunal must take appropriate steps to ensure that this information (or any information that would help identify this) is not revealed to other party.

## 3. **Tribunal procedures**

Both the First-tier and Upper Tribunal have procedural rules setting out their powers and how they should deal with appeals. There are also practice directions and practice statements, which set out how they should conduct themselves. The rules are similar for both the First-tier and Upper Tribunal and so this section applies to both (and explains where there are differences). The rules about hearings and decisions are also part of the procedural rules (see p217 and p219). Caselaw has also established a number of principles on how appeals should be conducted.

If the tribunal fails to follow the correct procedure, this may be grounds for appealing against a decision it reaches, as a breach of the procedural rules could mean that the decision is based on an error of law.[34] A complaint can also be made to HM Courts and Tribunals Service (HMCTS). For details of how to complain to HMCTS, see CPAG's *Welfare Benefits and Tax Credits Handbook*. A failure to follow procedure could also be challenged by a judicial review (see p190).

If a party to the appeal fails to comply with the rules, a practice direction or a direction, the tribunal may take any action which it considers just (including striking out the appeal – see p213).[35] The Upper Tribunal has more extensive powers to deal with failure to comply with the rules. The First-tier Tribunal may refer a person to the Upper Tribunal for it to deal with the issue.[36]

Legally qualified members of HMCTS staff ('registrars') and other appropriately trained staff ('caseworkers') can make many of the decisions about a case and how it is handled (but not final decisions on an appeal). They must act under the supervision of a judge and in accordance with relevant guidance. A party to the appeal can, within 14 days of being sent a notice of any decision made by a member of staff, apply in writing for the decision to be considered again by a judge.[37]

## The overriding objective: fair and just

The overriding objective of the procedural rules is to enable the tribunal to deal with appeals 'fairly and justly'.[38] Whenever the tribunal exercises a power under the rules (eg, to admit or not admit a late appeal, or to strike out an appeal), it must consider whether it would be fair and just. Similarly, when the tribunal interprets what the rules mean or what the practice directions say, it must try to come to the interpretation which enables an appeal to be dealt with in a way which is fair and just.[39]

It is therefore important to bear in mind this overriding objective in any dealings with the tribunal.

The rules set out some of the things that must be taken into account when deciding whether a particular interpretation of the rules is fair and just, or in deciding whether it would be fair and just to exercise a power in a particular way.[40] The tribunal should:

- deal with the case in a way which is proportionate to its importance, the complexity of the issues, the anticipated costs and the resources of the parties;
- avoid unnecessary formality and be flexible in the proceedings;
- ensure, so far as practicable, that all the parties are able to participate fully in the proceedings;
- use any special expertise of the tribunal effectively; *and*
- avoid delay, so far as it is compatible with the proper consideration of the issues.

**Note:** this list is not exhaustive. Other matters can still be taken into account when considering what is fair and just in a particular case.[41]

The parties to an appeal also have a duty to assist the tribunal in dealing with cases fairly and justly.[42]

## Directions

Tribunals can give a wide range of directions in order to manage an appeal. These must be consistent with the overriding objective to deal with cases fairly and justly (see above).

A direction can be given at any time, either on the initiative of the tribunal or following an application by a party to the proceedings.[43] An application for a direction can be made either orally at a hearing or by writing to the tribunal, and must include the reason for seeking it. Unless it considers there is a good reason not to do so, the tribunal must send a written notice of the direction to every party and to anyone else affected by it.

If a party is unhappy with a direction, s/he can apply for another direction which amends, suspends or sets aside the earlier direction.

If a party fails to comply with a direction, the appeal could be 'struck out' (see p213) or the party barred from any hearing (see p213).

It may be possible to appeal to the Upper Tribunal about the content of a particular direction – eg, to exclude or include certain evidence.[44]

The tribunal can give directions to:

- extend or shorten the time for complying with any rule or direction;
- consolidate or hear together two or more appeals that raise common issues, or treat one as a lead case;
- permit or require a party to amend a document;
- permit or require a party or another person to provide documents, information, evidence or submissions. There are more specific powers to obtain evidence (see below);
- deal with an issue in the proceedings as a preliminary issue – eg, to decide precisely what decision is under appeal or whether the tribunal has jurisdiction;
- hold a hearing to consider any matter. This could include, for example, a preliminary hearing to decide what further evidence is needed and who should provide it, how much time the final hearing needs or whether the appeal should be 'struck out' because of a failure to comply with a direction;
- decide the form of any hearing (eg, the order in which parties speak or give evidence and who questions the appellant), and how to manage the hearing if one parent is concerned s/he will be intimidated by the other – eg, warning all parties in advance about behaviour, or organising the hearing so that the parties are not in the same room at the same time;[45]
- postpone or adjourn a hearing – eg, to enable further evidence to be produced;
- require a party to produce a 'bundle' (an indexed set of documents relating to the appeal) for a hearing. The tribunal must take into account the resources of the parties when issuing a direction;
- 'stay' (or, in Scotland, 'sist') proceedings. This allows the tribunal to put the case on hold pending the outcome of another appeal in which it is expected that legal issues will be decided that are relevant to the outcome;
- transfer proceedings to another court or tribunal – eg, if parentage is being disputed;
- suspend the effect of its decision pending an application for permission to appeal against it.

## Evidence

The tribunal can give directions about:[46]

- issues on which it requires evidence or submissions;

- the nature of the evidence or submissions it requires, and the manner in which, and time at which, they are to be provided;
- whether the parties are permitted or required to provide expert evidence;
- any limit on the number of witnesses whose evidence a party may put forward.

The tribunal can exclude evidence if:
- it was not provided within a time limit in a direction or practice direction;
- it does not comply with a direction or a practice direction in some other way;
- it would be unfair to admit it.

## Harmful evidence

If a person with care or non-resident parent (or, in Scotland, a child applicant) has told the CMS or tribunal that s/he would like her/his address, or the address of a child, to be kept confidential, the tribunal and CMS must ensure that it (or information that could be used to identify it) is not revealed to other parties.[47] The tribunal can also order that documents or information should not be be disclosed, or that any matter which could allow the public to identify the people involved should not be disclosed.[48]

The tribunal can also direct that a particular person not get a document or information if this would be likely to cause her/him or another person serious harm.[49]

A party can request the tribunal to direct that a particular document or piece of information that s/he must provide be withheld from another party. S/he must send a copy of it to the tribunal and explain why it should not be disclosed.[50]

The tribunal can, however, disclose the document or information to the party's representative if it is satisfied that s/he will not disclose the document to another person without the consent of the tribunal and that such disclosure is in the interests of justice.[51] If any evidence is withheld, the tribunal must still ensure that there is a fair hearing and that each party has sufficient information to conduct the case. Evidence should not be withheld from the tribunal itself.[52]

## Witnesses

The tribunal can summon (in Scotland, 'cite') witnesses and order other documents to be produced.[53] The tribunal may require someone to attend as a witness at a hearing, and answer any questions and provide documents related to the proceedings.

The tribunal must give at least 14 days' notice of the hearing (or a shorter period if the tribunal directs this). If the person summoned is not a party to the proceedings, her/his expenses are paid.

**Note:** the tribunal cannot summon a child if this would be detrimental to her/his welfare. The tribunal must consider how to assist any children under 18, or vulnerable or sensitive witnesses, to give evidence (including, for example, by telephone or video link).[54]

## Costs

Neither the First-tier Tribunal nor the Upper Tribunal can award costs (except in a judicial review).[55]

## Striking out an appeal

In certain circumstances, the tribunal can dismiss an appeal, or part of an appeal, without considering it. This is known as **'striking out'** an appeal.

The tribunal *must* strike out an appeal, or part of an appeal, if:

- the appellant has failed to comply with a direction which stated that the appeal, or that part of the appeal, *would* be struck out for failure to comply;[56] *or*
- it does not have jurisdiction to decide the appeal (or that part of it) and has not transferred it to another tribunal or court.[57]

The tribunal *may* strike out an appeal, or part of an appeal, if:

- the appellant has failed to comply with a direction which stated that the appeal, or that part of the appeal, *could* be struck out for failure to comply; *or*
- the appellant has failed to co-operate with the tribunal to such an extent that the tribunal cannot deal with the proceedings fairly and justly;[58] *or*
- it considers that the appeal has no reasonable prospects of success.[59]

The tribunal must consider whether it would be fair and just to strike out the appeal.

The power to strike out an appeal because the appellant has failed to comply with a direction should be used in exceptional cases as a last resort.[60] If your appeal, or part of your appeal, is struck out for this reason, you can apply for it to be reinstated.[61] You should do this within one month of its sending you notice of the striking out.[62] This one-month time limit can be extended if the tribunal considers it to be fair and just to do so.[63] If an application to reinstate an appeal is rejected, a further application can be made if you have further evidence or circumstances have changed.[64]

It is not possible for an appeal, or part of it, to be reinstated if it is struck out for any reason other than a failure to comply with a direction. However, before striking out an appeal, the tribunal must invite you to make representations.[65]

The tribunal must give a written notice of its decision to strike out an appeal, or part of an appeal, and should explain why it is doing so.[66] A party to the appeal can ask for a written statement of reasons for the decision and can seek permission to appeal to the Upper Tribunal against a striking-out decision by the First-tier Tribunal.[67]

**Note:** as well as an appeal being struck out because of a failure by the appellant, a respondent to the appeal (ie, another party or the CMS) can be **'barred'** from taking any further part in the proceedings for failure to comply with a direction.[68] When the tribunal 'bars' a respondent, it need not consider any response or other submission made by that respondent, and can determine any or all issues against that respondent. A barred respondent can apply to be reinstated.

## Sending and receiving documents

If there is a time limit to provide a document, this starts to run from when the tribunal sends the request. The time limit is met when the tribunal receives the response. The tribunal can extend (or shorten) any time limit, and has powers to deal with any failure to comply with rules and directions (see p209).[69]

Anything that must be done by a particular day must be done by 5pm on that day.[70]

If a time limit ends on a day other than a working day, the act is treated as being in time if it is done on the next working day.[71]

Documents can be delivered to the tribunal by hand, post or fax to the address (or number) specified. The tribunal may give directions permitting documents to be sent by other methods.[72]

If a party provides a fax, email address or other method for receiving documents electronically, s/he must accept delivery of documents by that method unless s/he has explicitly stated that this is not acceptable.[73]

If a document is sent electronically, the recipient can request a hard copy and the sender must supply it. The request for a hard copy should be made as soon as reasonably practicable after receiving the document electronically.[74]

Each party should assume that the address provided by another party remains valid unless s/he has received written notice to the contrary.[75]

## Representatives

A party can appoint a representative (whether legally qualified or not) to represent her/him in the proceedings. Once appointed, a representative can do anything permitted or required to be done by the party (except sign a witness statement).[76]

The tribunal should notify all the other parties when a representative has been appointed. When the tribunal receives the notice of the appointment of a representative, it must provide her/him with any documents required to be issued to the represented party and need not send the documents to that party.[77] Any other party to the appeal must also be notified of the appointment and must send any documents required to the representative.

Even if a party has not appointed a representative, s/he can still be accompanied at the hearing. Her/his companion may act as a representative or otherwise assist in presenting the case at the hearing, provided the tribunal agrees.[78]

## Withdrawing an appeal

You can withdraw all, or part, of your appeal by writing to the tribunal before the hearing, or in person at the hearing.[79]

The tribunal's consent is not required for an appeal to be withdrawn before the hearing, unless it has already given a direction that withdrawal can only be with its consent.[80] If you wait until a hearing to withdraw, you can only do so with the tribunal's consent.[81] In the Upper Tribunal, consent is always needed to withdraw an appeal (even if the request is made in writing), unless the case is still at the stage of awaiting permission to appeal.[82]

Once an appeal has been withdrawn, it can be reinstated if you request this in writing within one month of the notice of withdrawal being received by the tribunal, or within a month of the date of the hearing at which the appeal was withdrawn.

When an appeal is withdrawn, the tribunal must notify the other parties.

# 4. Preparing a case

The First-tier Tribunal may be the first chance for an independent evaluation of the decision under appeal. It may also be the last chance because its decision can only be appealed further to the Upper Tribunal on a point of law. Therefore, each party (ie, person with care, non-resident parent and, in Scotland, a child applicant) should make sure that the First-tier Tribunal knows the facts and arguments about the case. Each may wish to attend the hearing (see p217) to put forward her/his views and evidence, even if s/he is not the person who appealed. Each party should also consider getting advice and asking an adviser to assist in preparing the case and to represent (see p214) her/him at the hearing.

## Considering the facts and law

- Read the response from the Child Maintenance Service (CMS) and any other documents to see whether it now accepts some of the arguments it previously rejected or ignored. Just because the CMS accepts part of a person's case does not mean that the tribunal will, especially if the other party disputes it.
- Check the law using this *Handbook, Child Support: The Legislation* (see Appendix 4) and other sources. If the CMS quotes a decision of the Upper Tribunal (or of the previous commissioners), consider getting a copy. HM Courts and Tribunals Service (HMCTS) does not have copies of unreported decisions (those considered less legally significant), so if an unreported decision is to be relied on by the CMS, a copy should be supplied to the parties and to the tribunal. If a party wishes to quote an unreported decision, s/he should supply copies to everyone, preferably by sending a copy to the tribunal clerk in advance of the hearing. A party (including the CMS) can quote the CMS's internal procedural guidance, but it is important to remember that this guidance is not legally binding.

- Check the documents attached to the response. If anything relevant is missing, write to the tribunal asking it to direct the CMS to provide it.

The CMS must provide a response to an appeal within 42 days (see p207). If the CMS delays producing its response, you can write to the tribunal, asking that your appeal be heard. This may mean that the tribunal does not have all the evidence the CMS has. However, you (or the other party) can ask the tribunal to direct the CMS (see p210) to provide copies of all the papers, explaining why these are needed.

## Further evidence

- Consider whether you have (or can get) any further relevant written evidence. This can be sent to the First-tier Tribunal at any stage, but it is best to do this soon after the response is sent out, so papers can be copied to the other parties. If evidence or unreported caselaw decisions are produced at the hearing or sent in shortly before, this may cause a postponement or an adjournment.
- Check how best to explain the facts and law at the hearing. For example, telling the tribunal 'I look after the child from Friday night to Monday night' may be the best evidence of those facts.
- Decide whether to call any witnesses at the hearing (see p212).

Information relating to court proceedings concerning children heard in private or ancillary relief proceedings (ie, dealing with money and property) can be disclosed to the tribunal by any party without permission being sought, provided the court does not direct otherwise.[83] This means that one parent can supply information about the finances of the other parent, to which s/he admitted in the course of divorce proceedings.

## Obtaining information and evidence

If you would like another person to provide further information or documents, you can write to the First-tier Tribunal requesting that s/he be directed to provide these. It is best to send a prepared list to HMCTS, which is as precise as possible and explains why the documents are needed. For example, if a parent with care believes that a non-resident parent has undisclosed income, s/he could ask for bank statements for a certain period. A person who is not a party (eg, an employer) cannot be directed to provide evidence, but can be ordered to attend as a witness and produce documents (see p212). This should be done before the full hearing so all the parties can consider that evidence.

If a person fails to comply without a good explanation, the tribunal may decide that s/he has something to hide and so may not believe her/his evidence.[84] If s/he is the person appealing, the appeal can be 'struck out' (see p213).

# 5. **Hearings**

*Future changes*

The government plans to make all First-tier Tribunals digital by default and to pilot online dispute resolution. Appeals will automatically be made online and appeal submissions and responses are likely to be produced electronically only. There will be online hearings and hearings by telephone or video conferences. The government also says that, in future, there will no longer be an automatic right to an oral hearing. Some of the procedures outlined in this section are, therefore, likely to change.

**The First-tier Tribunal** must hold an oral hearing before making a final decision in an appeal unless:[85]
- it is 'striking out' the proceedings (see p213);
- it considers that it can decide the matter fairly and justly without one, and none of the parties object;[86]
- it is deciding whether to accept an application for permission to appeal, set aside a decision or correct a decision;
- it is making a consent order (see p221).

An oral hearing includes one conducted by video link, telephone or other instant two-way communication.[87]

**The Upper Tribunal** may decide any case without a hearing, but must consider a party's views when deciding whether to hold a hearing.[88]

If there is not a hearing, the tribunal makes its decision by considering what has been said on the appeal form, any other evidence provided by the parties, and the response from the Child Maintenance Service (CMS). This is known as a 'paper hearing'.

## Notice

The tribunal must give reasonable notice of the time and place of the hearing and of any changes to the arrangements.[89] This must be at least 14 days, although shorter notice can be given with the parties' consent or in urgent or exceptional circumstances (if shorter notice is given, it must still be reasonable).[90] Papers, including evidence sent to the tribunal , should be sent to all the parties in good time before the hearing.[91]

## Attending a hearing

Generally, all hearings must be held in public and a party has a right to attend. However, the tribunal may direct that all or part of a hearing is to be held in private and may determine who is allowed to attend.

Even in a public hearing, the tribunal may exclude from all or part of it:[92]
- anyone whose conduct is disrupting, or is likely to disrupt, the hearing;
- anyone whose presence is likely to prevent another person from giving evidence or making submissions freely;
- anyone who should be excluded in order to prevent her/him hearing information that is likely to cause harm;
- anyone whose attendance would defeat the purpose of the hearing;
- a witness in the proceedings.

If a party fails to attend a hearing and the tribunal is satisfied that s/he has been notified or that reasonable steps to notify her/him have been taken, it may proceed with the hearing if it is in the interests of justice.[93] If a party arrives late, after the tribunal has decided to proceed in her/his absence, it should still consider whether to allow the person to participate or whether to adjourn the hearing to allow her/him the opportunity to attend.[94]

If a party chooses not to attend, s/he cannot then claim that the tribunal has acted unfairly if it decides the case on evidence given at the hearing that s/he has not had a chance to contest.[95]

## Composition of the tribunal

When the First-tier Tribunal deals with a case involving a child support decision, it usually comprises a single member, called a 'tribunal judge'.[96] The judge is legally qualified.[97] If the appeal raises difficult issues about financial accounts, the First-tier Tribunal can include a financially qualified member (a 'tribunal member') – ie, a chartered or certified accountant.[98] If there is one or more other members, the judge is the 'presiding member', can regulate the proceedings and has the casting vote.[99]

The Upper Tribunal almost always comprises a single judge, who is legally qualified. If the case is particularly difficult or there is conflicting caselaw, there may be a panel of two or three judges.[100]

If an appeal is meant to be heard by a tribunal of two or more members but some of them are absent, the hearing can still go ahead, but only if all the parties and the CMS agree.[101]

## The venue

There should normally be separate waiting rooms available at the hearing venue for the non-resident parent, parent with care and the CMS presenting officer. If you are worried about this, check with HM Courts and Tribunals Service (HMCTS) whether there are separate waiting areas available before the hearing and, if not, explain any problems this may cause. If the other party or witness could become violent, tell the tribunal clerk as soon as possible and ask what steps will be taken.

The hearing is usually held in the appellant's area. Expenses, including travel expenses, subsistence and some compensation for loss of earnings, are paid to those who attend as a party, witness or unpaid representative. You can claim certain travel and subsistence expenses for attending the hearing. The tribunal clerk will give you a claim form. Keep any receipts.

If it is difficult for you to attend the hearing (eg, because of disability), inform the tribunal clerk. An alternative venue may be possible, but convenience to the other parties to the appeal is also considered. If you are unable to attend a hearing at a venue, in rare cases a hearing may be arranged in your home. You may also be able to arrange to participate via video link, telephone or other means of instantaneous two-way electronic communication. Contact the tribunal to see whether this is possible.

## Conduct of the hearing

The First-tier Tribunal attempts to be informal. Its member(s) usually sit on one side of a table. The tribunal clerk (who does not take any part in making the decision) shows the parties into the room and they usually sit on the other side of the table, with the presenting officer (an official representing the CMS) between them. The judge introduces everyone and explains the tribunal's role.

Hearings can take an hour or longer. Each party can address the tribunal, give evidence, call witnesses and put questions to any other party, the presenting officer and witnesses. The order in which the parties present their cases is up to the judge. The CMS is there to explain the decision, not to argue for the CMS. The presenting officer has a role, for example, to inform the tribunal about CMS procedures. It is rare for the presenting officer to call any witnesses. The tribunal may require any witness, including a party, to take an oath or affirmation.

Ask the judge for clarification if you are unclear about what is happening or about anything that has been said.

If you need an interpreter, the tribunal will arrange this if you request it in good time.

The tribunal can adjourn a hearing at any point – eg, if more documents are needed. It should adjourn a hearing if, for example, one party is unable to attend and her/his evidence could play an important part in its reaching a decision.[102] If evidence has been taken, a new panel hearing the case must be made up of either exactly the same, or entirely different, members.

## 6. Decisions of the First-tier Tribunal

After the hearing, the First-tier Tribunal considers the case and makes its decision. If the appeal is allowed, the decision of the tribunal replaces that of the Child Maintenance Service (CMS). If the appeal is dismissed, the decision of the CMS remains in force. In making its decision, the tribunal looks afresh at the situation on the date of the CMS decision that is being appealed.[103]

It cannot take into account any change of circumstances that has occurred after the date of the decision, although it can take account of evidence that is relevant to the period up to the date of the decision, but which only became available later.[104] If it decides to allow the appeal because the decision was wrong on the facts at the time it was made, it cannot then direct how the CMS should deal with a later change of circumstances.

The whole appeal process can take some time, so if circumstances change while waiting for an appeal to be decided, a person with care or non-resident parent (or child applicant in Scotland) may wish to make a new child support application or request a supersession as well as pursuing the appeal.

The tribunal can consider any evidence and arguments, including those rejected or overlooked by the CMS and those which have not been used before.[105] The tribunal does not have to consider any issue not raised in the appeal.[106] However, it is 'inquisitorial', which means that it can consider legal arguments and factual questions on its own initiative, if appropriate, but should give its reasons for doing so.[107] The tribunal must decide what it believes are the relevant facts by evaluating all the relevant available evidence.[108] The tribunal can draw conclusions from the failure of a party to provide evidence.[109]

If the tribunal reaches a different conclusion from that of the CMS, it allows the appeal. **Note:** it may make a decision that is less advantageous to the person appealing.[110]

The tribunal can make a provisional decision, which will become final in specified circumstances. This may be done, for example, if it wants to give one last chance to a party to provide certain information within a specified time. The time limit for any further appeal runs from the date of the final decision.[111]

## Decision notices

Usually, the parties are invited to wait outside the hearing room and then asked back in to be told the decision. The First-tier Tribunal must also give a decision notice to the parties (unless it decides to withhold harmful information) as soon as reasonably practicable, stating:[112]

- its decision;
- any right to apply for reasons for the decision;
- any right of appeal against the decision, together with information about the time and manner in which such an appeal must be made.

The tribunal can decide to issue a full statement of the reasons for its decision, either verbally at the hearing or in writing to each party.[113] If it does not do this, you can apply for a written statement of reasons, provided this is received by the tribunal within a month of the decision notice being given or sent to the parties.[114]

Unless the decision was a consent order (see below), the tribunal must send this within one month of receiving the application, or as soon as reasonably practicable after that.[115]

## Record of proceedings

The presiding member of the First-tier Tribunal must keep a record of proceedings. This should include any evidence taken, submissions made and any procedural issues – eg, if a party asked for an adjournment.[116]

The record must be kept by HM Courts and Tribunals Service for at least six months from whichever is the later of:[117]

- the date of the decision;
- the date the reasons for the decision were given;
- the date the decision was corrected;
- the date a refusal to set aside was made; *or*
- the date of the determination of an application for permission to appeal (unless the documents are sent to the Upper Tribunal before the six months expire).

You can request a copy of the record of proceedings within this six-month period and it must be provided.

## Consent orders

If all the parties agree, they can request that the tribunal make an order disposing of (ie, cancelling) the proceedings with their consent. It only does so if it considers that it is appropriate.[118] The tribunal may simply make a decision on the appeal in the usual way. Dealing with an appeal by a consent order is only appropriate if it is clear that all parties have fully understood its implications.[119]

If a consent order is made, there does not have to be a hearing and no reasons for the order need to be given. Before agreeing to request a consent order, get independent advice.

---

## 7. Changing a First-tier Tribunal decision

A First-tier Tribunal can change its decision by:[120]

- correcting an accidental error (see p222);
- 'setting aside' the decision (see p222);
- reviewing the decision (see p222);
- allowing an appeal to the Upper Tribunal (see p223).

**Note:** an application for any of the above can be treated by the tribunal as an application for any of the others.

## Correcting an error

The First-tier Tribunal can, at any time, correct a clerical mistake or accidental slip or omission in a decision, direction or any document it produces (but not the decision itself) by sending a notice of the amended decision or direction to all parties.[121]

## Setting aside the decision

A decision, or part of a decision, can be 'set aside' (ie, cancelled) by the First-tier Tribunal if it considers it to be in the interests of justice to do so. It can do this if:[122]

- a document relating to the proceedings was not sent to or received by the tribunal, a party or representative at an appropriate time; *or*
- a party or representative was not present at the hearing; *or*
- there has been some other procedural irregularity.

An application for a set-aside must be received within one month of being sent the decision by the tribunal.

If the decision is set aside, the appeal is heard again, usually by a differently constituted tribunal, and a new decision is made. You should be given the opportunity to have an oral hearing, even if the appeal was previously decided on the papers.[123]

If an application for permission to appeal has been made to the First-tier Tribunal and all the parties argue that the decision is an error of law, it will be set aside and referred to a differently constituted First-tier Tribunal to determine.[124]

## Reviewing a decision

A First-tier Tribunal can 'review' its decision.[125] It must consider whether to do so before considering whether to grant permission to appeal to the Upper Tribunal and so, in practice, every application for permission to appeal is effectively an application for a review.

The tribunal may only review a decision if an application for permission to appeal has been made and it considers that there is an error of law.

If, on a review, the tribunal considers that it is appropriate to amend the reasons for its decision, the parties should be given an opportunity to make suitable representations. The notice to the parties should identify the error of law and the course of action the tribunal proposes to take.[126]

**Note:** a decision that has been reviewed can still be appealed to the Upper Tribunal. The First-tier Tribunal must notify the parties of the outcome of any review and of any right of appeal against it.

# 8. **Appealing to the Upper Tribunal**

Any party, including the Child Maintenance Service (CMS), can appeal to the Upper Tribunal against a final decision of the First-tier Tribunal. An appeal will only succeed if there is an error of law in the First-tier Tribunal's decision. See p197 and CPAG's *Welfare Benefits and Tax Credits Handbook* for information about when a decision contains an error of law. The tribunal's statement of reasons should include enough detail to allow all the parties to understand how the main issues in the case were decided.[127]

The Upper Tribunal can give the decision it thinks the First-tier Tribunal should have given. Alternatively (particularly if it thinks the First-tier Tribunal did not find all the relevant facts or consider the evidence properly), it may refer the case back to the First-tier Tribunal for a new decision to be made. If a case is referred back, the new First-tier Tribunal must apply the law in the way that the Upper Tribunal has instructed.

Before an appeal can be dealt with by the Upper Tribunal, you must apply for permission to appeal from the First-tier Tribunal. If this is refused, you can apply for permission directly to the Upper Tribunal. Permission should only be granted if it is arguable that there is an error of law in the First-tier Tribunal decision.

**Note:** a decision of the First-tier Tribunal which is a procedural decision or ruling (against which there is normally no right of appeal) can be challenged by judicial review. The case is normally heard by the Upper Tribunal. See CPAG's *Welfare Benefits and Tax Credits Handbook* for details.

## Applying for permission to appeal from the First-tier Tribunal

You must apply for permission to appeal to the Upper Tribunal from the First-tier Tribunal. An application must be in writing and be received by the tribunal within one month of being sent the following, whichever is the latest:[128]

- a written statement of reasons for the decision;
- following a review, a notice that the reasons for the decision were amended or the decision corrected;
- a notice that an application for the decision to be set aside made within the time limit was refused.

The application must state:[129]

- the decision of the First-tier Tribunal to which it relates;
- the alleged errors of law in the decision;
- the result sought.

If you apply late, you must explain why and include a request for an extension of time.[130] The First-tier Tribunal can only consider a late application if it has agreed to use its general power to extend the time for applying.

Usually, it is necessary to have obtained the full statement of reasons for a decision before seeking permission to appeal. If you have not requested a statement of reasons, the First-tier Tribunal must treat the application as an application for a statement of reasons rather than as an application for permission to appeal.[131] If reasons are issued, you must then make a new application for permission to appeal. If a request for a statement of reasons has been refused because it was made late, the First-tier Tribunal can only grant permission to appeal if it is in the interests of justice to do so.[132]

When considering an application, the First-tier Tribunal must consider whether to review its decision.[133] If it has not changed the decision (or part of it) on review, it must consider whether to grant permission to appeal in respect of its decision, or the unchanged part of it.

The First-tier Tribunal must send a record of its decision on the application for permission to appeal to the parties.[134] If permission is refused, in full or in part, the notice must include the reasons for this. It must also include notice of the right to apply directly to the Upper Tribunal for permission to appeal, and details of how to do so.[135]

The First-tier Tribunal may grant permission to appeal against part of a decision. If this is the case, you may wish to file that appeal with the Upper Tribunal, and also to seek permission to appeal directly from the Upper Tribunal in respect of the parts of the decision for which permission has not been granted by the First-tier Tribunal.

## Applying to the Upper Tribunal for permission to appeal

If permission to appeal has been refused (in whole or in part), or an application has not been admitted, by the First-tier Tribunal, you can apply to the Upper Tribunal for permission.[136]

The application to the Upper Tribunal must be made in writing and within one month of being sent the refusal of permission.[137] If made late, the application must include an explanation for why it is late, and it will not be considered unless the time limit is extended by the Upper Tribunal.[138] If the earlier application for a written statement of reasons to the First-tier Tribunal or the application for permission to appeal to the First-tier Tribunal was made late, an explanation must also be given and can only be considered if the Upper Tribunal considers it in the interests of justice to do so.[139]

The application must include details of:[140]
- the name and address of the appellant and any representative;
- an address for sending or delivering documents;
- details (including a full reference) of the decision challenged;
- the grounds for the appeal;
- whether you want a hearing of the application.

The application must include copies of:[141]
- the written record of the decision challenged;
- the written statement of reasons for the decision (if it exists);
- the First-tier Tribunal's notice refusing permission to appeal or refusing to admit the application.

Using Form UT1, *Application for Permission to Appeal to an Upper Tribunal Judge and Notice of Appeal,* should ensure that your application is correctly made.[142]

The Upper Tribunal must send you (but not the other parties) its reasons for refusing an application.[143] There is no right of appeal against a decision of the Upper Tribunal to refuse permission to appeal.[144]

The Upper Tribunal must send notice of permission to appeal to all the parties.[145] If this happens, generally the application for permission is treated as the notice of appeal. The Upper Tribunal sends a copy of this to all the parties and explains that it is treating the application for permission as the actual appeal.[146] If the parties agree, the Upper Tribunal can then determine the appeal without a need for any further response from them.[147]

## Notice of appeal

If the First-tier Tribunal grants you permission to appeal, you should send a notice of appeal to the Upper Tribunal. If you have received permission to appeal directly from the Upper Tribunal, this is usually treated as the notice of appeal, unless the Upper Tribunal directs otherwise.[148]

The notice of appeal must be received by the Upper Tribunal within one month of your being sent the notice of permission to appeal by the First-tier Tribunal.[149]

The same information and documents must be included with the notice of appeal as for an application for permission to appeal.[150]

Late notices of appeal must include a request for an extension of time and the reasons why the notice was not provided in time, and cannot be admitted unless the time limit is extended by the Upper Tribunal.[151]

The Upper Tribunal must send a copy of the notice of appeal and accompanying documents to each party and to the CMS.[152]

## Responses and replies

The other party can respond to the appeal, but does not have to unless the Upper Tribunal so directs.[153]

A response must be in writing and received by the Upper Tribunal within one month of being sent the notice of appeal (or the notice of a grant of permission to appeal, if this is treated as the notice of appeal). A late response must request an extension of the time limit and explain why it is late.[154]

The response must state:[155]
- the name and address of the respondent and any representative;
- an address for sending or delivering documents;
- whether the respondent opposes the appeal;
- the grounds on which the respondent intends to rely in the appeal;
- whether the respondent wants a hearing.

The Upper Tribunal must provide a copy of the response to the appellant and the other parties.[156]

The appellant may then reply to the response, but does not have to unless the Upper Tribunal so directs. The reply must be received within one month of being sent the response and is then copied to the other parties by the Upper Tribunal.[157]

## Decisions of the Upper Tribunal

The Upper Tribunal's decision may replace the decision of the First-tier Tribunal (or it can direct that the case be reconsidered by a new First-tier Tribunal).

The Upper Tribunal may announce its final decision verbally at a hearing (although this is far less common than at the First-tier Tribunal) and must then (unless it decides to withold harmful information) provide the parties with a notice stating its decision and details of any further rights of review and appeal. The Upper Tribunal must always give reasons for its decision, unless it was made with the consent of the parties or the parties have consented to a decision being given without reasons.[158]

If the proceedings are recorded, this should be kept for six months. A party can apply for a transcript, but will have to pay for it unless s/he has challenged or intends to challenge the decision, the transcript is necessary in order to bring that challenge, and the Upper Tribunal is satisfied that s/he cannot afford to pay.

## Challenging an Upper Tribunal decision

**Note:** you should get legal advice if you are considering whether to challenge an Upper Tribunal decision.

Upper Tribunal decisions can be changed by:
- correcting an accidental error (see p222);[159]
- 'setting aside' the decision (see p222);[160]
- appealing to the Court of Appeal (in Scotland, the Court of Session). Permission is needed for this, and the appeal must be on the grounds that the Upper Tribunal made an error of law. An application for permission must first be made to the Upper Tribunal.[161] This is similar to the procedure for applying for permission from the First-tier Tribunal, except that the time limit is three months. The Upper Tribunal must consider a review (see p227) before deciding whether to grant permission. If the Upper Tribunal refuses permission, the request can be made directly to the Court of Appeal/Court of Session. The

Upper Tribunal's refusal decision should include a statement of reasons, details of the relevant court and the time limit for applying.[162] Permission can only be granted if the Upper Tribunal or court considers the appeal would raise an important point of principle or practice, or there is some other compelling reason to grant it;[163]

- reviewing the decision (see p222). The procedure is as for the First-tier Tribunal, except that the Upper Tribunal can only review the decision if it overlooked a legislative decision or binding legal authority which could have affected it or, since giving its decision, a court has made a decision that could have affected it.[164]

The Upper Tribunal may treat an application for a decision to be corrected, set aside or reviewed, or an application for permission to appeal against a decision, as an application for any one of these things.[165]

A decision of the Upper Tribunal that cannot be appealed against (eg, a refusal to grant leave to appeal from the First-tier Tribunal to the Upper Tribunal) can be challenged by applying for judicial review to the High Court (in England and Wales) or the Court of Session (in Scotland). This can only be done if the case would raise some important point of principle or practice, or if there is some other compelling reason.[166]

For further details about challenging Upper Tribunal decisions, see CPAG's *Welfare Benefits and Tax Credits Handbook.*

# 9. **Test case rules**

Special rules apply if a court or Upper Tribunal decision on a 'test case' is pending, or an Upper Tribunal or court decision on a test case has been made. A 'test case' is one in which a person is challenging the Child Maintenance Service's (CMS's) interpretation of the law in a way that affects other cases more generally, even if it is the CMS's own appeal and even if the person does not consider the case to be a test case.

These rules apply to child support calculation decisions, revision and supersession decisions, and appeals to the First-tier or Upper Tribunal.

## If there is a test case pending

If a test case is decided against the CMS, the CMS must usually follow the law as decided in that case in all other cases. However, if an appeal is still pending before the Upper Tribunal or a court, the CMS can:[167]

- postpone making a decision on the application, revision or supersession in any other case which might be affected by the decision in that appeal until the test case appeal has been decided; *or*

- make a decision as if the test case had already been decided in a way that would result in the lowest possible amount of child support being payable in a case that might be affected by the decision. This only applies if there is no calculation in force in the case that might be affected by the test case decision.[168]

An appeal is 'pending' before a court if:[169]
- an appeal (including an application for judicial review) about child support has been made to the High Court, Court of Appeal, Court of Session or Supreme Court but has not been determined;
- an application for permission to make such an appeal (or judicial review) has been made, but has not been determined;
- the CMS has certified in writing that it is considering making such an appeal or application and the time for appealing or applying has not expired, and the CMS considers that the appeal might result in the non-resident parent having no, or less, liability for child support.[170]

An appeal also counts as pending if a court (but not the Upper Tribunal) has referred a question to the Court of Justice of the European Union for a preliminary ruling.

If the CMS does not make an application or appeal in time, it can no longer postpone making a decision.

A decision to suspend or make a decision on the assumption that the CMS will win the test case is a discretionary one. The CMS must, therefore, take into account the welfare of any child likely to be affected by the decision when making it.

## How a pending test case affects similar cases

If a test case pending before a court may affect a similar case awaiting a decision from the First-tier Tribunal or Upper Tribunal, or there is a possibility that the CMS may appeal, the CMS may:[171]
- direct the tribunal to refer the similar case to the CMS. The CMS makes no decision until the test case is decided. It then revises the CMS decision under appeal or supersedes the tribunal decision under appeal; *or*
- direct the tribunal to deal with the case itself. The tribunal must then either:
  - postpone its decision until the test case is decided; *or*
  - decide the appeal as if the test case appeal has already been decided against the person who appealed in the similar case. It should only do this if it considers that it is in the appellant's interests. If the test case is later decided in that person's favour, the CMS supersedes the tribunal decision in the similar case.

## Test case decisions

If a decision of the Upper Tribunal or court interprets child support law, the CMS must usually apply that interpretation in the period before the decision was given. This usually requires the CMS to supersede all decisions which are affected.

However, if the Upper Tribunal/court rejects the CMS's interpretation of the law, that test case decision only has effect from the date it is made.[172] For the period before that date, the CMS (and either tribunal) assumes that it was right in its interpretation of the law when making the original decision which led to the appeal.[173]

This rule does not apply to:

- an application for child support (or a reduced benefit decision) made before 1 June 1999;[174]
- a revision or supersession of any decision made before 1 June 1999;[175]
- a decision in a case where the CMS had suspended a decision under the test case pending rules (see p227);[176]
- a revision or supersession decision in a case where the CMS had required the First-tier or Upper Tribunal to refer the case to the CMS, or deal with it on the assumption that the test case had already been decided against the appellant.[177]

# Notes

**1. Considering an appeal**
1   s20(4)(c) CSA 1991; reg 14A(4) CSMC Regs
2   Reg 27A(1) CSMC Regs
3   s20 CSA 1991
4   Reg 12(1) CS(MPA) Regs
5   **EW** Arts 3 and 4 CSA(JC)O
   **S** Arts 2, 3 and 4 CSA(JC)(S)O
6   r5(3)(k) TP(FT) Rules

**2. Appealing to the First-tier Tribunal**
7   s20(3) CSA 1991; regs 24-26 CSMC Regs
8   www.gov.uk/government/organisations/hm-courts-and-tribunals-service
9   r22(3) TP(FT) Rules
10  r22(4) TP(FT) Rules
11  *MM v SSWP (PIP)* [2016] UKUT 36 (AAC)
12  CMS leaflet CMSB011GB, *What To Do If You're Unhappy With the Child Maintenance Service*, April 2017

13  r22(2)(d) and Sch 1 TP(FT) Rules
14  R(IB) 4/02
15  r12 TP(FT) Rules
16  Reg 7(2) CSMC Regs
17  r22(8) TP(FT) Rules
18  r22(8) TP(FT) Rules
19  *KK v Sheffield City Council (CTB)* [2015] UKUT 367 (AAC); *PM v SSD (AFCS)* [2015] UKUT 647 (AAC)
20  rr2(1), (2) and (3)(a) and 5(3)(a) TP(FT) Rules; *Information Commissioner v PS* [2011] UKUT 94 (AAC); *CD v First-tier Tribunal (CICA)* [2010] UKUT 181 (AAC), reported as [2011] AACR 1
21  r22(6) TP(FT) Rules
22  *LS v London Borough of Lambeth (HB)* [2010] UKUT 461 (AAC)
23  r22(7) TP(FT) Rules
24  CMS leaflet CMSB011GB, *What To Do If You're Unhappy With the Child Maintenance Service,* April 2017

25 CMS leaflet CMSB011GB, *What To Do If You're Unhappy With the Child Maintenance Service*, April 2017
26 r24(1)(b)(ii) TP(FT) Rules
27 r24(2)(a)-(d) TP(FT) Rules
28 r24(2)(e) TP(FT) Rules
29 r24(3) TP(FT) Rules
30 r24(4) TP(FT) Rules
31 *TR v SSWP and PW(CSM)* [2013] UKUT 80 (AAC)
32 r24(6) and (7) TP(FT) Rules
33 r19(2) and (3) TP(FT) Rules

**3. Tribunal procedures**
34 R(IS) 11/99; *KB v SSWP (DLA)* [2011] UKUT 388 (AAC)
35 r7 TP(FT) Rules; r7 TP(UT) Rules
36 s25 TCEA 2007; r7(3) TP(FT) Rules; r7(3) and (4) TP(UT) Rules
37 r4 TP(FT) Rules; Courts and Tribunals Judiciary Practice Statement, *Delegation of Functions to Tribunal Caseworkers First-tier Tribunal (Social Entitlement Chamber)*, 5 June 2017; Courts and Tribunals Judiciary Practice Statement, *Delegation of Functions to Registrars First-tier Tribunal (Social Entitlement Chamber)*, 1 December 2016
38 r2 TP(FT) Rules; r2 TP(UT) Rules
39 r2(3) TP(FT) Rules; r2(3) TP(UT) Rules
40 r2(2) TP(FT) Rules; r2(2) TP(UT) Rules
41 *MS v SSWP* [2009] UKUT 211 (AAC)
42 r2(4) TP(FT) Rules; r2(4) TP(UT) Rules
43 r6(1) TP(FT) Rules; r6(1) TP(UT) Rules
44 *LM v London Borough of Lewisham* [2009] UKUT 204 (AAC)
45 *WA v SSWP and P (CSM)* [2016] UKUT 86 (AAC)
46 r15 TP(FT) Rules; r15 TP(UT) Rules
47 r19(3) TP(FT) Rules; r19(2) and (4) TP(UT) Rules
48 r14(1) TP(FT) Rules; r14(1) TP(UT) Rules
49 r14(2) TP(FT) Rules; r14(2) TP(UT) Rules
50 r14(3) TP(FT) Rules; r14(3) TP(UT) Rules
51 r14(5) and (6) TP(FT) Rules; r14(5) and (6) TP(UT) Rules
52 R(CS) 3/06
53 r17 TP(FT) Rules; r17 TP(UT) Rules
54 Tribunals Judiciary Practice Direction, *First-tier and Upper Tribunal, Child, Vulnerable Adult and Sensitive Witnesses*, 30 October 2008; *SW v SSWP (DLA)* [2015] UKUT 319 (AAC); *LO'L v SSWP (ESA)* [2016] UKUT 10 (AAC), reported as [2016] AACR 31
55 r10 TP(FT) Rules; r10 TP(UT) Rules
56 r8(1) TP(FT) Rules; r8(1) TP(UT) Rules
57 r8(2) TP(FT) Rules; r8(2) TP(UT) Rules

58 r8(3)(b) TP(FT) Rules; r8(3)(b) TP(UT) Rules
59 r8(3)(c) TP(FT) Rules; r8(3)(c) TP(UT) Rules
60 *DTM v Kettering Borough Council (CTB)* [2013] UKUT 625 (AAC)
61 r8(5) TP(FT) Rules; r8(5) TP(UT) Rules
62 r8(6) TP(FT) Rules; r8(6) TP(UT) Rules
63 rr2(1) and (3)(a) and 5(3)(a) TP(FT) Rules; rr2(1), 3(a) and 5(3)(a) TP(UT) Rules
64 *R(BD) v First-tier Tribunal (CIC)* [2013] UKUT 332 (AAC)
65 r8(4) TP(FT) Rules; r8(4) TP(UT) Rules
66 *RN v SSWP (RP)* [2013] UKUT 461 (AAC)
67 *Synergy Child Services Ltd v Ofsted* [2009] UKUT 125 (AAC); *LS v London Borough of Lambeth (HB)* [2010] UKUT 461 (AAC), reported as [2011] AACR 27
68 r8(7) and (8) TP(FT) Rules; r8(7) and (8) TP(UT) Rules
69 rr5(3)(a) and 7 TP(FT) Rules; rr5(3)(a) and 7 TP(UT) Rules
70 r12(1) TP(FT) Rules; r12(1) TP(UT) Rules
71 r12(2) and (3) TP(FT) Rules; r12(2) and (3) TP(UT) Rules
72 r13(1) TP(FT) Rules; r13(1) TP(UT) Rules
73 r13(2) and (3) TP(FT) Rules; r13(2) and (3) TP(UT) Rules
74 r13(4) TP(FT) Rules; r13(4) TP(UT) Rules
75 r13(5) TP(FT) Rules; r13(5) TP(UT) Rules
76 r11(5) TP(FT) Rules; r11(3) TP(UT) Rules
77 r11(6) TP(FT) Rules; r11(4) TP(UT) Rules
78 r11(7) and (8) TP(FT) Rules; r11(5) and (6) TP(UT) Rules
79 r17 TP(FT) Rules; r17 TP(UT) Rules
80 *WM v SSWP (DLA)* [2015] UKUT 642 (AAC)
81 r17(1)(b), (2) and (3)(b) TP(FT) Rules
82 r17(1) and (2) TP(UT) Rules

**4. Preparing a case**
83 r5 Family Proceedings Courts (Child Support Act 1991) Rules 1993, No.627; r10.21A Family Proceedings Rules 1991, No.1247
84 CCS/3757/2004

**5. Hearings**
85 r27 TP(FT) Rules
86 *MM v SSWP (ESA)* [2011] UKUT 334 (AAC); *JP v SSWP (IB)* [2011] UKUT 459 (AAC)
87 r1(3) TP(FT) Rules; r1(3) TP(UT) Rules
88 r34 TP(UT) Rules
89 r29(1) TP(FT) Rules; r36(1) TP(UT) Rules

90 r29(2) TP(FT) Rules; r36(2)(b) TP(UT) Rules. The only other exception to this is when the Upper Tribunal is conducting a hearing of an application for permission to bring judicial review, in which at least two working days' notice must be given. Such proceedings are outside the scope of this *Handbook*.
91 CCS/1925/2002
92 r30 TP(FT) Rules; r37 TP(UT) Rules
93 r31 TP(FT) Rules; r38 TP(UT) Rules
94 *AK v HMRC (TC)* [2016] UKUT 98 (AAC)
95 CCS/1689/2007; CCS/2901/2001; CCS/2676/2001
96 Art 2 FT&UT(CT)O; Tribunals Judiciary Practice Statement, *Composition of Tribunals in Social Security and Child Support Cases in the Social Entitlement Chamber on or after 1 August 2013*, July 2013, para 6
97 Sch 2 para 1(2) TCEA 2007
98 Tribunals Judiciary Practice Statement, *Composition of Tribunals in Social Security and Child Support Cases in the Social Entitlement Chamber on or after 1 August 2013*, July 2013, para 7
99 Tribunals Judiciary Practice Statement, *Composition of Tribunals in Social Security and Child Support Cases in the Social Entitlement Chamber on or after 1 August 2013*, July 2013, para 12; Art 8 FT&UT(CT)O
100 Tribunals Judiciary Practice Statement, *Composition of Tribunals in Relation to Matters that Fall to be Decided by the Administrative Appeals Chamber of the Upper Tribunal on or after 26 March 2014*, March 2014, para 3a; Arts 3 and 4 FT&UT(CT)O
101 Sch 4 para 15(6) TCEA 2007; *PF v SSWP (ESA)* [2015] UKUT 553 (AAC)
102 *DC v SSWP (ESA)* [2015] UKUT 150 (AAC)

### 6. Decisions of the First-tier Tribunal
103 s20(7) CSA 1991
104 s20(7)(b) CSA 1991; R(CS) 1/03; *MT v SSWP and MB (CSM)* [2015] UKUT 492 (AAC)
105 CCS/16351/1996; *MB v CMEC* [2009] UKUT 29 (AAC), para 16
106 s20(7)(a) CSA 1991
107 R(IB) 2/04; *A P-H v SSWP (DLA)* [2010] UKUT 183 (AAC); *JW v SSWP & MC & JC (CSM)* [2013] UKUT 407 (AAC), reported as [2014] AACR 8; *JR v SSWP and TR (CSM)* [2015] UKUT 582 (AAC); *ET v SSWP (PIP)* [2017] UKUT 478 (AAC)

108 CCS/2861/2001
109 CCS/3757/2004
110 R(IB) 2/04
111 *AB v CMEC (CSM)* [2010] UKUT 385 (AAC)
112 r33 TP(FT) Rules
113 r34(2)(b) TP(FT) Rules
114 r34(3) and (4) TP(FT) Rules
115 r34(5) TP(FT) Rules
116 Tribunals Judiciary Practice Statement, *Record of Proceedings in Social Security and Child Support Cases in the Social Entitlement Chamber on or after 3 November 2008*, November 2008
117 *DT v SSWP* [2015] UKUT 509 (AAC)
118 r32 TP(FT) Rules; r39 TP(UT) Rules; *AW v SSWP and AL (CSM)* [2017] UKUT 235 (AAC)
119 *MM v SSWP and IJ (CSM)* [2015] UKUT 590 (AAC)

### 7. Changing a First-tier Tribunal decision
120 Not including judicial review of non-appealable decisions.
121 r42 TP(FT) Rules; *AS v SSWP (ESA)* [2011] UKUT 159 (AAC); *CG v SSWP (DLA)* [2011] UKUT 453 (AAC)
122 r37 TP(FT) Rules
123 CIB/4193/2003
124 s23A CSA 1991
125 Introduced by s9 TCEA 2007; see also r40 TP(FT) Rules
126 *JS v SSWP (DLA)* [2013] UKUT 100 (AAC), reported as [2013] AACR 30

### 8. Appealing to the Upper Tribunal
127 *MW v SSWP (II)* [2011] UKUT 465 (AAC)
128 r38(2) and (3) TP(FT) Rules
129 r38(6) TP(FT) Rules
130 r38(5) TP(FT) Rules
131 r38(7) TP(FT) Rules
132 r38(7)(c) TP(FT) Rules
133 r39(1) TP(FT) Rules
134 r39(3) TP(FT) Rules
135 r39(4) TP(FT) Rules
136 r21(2) TP(UT) Rules
137 r21(3)(b) TP(UT) Rules
138 r21(6) TP(UT) Rules
139 r21(7) TP(UT) Rules
140 r21(4) TP(UT) Rules
141 r21(5) TP(UT) Rules
142 Form UT1 is available from http://hmctsformfinder.justice.gov.uk/HMCTS/FormFinder.do
143 r22(1) TP(UT) Rules

144 *R (Cart) v Upper Tribunal and R (MR*
*(Pakistan)) v Upper Tribunal and SSHD*
[2011] UKSC 28, reported as [2011]
AACR 38
145 r22(2)(a) TP(UT) Rules
146 r22(2)(b) TP(UT) Rules
147 r22(2)(c) TP(UT) Rules
148 r23(1) TP(UT) Rules
149 r23(2) TP(UT) Rules
150 r23(3) and (4) TP(UT) Rules
151 r23(5) TP(UT) Rules
152 r23(6) TP(UT) Rules
153 r24(1) TP(UT) Rules
154 r24(2) and (4) TP(UT) Rules
155 r24(3) TP(UT) Rules
156 r24(5) TP(UT) Rules
157 r25 TP(UT) Rules
158 r40 TP(UT) Rules
159 r42 TP(UT) Rules
160 r43 TP(UT) Rules
161 s13 TCEA 2007; rr44 and 45 TP(UT)
Rules
162 r45(4) TP(UT) Rules
163 s13(6) and (6A) TCEA 2007; AUTCAO;
r41.57(2) Rules of the Court of Session
164 r46 TP(UT) Rules
165 r48 TP(UT) Rules
166 *Eba v Advocate General for Scotland*
[2011] UKSC 29; *R (Cart) v Upper*
*Tribunal and R (MR (Pakistan)) v Upper*
*Tribunal and SSHD* [2011] UKSC 28,
reported as [2011] AACR 38

## 9. Test case rules
167 s28ZA(1) and (2) CSA 1991
168 Reg 28(1) CSMC Regs
169 s28ZA(4) and (5) CSA 1991
170 s28ZA(4)(c) CSA 1991; reg 28(2) CSMC
Regs
171 s28ZB CSA 1991
172 s28ZC(1) and (3) CSA 1991; regs 30-32
CSMC Regs
173 s28ZC(1) and (3) CSA 1991
174 s28ZC(1)(b)(i) CSA 1991
175 s28ZC(1)(b)(ii) and (iii) CSA 1991
176 s28ZC(2)(a) CSA 1991
177 s28ZC(2)(b) CSA 1991

# Chapter 11

# Complaints

This chapter covers:
1. Grounds for a complaint (below)
2. Compensation payments (p234)
3. Complaining about the Child Maintenance Service (p235)
4. Complaining about Child Maintenance Options (p236)
5. Complaining about Jobcentre Plus (p237)
6. Complaining to the Independent Case Examiner (p238)
7. Using your MP (p239)
8. Complaining to the Ombudsman (p239)

## 1. Grounds for a complaint

A decision about child support can usually be challenged by applying for a revision and then an appeal (see Chapters 9 and 10).

A complaint is a separate process and does not necessarily lead to a decision being changed. A complaint can be made about any aspect of the administration of the statutory child support scheme – eg, a delay in dealing with a case, poor administration, the behaviour of staff, incorrect information or advice provided by officials or the way in which a particular policy or practice has affected you.

In some cases, it may be appropriate to challenge a decision as well as making a complaint – eg, if you think that child support has been wrongly calculated and challenge the decision, but you also wish to complain about a delay in making the calculation or some other aspect of the way your case has been handled or you have been treated.

A complaint may be appropriate if there is no right to appeal against the decision in question (see p190). In this situation, judicial review may also be possible (instead of, or as well as, making a complaint). Get legal advice if you are considering a judicial review (see also p190).

It may be appropriate to seek a compensation payment for any loss related to a complaint (see p234).

The Parliamentary and Health Service Ombudsman (see p239) has a website (www.ombudsman.org.uk/making-complaint/before-you-come-to-us/complain-change) to encourage and assist people to complain about government departments and agencies.[1]

## Who the complaint is about

It is important to be clear which organisation has caused the problem. In most cases, this will be the Child Maintenance Service. However, problems concerning the deduction of payments from benefits may be caused by Jobcentre Plus, and complaints about any of its functions should be made to the Department for Work and Pensions. If there is a delay or poor administration of an appeal by HM Courts and Tribunals Service (HMCTS), the complaint should be made to HMCTS. For information about making complaints to HMCTS, see CPAG's *Welfare Benefits and Tax Credits Handbook*.

# 2. Compensation payments

If you have not received prompt, courteous and efficient service, or have lost out because of an error, delay or poor standard of service by the Child Maintenance Service (CMS) or Jobcentre Plus, it may be appropriate to request compensation or a consolatory payment (see p235) when making a complaint. Ex gratia payments can be made if someone has experienced a financial loss or significant delay, or has been caused severe distress or inconvenience.

A Department for Work and Pensions guide (*Financial Redress for Maladministration: special payment scheme – policy and guiding principles*) explains the rules on whether financial compensation should be paid and, if so, how much is appropriate. It is available on the www.gov.uk website[2] or on request from the CMS and Jobcentre Plus.

There is no legal right to these payments, but it can sometimes be useful to make it clear that financial compensation would help to resolve the complaint. The CMS cannot be sued for negligence.[3]

Compensation payments may be appropriate if there has been:
- significant delay – eg, in making calculations or reviewing liability. It is useful to refer to what the CMS and Jobcentre Plus say about their service standards when assessing how severe a delay has been;
- delays or errors in enforcement;
- delays in passing child support payments to the person with care;
- wrong identification of a non-resident parent;
- financial loss because of CMS or Jobcentre Plus error – eg, in bank, postal or telephone charges;
- other examples of gross inconvenience, embarrassment, breach of confidentiality or severe distress.

If you are not offered compensation, or you are not offered as much as you consider appropriate, you could consider taking the complaint further – ie, to the Independent Case Examiner (see p238) or the Ombudsman (see p239).

## Consolatory payments

Consolatory payments are smaller payments than compensation payments that can be made if action by the CMS or Jobcentre Plus has caused serious inconvenience because the same mistakes were made more than once, or the mistakes caused severe embarrassment or humiliation. Evidence of your (or a family member's) health being affected as a result may also be considered if it can be shown to be a direct result of errors made by the CMS or Jobcentre Plus. Consolatory payments are made in recognition of the effect of an error on someone's life and, therefore, it is possible to claim them even if there is no financial loss.

Many people experience inconvenience and frustration when using the CMS and Jobcentre Plus, and this alone is not enough to secure a consolatory payment.

Separate decisions are made on whether to award compensation or a consolatory payment, based on the facts of each case. In some cases, both may be paid. The *Financial Redress for Maladministration* staff guide covers both compensation and consolatory payments.

---

## 3. Complaining about the Child Maintenance Service

Most complaints involving child support are made to the Child Maintenance Service (CMS). Complaints are likely to be about:
- standards of service, including delays, staff communications, poor administration and lost papers; *or*
- how discretionary decisions are made – eg, failure to follow guidance, following it too strictly or failing to take all the relevant circumstances into account. It may be appropriate to get advice on whether judicial review is also possible.

A complaint should be started by contacting the person who has been dealing with your case, or her/his manager. This information should be in letters sent by the CMS, along with telephone contact information. The complaint can be made by telephone or in writing. Records of all communications should be kept in case the complaint is taken further. A complaint made by letter should be clearly headed 'Complaint'.

If the CMS officer or manager cannot resolve the complaint, it can be taken further by contacting the complaints resolution team at the office handling your case. Contact details should be given in any letters sent.

If you are still not satisfied with the outcome or if there has been an unreasonable delay, you can ask for a review (which will be arranged by a senior Department for Work and Pensions manager). The CMS calls this review the 'complaints stage 2'. The review considers whether the complaint was dealt with properly and if anything else can be done. Contact details for requesting a review should be given in the letter from the complaints resolution team.

At each of these stages of the complaints procedure, your complaint should be acknowledged within two days and the CMS should normally resolve it within 15 working days. If it is expected to take longer, the CMS should keep you informed and agree a timescale with you.

More information about the complaints procedure is available in a CMS leaflet[4] or on the www.gov.uk/child-maintenance website.

If you are not satisfied that the complaint has been resolved, you can contact the Independent Case Examiner (see p238).

The final option in the complaints procedure is the Parliamentary and Health Service Ombudsman (see p239).

## Standards of service

When considering whether, or at what point, to make a complaint, it may be useful to be aware of the standards of service that the CMS says it will meet.

The CMS no longer publishes detailed information about its service standards, although some information is published in various documents. Standards that should be expected include the following. The CMS aims to:

- start gathering information from the non-resident parent within four weeks of a child support application, if it has contact details;
- make an accurate decision on an application within 12 weeks (but in some cases, a decision may take up to 26 weeks);
- make payments to the person with care within a week of receiving the money from the non-resident parent, if the collection service is being used;
- take action to use a deduction from earnings order, where appropriate, within four months of a non-resident parent's first being informed of her/his liability;
- answer telephone calls within one minute;
- respond to letters, and either resolve complaints or agree on the next course of action, within three weeks of receiving them.

## 4. Complaining about Child Maintenance Options

The complaints process for the Child Maintenance Options service is similar to that for the Child Maintenance Service (see p235). A complaint should be started by talking to the person dealing with the enquiry, or to her/his manager. If the matter cannot be resolved, a complaint can be made by phone, in writing or by email via www.cmoptions.org. If made online or by letter, it should be clearly headed 'Complaint'. Child Maintenance Options will confirm that a complaint made by email or letter has been received.

If you are not satisfied after following this procedure, you can ask for a review. The complaints review team should look at the complaint again to see whether there is more that can be done. The review team aims to resolve complaints within 15 days.

A leaflet with further details of the complaints process is available from the above website or by telephoning 0800 988 0988 (Child Maintenance Choices in Northern Ireland, 0800 028 7439).[5]

If you have gone through every stage of the complaints procedure and you are still not satisfied, you can complain to the Independent Case Examiner (see p238), or, via her/his MP, to the Parliamentary and Health Service Ombudsman (see p239).

# 5. **Complaining about Jobcentre Plus**

As part of the Department for Work and Pensions (DWP), Jobcentre Plus has a similar complaints procedure to the Child Maintenance Service (CMS). A non-resident parent may want to complain about the way in which child support payments have (or have not) been deducted from her/his benefit. However, a non-resident parent receiving benefits who disagrees with the rate of child support s/he should be paying (and therefore with the deduction being made from benefit) should challenge the decision of the CMS, not complain to Jobcentre Plus. A complaint to Jobcentre Plus can be made if it is about the administration of the deductions. Jobcentre Plus can make compensatory payments if appropriate.

See CPAG's *Welfare Benefits and Tax Credits Handbook* for more information about how to complain about Jobcentre Plus.

If you have gone through every stage of the Jobcentre Plus complaints procedure and you are still not satisfied, you can complain to the Independent Case Examiner (see p238) or, via your MP, to the Parliamentary and Health Service Ombudsman (see p239).

**Note:** remember that some decisions about benefits can be challenged. It may be necessary to do this as well as, or instead of, complaining.

## 6. Complaining to the Independent Case Examiner

The Independent Case Examiner's (ICE's) office can help resolve situations where people believe that certain government agencies have not dealt with them fairly or resolved complaints to their satisfaction. ICE is an independent referee, completely separate from the Child Maintenance Service (CMS), Child Maintenance Options service or any other government department.

A complaint can only go to ICE after the CMS's (or other agency's) complaints procedure has been used and a final response received – ie, a decision on a review of the complaint (ie, a stage 2 complaint), which advises that the complaint can be made to ICE. The complaint to ICE must be made within six months of the final response. ICE cannot look at complaints made after this date.

ICE cannot consider a complaint which is being investigated, or which has been investigated, by the Parliamentary and Health Service Ombudsman (see p239). There may be a choice of complaining directly to the Ombudsman via an MP, but the Ombudsman's office usually encourages people to use ICE first.

Complaints can be made in writing or by telephone on 0800 414 8529. Contact details can be found on the ICE website.[6] Include all the relevant facts, including the CMS (or Jobcentre Plus) office being complained about, together with details of the complaint and the response. ICE can give further advice on making a complaint, or appoint a representative to act on your behalf, if required.

ICE first investigates and decides whether or not it can accept the complaint. It aims to decide this within two weeks. If ICE accepts the complaint, it attempts to settle it by suggesting ways in which you could come to an agreement with the CMS or Jobcentre Plus. It aims to resolve complaints this way within eight weeks of accepting them.

If this fails, ICE can then ask for all relevant information and attempts to settle the complaint. If this is not possible, an investigation is carried out and a formal report prepared setting out how the complaint arose and how it believes it should be settled. ICE aims to do this within 15 weeks, or 20 weeks if a report by ICE is required.

In 2016/17, ICE upheld some aspects of over three-quarters of the complaints relating to child support that it investigated.[7] If it makes a recommendation of action to the CMS or Jobcentre Plus, this is almost always followed.

If you are unhappy with the way that ICE has dealt with a complaint, you can use ICE's own complaints process. Details of ICE's standards of service are available on its website. If you remain unhappy, you can ask your MP to consider referring the case to the Parliamentary and Health Service Ombudsman (see p239).

# 7. Using your MP

It may be appropriate to consult your MP at any stage of the complaints process. An MP may be able to provide advocacy or other support to get the matter resolved more quickly. However, consulting an MP is particularly important if you have been through the complaints process of the Child Maintenance Service (or Child Maintenance Options or Jobcentre Plus) without a satisfactory resolution, and even more so if you have used the Independent Case Examiner but still want to take matters further.

An MP may be able to advise on whether taking the complaint further is worthwhile. It may be that you are unhappy about an aspect of child support law, in which case a complaint is not appropriate. Whether the issue concerns law or procedure, an MP may be willing to take matters further to try to get legislation changed or practice improved. An MP may also refer the complaint to the Parliamentary and Health Service Ombudsman (see below).

You can find out who your MP is by using the constituency locator on the UK Parliament website, by phoning 020 7219 4272 or emailing hcenquiries @parliament.uk. Most MPs have local surgeries where they meet constituents. Alternatively, a complaint can be passed to the MP in writing. Contact details, including email addresses, for MPs are available on the UK Parliament website.[8]

# 8. Complaining to the Ombudsman

The Parliamentary and Health Service Ombudsman investigates complaints about a range of government departments and other public bodies.

Before using the Ombudsman, the organisation should have a full opportunity to respond to your complaint and put things right. For complaints about the Child Maintenance Service, Child Maintenance Options and Jobcentre Plus, the Independent Case Examiner (ICE) (see p238) can also be used. This does not need a referral from an MP, and the Ombudsman's office encourages people to use ICE first.

The first stage of using the Ombudsman is to download a complaints form from the Ombudsman website and send the complaint to your MP, asking her/ him to consider the complaint, sign the form and send it to the Ombudsman. Normally, the Ombudsman does not investigate if the complaint is passed to an MP more than 12 months after the complainant became aware that s/he had a good reason to complain – ie, that there was a need to take the complaint further.

If the complaint is investigated, the MP is sent a full report. The Ombudsman may recommend an apology and possibly compensation. Ombudsman reports can also lead to changed practices and procedures in the agencies under investigation.

More information about the Ombudsman is available at www.ombudsman.org.uk, or from the helpline on 0345 015 4033.

# Notes

### 1. Grounds for a complaint
1 www.ombudsman.org.uk/making-complaint/before-you-come-to-us/complain-change

### 2. Compensation payments
2 www.gov.uk/government/publications/compensation-for-poor-service-a-guide-for-dwp-staff
3 *Rowley and Others v SSWP* [2007] EWCA Civ 598

### 3. Complaining about the Child Maintenance Service
4 CMS leaflet CMSB011GB, *What to Do if You're Unhappy With the Child Maintenance Service*, April 2017

### 4. Complaining about Child Maintenance Options
5 Child Maintenance Options leaflet, *How to Complain About Child Maintenance Options*, November 2013

### 6. Complaining to the Independent Case Examiner
6 www.gov.uk/government/organisations/independent-case-examiner
7 Independent Case Examiner for the DWP, *Annual Report, April 2016 – 31 March 2017*, September 2017

### 7. Using your MP
8 www.parliament.uk/mps-lords-and-offices/mps

# Appendix 1

## Useful addresses

### Department for Work and Pensions

www.gov.uk/government/
organisations/department-for-work-
pensions

### Child Maintenance Options

(England, Wales and Scotland)
PO Box 578
Rotherham S63 3FP
Tel: 0800 988 0988
Welsh language line: 0800 408 0308
www.cmoptions.org

### Child Maintenance Choices

(Northern Ireland)
Tel: 0800 028 7439
Textphone: 08001 0800 028 7439
cms_choices@nidirect.gsi.gov.uk
www.nidirect.gov.uk/information-
and-services/child-maintenance-
service/child-maintenance-choices

### Child Maintenance Service

PO Box 249
Mitcheldean GL17 1AJ
National enquiry line: 0345 266 8792
Textphone: 0345 266 8795
www.gov.uk/child-maintenance

### Child Support Agency

Tel: 0800 171 2033
Textphone: 0800 171 2162
Welsh language helpline:
0800 171 2159
www.gov.uk/child-maintenance

Further contact details, including
full postal details for Child Support
Agency offices dealing with '2003
rules' and '1993 rules' cases for the
different regions, are available at:
www.gov.uk/child-maintenance/
contact.

### Northern Ireland Child Maintenance Service

PO Box 252
Mitcheldean GL17 1AP
'2012 rules': 0800 232 1956
www.communities-ni.gov.uk/
contacts/child-maintenance-service

### HM Courts and Tribunals Service

Appeals should be sent to:

### England and Wales

HMCTS SSCS Appeals Centre
PO Box 1203
Bradford BD1 9WP
Fax: 0870 739 4108

**Scotland**
HMCTS SSCS Appeals Centre
PO Box 27080
Glasgow G2 9HQ
Fax: 0870 324 0164

The offices below are the regional
offices for social security and child
support appeals. They can advise
about your nearest tribunal venue.

**Leeds**
York House
31–36 York Place
Leeds LS1 2ED
Tel: 0300 123 1142
Textphone: 0300 123 1264
SSCSA-Leeds@hmcts.gsi.gov.uk

**Liverpool**
36 Dale Street
Liverpool L2 5UZ
Tel: 0300 123 1142
Textphone: 0300 123 1264
SSCSA-Liverpool@hmcts.gsi.gov.uk

**Newcastle**
Manorview House
Newcastle upon Tyne NE1 6PA
Tel: 0300 123 1142
Textphone: 0300 123 1264
SSCSA-Newcastle@hmcts.gsi.gov.uk

**Sutton**
Copthall House
9 The Pavement
Grove Road
Sutton SM1 1DA
Tel: 0300 123 1142
Textphone: 0300 123 1264
SSCSA-Sutton@hmcts.gsi.gov.uk

**Birmingham**
Administrative Support Centre
PO Box 14620
Birmingham B16 6FR
Tel: 0300 123 1142
ASCBirmingham@hmcts.gsi.gov.uk

**Cardiff**
Eastgate House
35–43 Newport Road
Cardiff CF24 0AB
Tel: 0300 123 1142
Textphone: 0300 123 1264
SSCSA-cardiff@hmcts.gsi.gov.uk

**Glasgow**
20 York Street
Glasgow G2 2GT
Tel: 0300 790 6234
Textphone: 0141 354 8413
SSCSA-Glasgow@justice.gov.uk

**Upper Tribunal (Adminstrative Appeals Chamber)**
www.gov.uk/courts-tribunals/upper-
tribunal-administrative-appeals-
chamber

**England**
5th Floor
7 Rolls Buildings
Fetter Lane
London EC4A 1NL
Tel: 020 7071 5662
TypeTalk: 18001 020 7071 5662
Fax: 0870 324 0028
adminappeals@hmcts.gsi.gov.uk

**Scotland**
George House
126 George Street
Edinburgh EH2 4HH
Tel: 0131 271 4310
Fax: 0131 271 4398
utaacmailbox@scotland.gsi.gov.uk

**Wales**
As for England or:
The Administrative Appeals Chamber
of the Upper Tribunal (Wales)
Civil Justice Centre
2 Park Street
Cardiff CF10 1ET
Tel: 029 2037 6460
Fax: 029 2037 6461

**Northern Ireland**
Tribunal Hearing Centre
2nd Floor
Royal Courts of Justice
Chichester Street
Belfast BT1 3JT
Tel: 028 9072 4883
tribunalsunit@courtsni.gov.uk
www.courtsni.gov.uk/en-GB/tribu-
nals/ossc

**Independent Case Examiner**
PO Box 209
Bootle L20 7WA
Tel: 0800 414 8529
Textphone: 18001 0800 414 8529
Fax: 0151 221 6601
ice@dwp.gsi.gov.uk
www.gov.uk/government/
organisations/independent-case-
examiner

**The Parliamentary and Health
Service Ombudsman**
Citygate
Mosley Street
Manchester M2 3HQ
Tel: 0345 015 4033
Text 'call back' service:
07624 813 005
phso.enquiries@ombudsman.org.uk
www.ombudsman.org.uk

# Appendix 2

## Statutes

A man is assumed to be the father of a child for child support purposes if he is found to be the father by a court in England or Wales in proceedings under one of the following statutes.

s42 National Assistance Act 1948

Affiliation Proceedings Act 1957

s6 Family Law Reform Act 1969

Guardianship of Minors Act 1971

Children Act 1975

Child Care Act 1980

Children Act 1989

s26 Social Security Act 1986

s4 Family Law Reform Act 1987

s105 Social Security Administration Act 1992

A maintenance order only prevents an application to the Child Maintenance Service under section 4 or 7 of the Child Support Act 1991 if it was made in proceedings under one of the following statutes.

Conjugal Rights (Scotland) Amendment Act 1861

Court of Session Act 1868

Sheriff Courts (Scotland) Act 1907

Guardianship of Infants Act 1925

Illegitimate Children (Scotland) Act 1930

Children and Young Persons (Scotland) Act 1932

Children and Young Persons (Scotland) Act 1937

Custody of Children (Scotland) Act 1939

National Assistance Act 1948

Affiliation Orders Act 1952

Affiliation Proceedings Act 1957

Matrimonial Proceedings (Children) Act 1958

Guardianship of Minors Act 1971

Part II Matrimonial Causes Act 1973
Guardianship Act 1973
Children Act 1975
Supplementary Benefits Act 1976
Domestic Proceedings and Magistrates' Courts Act 1978
Part III Matrimonial and Family Proceedings Act 1984
Family Law (Scotland) Act 1985
Social Security Act 1986
Schedule 1 Children Act 1989
Social Security Administration Act 1992
Schedule 5, 6 or 7 Civil Partnership Act 2004

The court order usually states the legal provisions under which it was made.

# Appendix 3

# Information and advice

It may be easier to get a positive response from the Child Maintenance Service if you have obtained advice about your rights or have an adviser assisting you.

Unfortunately, CPAG is unable to deal with enquiries, either from advisers or members of the public, on child support issues.

The following may be able to help.

- Citizens Advice and other local advice centres provide information, and may be able to represent you. You can find your nearest office from www.citizensadvice.org.uk.
- Law centres can help with advice and representation, but may not cover child support problems and may limit their help to people who live and work in certain areas. You can check whether you are near a law centre from www.lawcentres.org.uk.
- Solicitors can give free legal advice to people on low incomes under the 'legal help' scheme (advice and assistance scheme in Scotland). This does not cover the cost of representation at an appeal hearing, but can cover the cost of preparing written submissions and obtaining evidence such as medical reports. However, solicitors do not always have a good working knowledge of the child support rules and you may need to shop around until you find one who does.
- http://find-legal-advice.justice.gov.uk can be used to find high quality legal advisers in England and Wales, including advice agencies and solicitors.
- Local authority welfare rights workers provide an advice and representation service for benefit claimants in many areas.
- Lone-parent organisations may offer help and advice about child support, or it may help to talk to other parents about their experiences. For details of your local group and for helpline advice, contact: Single Parent Action Network (0117 955 6971; www.spanuk.org.uk); Gingerbread ( helpline: 0808 802 0925; www.gingerbread.org.uk); One Parent Families Scotland (helpline: 0808 801 0323; www.opfs.org.uk).
- There are some groups supporting parents who may be able to provide advice. These include the National Association for Child Support Action (NACSA), Loverock House, Brettell Lane, Brierley Hill, West Midlands DY5 3JN (http://nacsa.co.uk). For general enquiry support, you can write, phone (01384 572525) or email (admin@nacsa.co.uk). A telephone advice line for advice on individual cases is available to subscribers.

- Many trade unions provide advice to members on child support.
- Local organisations for particular groups of people may offer help.

## Representation at appeals

Some parents may find it difficult to obtain representation at appeal hearings. Although many parents, especially with the help of Chapter 10, will be able to present their own case, it can be invaluable to obtain objective independent advice which draws on the legislation. An advice centre which has a copy of the legislation (see Appendix 4) and experience of representing at tribunals in other sorts of cases (eg, social security) may be able to provide a representative for a child support appeal.

# Appendix 4

## Useful publications

Stationery Office books are available from Stationery Office bookshops or can be ordered from TSO Orders, PO Box 29, Norwich NR3 1GN (tel: 0333 202 5070; email: customer.services@tso.co.uk; web: www.tsoshop.co.uk). Many publications listed are available from CPAG. See below for order details, or order from www.shop.cpag.org.uk.

### 1. Caselaw and legislation

All the legislation listed in Appendix 5 can be found at www.legislation.gov.uk. Most is updated.

*Child Support: the legislation*, E Jacobs (CPAG)
Legislation with detailed commentary. 13th edition main volume (January 2018): £99 (£84.15 for members and Citizens Advice).

*Social Security Legislation, Volume I: Non-Means-Tested Benefits and Employment and Support Allowance*, D Bonner, I Hooker and R White (Sweet & Maxwell)
Legislation with commentary. 2018/19 edition (September 2018): £116.

*Social Security Legislation, Volume II: Income Support, Jobseeker's Allowance, State Pension Credit and the Social Fund*, J Mesher, P Wood, R Poynter, N Wikeley and D Bonner (Sweet & Maxwell)
Legislation with commentary. 2018/19 edition (September 2018): £116.

*Social Security Legislation, Volume III: Administration, Adjudication and the European Dimension*, M Rowland and R White (Sweet & Maxwell)
Legislation with commentary. 2018/19 edition (September 2018): £116.

*Social Security Legislation, Volume IV: Tax Credits and HMRC-administered Social Security Benefits*, N Wikeley and D Williams (Sweet & Maxwell)
Legislation with commentary. 2018/19 edition (September 2018): £116.

*Social Security Legislation, Volume V: Universal Credit*, R Poynter, N Wikeley and P Wood (Sweet & Maxwell)
Legislation with commentary. 2018/19 edition (September 2018): £116.

*Social Security Legislation – updating supplement*, (Sweet & Maxwell)
The spring 2018 update to the 2017/18 main volumes: £75.

*CPAG's Housing Benefit and Council Tax Reduction Legislation*, L Findlay, R Poynter, C George, S Wright, M Williams, S Mitchell and M Brough (CPAG)
Legislation with detailed commentary.
2018/19 31st edition (winter 2018): £128 (£108.30 members and Citizens Advice) including Supplement.

## 2. Periodicals

*Welfare Rights Bulletin* (CPAG, bimonthly).
Covers developments in social security law, including decisions of the courts and the Upper Tribunal, and updates CPAG's *Welfare Benefits and Tax Credits Handbook*. The annual subscription is £40 (£34 for members and Citizens Advice) and it is included in CPAG's Welfare Rights subscription (see www.cpag.org.uk/membership for details).

Articles on social security can also be found in *Legal Action* (Legal Action Group), *Adviser* (Citizens Advice) and the *Journal of Social Security Law* (Sweet & Maxwell).

## 3. Department for Work and Pensions publications

Many leaflets and factsheets explaining the statutory child support schemes are available through the gov.uk website (www.gov.uk/child-maintenance). Other leaflets on child maintenance issues are available from Child Maintenance Options on 0800 988 0988 (www.cmoptions.org).
Leaflets and most other Child Maintenance Service publications can also be obtained from the national enquiry line: 0345 266 8792.

Bulk copies of leaflets (more than 50 copies) can be ordered by advice agencies from APS. An order form is available at www.gov.uk/government/publications/dwp-leaflets-order-form.
Leaflets cover a wide range of subjects, including:

- how to apply;
- how child support is worked out and paid;
- how shared care and split care affect child support;
- what happens if someone denies s/he is a parent of a child;
- how the statutory child support services use personal information;
- what happens if the non-resident parent does not pay child support;
- information for a non-resident parent's employer;
- disputing decisions, making a complaint and appealing;
- changes that must be reported.

Where rules differ for each of the three statutory child support schemes, there are specific versions of the leaflets for each scheme.

## 4. Other publications: general

*Welfare Benefits and Tax Credits Handbook* (CPAG)
2018/19, April 2018: £61 (£51.85 members and Citizens Advice)/£15 for claimants.

*Welfare Benefits and Tax Credits Handbook Online* (CPAG)
Includes the full text of the *Welfare Benefits and Tax Credits Handbook* updated throughout the year.
Annual subscription £61 per concurrent user (£51.85 members and Citizens Advice). Bulk discounts are available. More information at www.shop.cpag.org.uk.

Council Tax Handbook (CPAG)
12th edition, summer 2018: £26
(£22.10 members and Citizens
Advice).

Debt Advice Handbook (CPAG)
12th edition, January 2018: £26
(£22.10 members and Citizens
Advice).

Fuel Rights Handbook (CPAG)
19th edition, winter 2018: £29
(£24.65 members and Citizens
Advice).

Benefits for Migrants Handbook
(CPAG)
10th edition, autumn 2018: £36
(£30.60 members and Citizens
Advice).

Student Support and Benefits Handbook
(CPAG)
15th edition, autumn 2018: £27
(£22.95 members and Citizens
Advice).

Benefits for Students in Scotland
Handbook (CPAG)
16th edition, autumn 2018: £22
(£18.70 members and Citizens
Advice).

Children's Handbook Scotland: a
benefits guide for children living away
from their parents (CPAG)
11th edition, autumn 2018: £24
(£20.40 members and Citizens
Advice).

Universal Credit: what you need to
know (CPAG)
5th edition, summer 2018: £15
(£12.75 members and Citizens
Advice).

Financial Help for Families: what you
need to know
1st edition, January 2018: £15
(£12.75 members and Citizens
Advice).

Personal Independence Payment: what
you need to know (CPAG)
2nd edition, August 2016: £15
(£12.75 members and Citizens
Advice).

Winning Your Benefit Appeal: what you
need to know (CPAG)
2nd edition, December 2016: £15
(£12.75 members and Citizens
Advice).

Help with Housing Costs Vol 1: Guide
to Universal Credit and Council Tax
Rebates 2018/19 (Shelter/CIH)
June 2018: £41.

Help with Housing Costs Vol 2: Guide
to Housing Benefit 2018/19 (Shelter/
CIH)
June 2018: £41.

Disability Rights Handbook 2018/19
(Disability Rights UK)
April 2018: £33.99.

Tribunal Practice and Procedure (Legal
Action Group)
4th edition, autumn 2016: £65.

Big Book of Benefits and Mental Health
17th edition, May 2017: £25.

Big Book of Benefits and Money for
Older People
1st edition, May 2017: £35.

**For CPAG publications and most of
those in Sections 1 and 4 contact:**
CPAG, 30 Micawber Street, London
N1 7TB, tel: 020 7812 5227, email:
bookorders@cpag.org.uk,
www.shop.cpag.org.uk.

# Appendix 5

## Abbreviations used in the notes

| | |
|---|---|
| AAC | Administrative Appeals Chamber |
| AACR | Administrative Appeals Chamber Reports |
| AC | Appeal Cases |
| All ER | All England Reports |
| Art(s) | Article(s) |
| CMLR | Common Market Law Reports |
| col | column |
| EC | European Commission |
| EHRR | European Human Rights Reports |
| EWCA Civ | England and Wales Court of Appeal (Civil Division) |
| EWHC | England and Wales High Court |
| FCR | Family Court Reports |
| FLR | Family Law Reports |
| GWD | Greens Weekly Digest |
| HL | House of Lords |
| para(s) | paragraph(s) |
| r(r) | rule(s) |
| Reg(s) | Regulation(s) |
| s(s) | section(s) |
| SC | Supreme Court |
| Sch(s) | Schedule(s) |
| SCLR | Scottish Civil Law Reports |
| SLT | Scots Law Times |
| UKHL | United Kingdom House of Lords |
| UKSC | United Kingdom Supreme Court |
| UKUT | United Kingdom Upper Tribunal |
| WLR | Weekly Law Reports |

## Acts of Parliament

Unless information in this *Handbook* specifically relates to '1993 rules' cases, legislative references are for '2003 rules' and '2012 rules' cases only. Provisions for '1993 rules' cases are as the law stood before the Child Support, Pensions and Social Security Act 2000 came into force. Full legislative referencing for '1993 rules' cases can be found in the 2001/02 and 2002/03 editions of this *Handbook*.

| | |
|---|---|
| AA 1976 | Adoption Act 1976 |
| A(S)A 1978 | Adoption (Scotland) Act 1978 |
| A&CA 2002 | Adoption and Children Act 2002 |
| A&C(S)A 2007 | Adoption and Children (Scotland) Act 2007 |
| CA 1989 | Children Act 1989 |
| C(S)A 1995 | Children (Scotland) Act 1995 |
| CMOPA 2008 | Child Maintenance and Other Payments Act 2008 |
| CPA 2004 | Civil Partnership Act 2004 |
| CSA 1991 | Child Support Act 1991 |
| CSPSSA 2000 | Child Support, Pensions and Social Security Act 2000 |
| DPMCA 1978 | Domestic Proceedings and Magistrates' Courts Act 1978 |
| ERA 1996 | Employment Rights Act 1996 |
| FL(S)A 1985 | Family Law (Scotland) Act 1985 |
| FLRA 1969 | Family Law Reform Act 1969 |
| HF&EA 1990 | Human Fertilisation and Embryology Act 1990 |
| HF&EA 2008 | Human Fertilisation and Embryology Act 2008 |
| HRA 1998 | Human Rights Act 1998 |
| ICTA 1988 | Income and Corporation Taxes Act 1988 |
| ITA 2007 | Income Tax Act 2007 |
| IT(EP)A 2003 | Income Tax (Earnings and Pensions) Act 2003 |
| IT(TOI)A 2005 | Income Tax (Trading and Other Income) Act 2005 |
| LR(PC)(S)A 1986 | Law Reform (Parent and Child) (Scotland) Act 1986 |
| MCA 1973 | Matrimonial Causes Act 1973 |
| MO(RE)A 1992 | Maintenance Orders (Reciprocal Enforcement) Act 1992 |
| SSA 1998 | Social Security Act 1998 |
| SSAA 1992 | Social Security Administration Act 1992 |
| SSCBA 1992 | Social Security Contributions and Benefits Act 1992 |
| TCEA 2007 | Tribunals, Courts and Enforcement Act 2007 |
| WRA 2012 | Welfare Reform Act 2012 |

## Regulations and other statutory instruments

Most provisions in regulations have equivalents for each of the three statutory child support schemes. For example, the CS(MASC) Regs contain the '1993 rules' equivalent of the '2003 rules' provisions in the CS(MCSC) Regs, and the CSMC Regs include equivalent provision where appropriate for the '2012 rules'. Unless information specifically relates to '1993 rules' cases, the legislative references in this *Handbook* do not generally relate to '1993 rules' cases. Full legislative referencing for '1993 rules' cases can be found in the 2001/02 and 2002/03 editions of this *Handbook*. If you are unsure of the correct '1993 rules' legislative reference, seek advice.

| | |
|---|---|
| AS(CSA)(AOCSCR) | Act of Sederunt (Child Support Act 1991) (Amendment of Ordinary Cause and Summary Cause Rules) 1993 No.919 |
| AS(CSR) | Act of Sederunt (Child Support Rules) 1993 No.920 |
| AUTCAO | The Appeals from the Upper Tribunal to the Court of Appeal Order 2008 No.2834 |
| CB Regs | The Child Benefit (General) Regulations 2006 No.223 |
| CS(AIAMA) Regs | The Child Support (Arrears, Interest and Adjustment of Maintenance Assessments) Regulations 1992 No.1816 |
| CS(APD) Regs | The Child Support (Applications: Prescribed Date) Regulations 2003 No.194 |
| CS(C&E) Regs | The Child Support (Collection and Enforcement) Regulations 1992 No.1989 |
| CS(CEMA) Regs | The Child Support (Collection and Enforcement and Miscellaneous Amendments) Regulations 2000 No.2001/162 |
| CS(CEOFM) Regs | The Child Support (Collection and Enforcement of Other Forms of Maintenance) Regulations 1992 No.2643 |
| CS(DEOAMMA) Regs | Child Support (Deduction from Earnings Orders Amendment and Modification and Miscellaneous Amendments) Regulations 2016 No.982 |
| CS(DOF) Regs | The Child Support (Deduction Orders and Fees) (Amendment and Modification) Regulations 2016 No.439 |
| CS(ELEC) Regs | The Child Support (Ending Liability in Existing Cases and Transition to New Calculation Rules) Regulations 2014 No.614 |
| CS(MAJ) Regs | The Child Support (Maintenance Arrangements and Jurisdiction) Regulations 1992 No.2645 |

| | |
|---|---|
| CS(MCP) Regs | Child Support (Maintenance Calculation Procedure) Regulations 2000 No.2001/157 |
| CS(MOC&NCR) Regs | The Child Support (Meaning of Child and New Calculation Rules) (Consequential and Miscellaneous Amendment) Regulations 2012 No.2785 |
| CS(MPA) Regs | The Child Support (Management of Payments and Arrears) Regulations 2009 No.3151 |
| CS(NIRA) Regs | The Child Support (Northern Ireland Reciprocal Arrangements) Regulations 1993 No.584 |
| CS(NIRA)(A) Regs 2014 | The Child Support (Northern Ireland Reciprocal Arrangements) Amendment Regulations 2014 No.1423 |
| CS(V) Regs | The Child Support (Variations) Regulations 2000 No.2001/156 |
| CS(V)(MSP) Regs | The Child Support (Variations) (Modification of Statutory Provisions) Regulations 2000 No.3173 |
| CS(VP) Regs | The Child Support (Voluntary Payments) Regulations 2000 No.3177 |
| CSA(CA)O | The Child Support Act 1991 (Consequential Amendments) Order 1993 No.785 |
| CSA(JC)O | The Child Support Appeals (Jurisdiction of Courts) Order 2002 No.1915 |
| CSA(JC)(S)O | Child Support Appeals (Jurisdiction of Courts) (Scotland) Order 2003 No.96 |
| CSF Regs | The Child Support Fees Regulations 1992 No.3094 |
| CSF Regs 2014 | The Child Support Fees Regulations 2014 No.612 |
| CSI Regs | The Child Support Information Regulations 2008 No.2551 |
| CSM(CBR) Regs | The Child Support Maintenance (Changes to Basic Rate Calculation and Minimum Amount of Liability) Regulations 2012 No.2678 |
| CSMC Regs | The Child Support Maintenance Calculation Regulations 2012 No.2677 |
| FT&UT(CT)O | The First-tier Tribunal and Upper Tribunal (Composition of Tribunal) Order 2008 No.2835 |
| SS(C&P) Regs | The Social Security (Claims and Payments) Regulations 1987 No.1968 |
| SS&CS(DA) Regs | The Social Security and Child Support (Decisions and Appeals) Regulations 1999 No.991 |
| TP(FT) Rules | The Tribunal Procedure (First-tier Tribunal) (Social Entitlement Chamber) Rules 2008 No.2685 |
| TP(UT) Rules | The Tribunal Procedure (Upper Tribunal) Rules 2008 No.2698 |

| | |
|---|---|
| UC,PIP,JSA&ESA(C&P) Regs | The Universal Credit, Personal Independence Payment, Jobseeker's Allowance and Employment and Support Allowance (Claims and Payments) Regulations 2013 No.380 |

# Index